JOGO
BONITO

JOGO BONITO

Pelé, Neymar and Brazil's Beautiful Game

HENRIK BRANDÃO JÖNSSON

Translated by Nichola Smalley

YELLOW JERSEY PRESS
LONDON

Published by Yellow Jersey Press 2014

2 4 6 8 10 9 7 5 3 1

First published as *Gräset är alltid grönare i Brasilien* in 2013
by Offside Press AB, Sweden

First published in Great Britain in 2014 by
Yellow Jersey Press
Random House, 20 Vauxhall Bridge Road,
London SW1V 2SA

www.randomhouse.co.uk

Addresses for companies within The Random House Group Limited
can be found at: www.randomhouse.co.uk/offices.htm

The Random House Group Limited Reg. No. 954009

A CIP catalogue record for this book
is available from the British Library

ISBN 9780224099899

The Random House Group Limited supports the Forest Stewardship Council®
(FSC®), the leading international forest-certification organisation. Our books
carrying the FSC label are printed on FSC®-certified paper. FSC is the only
forest-certification scheme supported by the leading environmental
organisations, including Greenpeace. Our paper procurement policy can be
found at www.randomhouse.co.uk/environment

Typeset in ITC Galliard by Palimpsest Book Production Limited,
Falkirk, Stirlingshire

Printed and bound in Great Britain by
Clays Ltd, St Ives plc

For Clara, who was born
in the football republic

contents

FOREWORD

The concierge stared at me as if I'd just landed from outer space.

'What, *you've* got a team?'

For three months I'd been living in my girlfriend's little flat in Rua Dois de Dezembro in Rio de Janeiro. The location was excellent: a block away from Flamengo beach, and the street was named after Brazil's national samba day, 2 December. 'The best possible start to my life in Brazil,' I thought as my plane landed.

But during those first months, I was met mostly with suspicion. The concierges in my apartment block saw me as just another gringo who'd come to Rio to soak up the city's magic. The fact that my girlfriend was a tall, beautiful *mulata* just reinforced their image of me as a pleasure-seeker.

Now the concierge caught sight of the black and white striped Botafogo shirt I was wearing for the first time since moving into the building.

'I didn't know you had a club,' he said, smiling.

I kissed the shirt theatrically and went out to my friend, who was waiting in the car. We drove across the bridge to the neighbouring city, Niterói, to see the first home game for Botafogo, who, for the first time in the club's one-hundred-year history, had been relegated to Segundona, the Brazilian second division. The opponents were Vila Nova, who'd just been promoted from division three, and the match was played in a grotty little stadium from 1941. The standing-room-only terraces were made of scaffolding, and the power went during the second half. Botafogo played abysmally and the foreboding of another bad season spread through the stands. Botafogo lost 2-1.

When I got home, the concierge rushed to open the door for me.

'Poor you,' he said, giving me a bear hug.

It meant nothing that I supported bohemian Botafogo, the smallest of Rio's four major clubs, and that he rooted for Flamengo, Brazil's biggest club. I was no longer an anonymous gringo. I had shown my colours. I had a club. Over the next few weeks, I was introduced to all the neighbours and integrated into the neighbourhood. From that day on I always had someone to talk to in the building. I only understood later that I had gone through an initiation ritual.

I'd become a citizen of the football republic.

Since I first moved to Rio, just after the millennium, I'd been thinking about writing a book about football in Brazil. I wrote a few well-received pieces for the Swedish football magazine *Offside*, which then found their way into *FourFourTwo*, Germany's *11 Freunde*, France's *Courier International*, and a few Asian magazines I can't even remember the names of. But my day-to-day job as Latin America correspondent took up most of my time. The book never happened. Now, with the 2014 World Cup around the corner, I saw my chance.

Over the last year, I've travelled the country in search of the best tales of Brazil's national passion. I've met a four-time World Cup winner, who, alone in his skyscraper, ponders the importance of superstition in football. I've visited the home of Romário, the bad boy of Brazilian football who's become an exemplary congressman. I've rummaged in the dark history of Garrincha, taken the bus with Brazil's most dangerous supporters' club, drained a bottle of hazelnut liqueur with the world's most famous football commentator and handed out medals to football-playing Indians in the Amazon.

The result is a book that not only tells the story of Brazilian football, but also of today's Brazil. Few countries have developed as fast during the 2000s. When I moved here, the biggest country in the southern hemisphere had one of the world's highest national debts, unemployment was widespread and violence claimed more victims than the war in Iraq. Now, Brazil is lending money to the European Central Bank, offering work to Portuguese job-seekers and disarming its favelas.

In my job as a correspondent, I often struggle with the strong preconceptions that readers have about Brazil. They either see a country with an unequalled lust for life, with green palms and beautiful bodies, samba and carnival. Or they think of guns in impoverished favelas, corrupt politicians and disappearing rain-forests. The hardest aspect of my task is that these images do stand up. Brazil is both heaven and hell. Often at the same time.

Nowhere is this more evident than in football.

When I started writing this book I was sure of two things: the Brazilian national football team had never been doing so badly, and Brazilian society had never been doing so well. But in this land of breathtaking contrasts, you never know what's waiting around the corner. When I was about to write the last chapter, everything was turned upside-down. During the dress rehearsal for the 2014 World Cup, the 2013 Confederations Cup, two million Brazilians took to the streets; they burned buses, smashed bank windows and protested against corruption and the abuse of power. At the same time, the Brazilian team were playing their best football in at least ten years. *A Seleção*, the Selection, outclassed the world champions Spain 3-0 in the final.

And with that, Brazilians' longing for a sixth World Cup success rests heavily on the shoulders of the young, inexperienced generation, with Barcelona's Neymar at their head. It's he who must heal the football nation's deepest wound – losing against Uruguay at the Maracanã in the 1950 World Cup. That humiliation still sticks in people's throats and makes Brazil the only winning nation to have lost a World Cup final on home turf.

It can never be allowed to happen again.

On 13 July 2014, the World Cup final will be played in Rio, at the newly renovated Maracanã. Challenges are always a little bigger in Brazil.

Life is always a bit more colourful in Brazil.

The grass is always greener in Brazil.

Happy reading.

Henrik Brandão Jönsson

1

'We refined football and turned it into an art form'
On Pelé, Neymar and the birth of Brazilian football

I'm standing in the sweat-scented dressing room, feeling both proud and reverential. Proud because I have just, with a beseeching look, convinced one of the guides at Santos football museum to open an emergency exit, meaning I am able to wander into the nearly one-hundred-year-old ground Vila Belmiro and then into the dressing room. Reverential because I have found my way into the holiest of holies, to a place where the birth, the apex and the future of Brazilian football flow together. It feels like meeting the Father, the Son and the Holy Ghost all at the same time.

The dressing room is empty and silent. The whitewashed walls, the worn wooden benches and the tactics board have all been here since the 1960s, when Santos FC were the world's best football club. I come to a halt in front of two lockers.

One of them is locked, and will always stay locked. The museum attendant doesn't even know where the key is.

The one beside it, however, is ajar. Santos are playing away in the Copa Libertadores, South America's Champions League, and the team's biggest star, Neymar, was obviously in a hurry as he left. I look into the locker. A few girls have left notes with red hearts drawn on them. One of them asks him to ring her as soon as he's back. Another note sends thanks for the latest goals in the Paulista, the hard-won state championships in São Paulo. A plumber, who's fixed the showers in the old dressing room, has left his card. I think it would be a shame not to follow suit. If it is the case that Neymar is going to be the world's best footballer, I might as well get in early and ask for an interview.

I prop up my card on a ledge in the depths of the locker and leave the stadium.

Brazilian football literally took its first steps here in Santos.

Charles Miller was the son of a Scottish man and an English woman who had emigrated to Brazil. At the age of ten, Charles was sent back to England to go to boarding school in Southampton, and, a decade later, when it was time to return to his parents in Brazil, he had become one of the town's best, most enthusiastic footballers. On 24 September 1894, the *Southampton Observer* wrote: 'We had hoped that Charles Miller, the intelligent right-winger from Banister Court School, would be helping his team during the coming season, but according to what I've heard, today's match is to be his last in England. Next Friday he returns to South America. We will truly miss this dedicated, talented player. On behalf of myself and my readers, I wish him a pleasant journey and hope he finds great success in his home country.'

When the steamship SS *Magdalena* docked in Santos harbour, Charles Miller was carrying two leather balls, a rulebook from the English football association, two football shirts, a pair of football boots and a pump. Miller and his luggage came to fundamentally change Brazil. The young Englishman founded the country's first football team, an amateur team from São Paulo Railway Company where his father worked.

The founding of the first proper football clubs took another ten years, and coincided with the wealth brought about in Brazil by European coffee drinking. On Sunday 14 April 1912, the day the *Titanic* sank, three men from Santos's upper middle class created the port town's first genuine football club. Because an Englishman had been the one to bring football to the country, the club was given an English name – Santos Football Club.

Almost thirty years later, 700 kilometres north of Santos, a match took place which seemed like any other, but which was to have fundamental consequences for the club's future. In Belo Horizonte, at that time Brazil's third-biggest city, the home team, Atlético Mineiro, were to meet São Cristóvão from Rio de Janeiro. Atlético had lost their star striker in a work accident the previous year, and were searching feverishly for a replacement. The club had heard of Dondinho, a promising striker from a local rural club. The new talent got to play a trial against São Cristóvão, and he scored in the first half. In the second, Dondinho was even more impressive, and rushed into the penalty area, which was patrolled by the bullish centre-back Augusto. There was a nasty collision, in which Dondinho came off worst, falling to the ground. He clutched his knee and had to be helped off the pitch.

Dondinho, who was descended from slaves and was illiterate, had told his pregnant wife that the trial was his big chance – he would be able to support his family on his talent for scoring goals. But it turned out that the ligament in his knee had been badly torn. No contract was signed and his professional career was over before it had begun. When the couple's first baby was born six months later, the family had no money. The following year, their second son was born, and when their daughter came into the world there was no food on the family's table. Dondinho was desperate and pulled the few strings he could. Finally, he got an offer from one of the new towns in the state of São Paulo. The mayor promised to employ him if he signed for the town's club. Despite the fact that his knee ached and swelled up every time he played, Dondinho accepted and moved with his family to Bauru.

When the time came to sign his employment contract, it turned out that the new mayor had no interest in acknowledging his predecessor's agreement. Dondinho remained without work and the family's situation went from bad to catastrophic. The three children went barefoot in ragged clothes, and they survived on bread, bananas and handouts from relatives. Dondinho's only chance to earn money was to score goals for Bauru AC and hope that someone gave him a few coins afterwards. In the evenings the firstborn son tended his injured knee with ice while his father cursed the centre-back from São Cristóvão. If it hadn't been for that Augusto, Dondinho complained, he would have had a shining football career and the family would have lived in a beautiful house in Belo Horizonte.

To make up for his father's lack of income, the eight-year-old, who'd been christened Edson after the inventor of the light bulb, Thomas Edison, went every day to the train station to shine businessmen's shoes. When he came home, he gave the coins to his mother and was grudgingly allowed to kick a ball around on the gravel outside their home for a few hours – his mother thought football had been a curse for the family and would rather Edson had set a good example to his younger siblings and put his spare time into studying.

But it made no difference what his mother said. Edson had inherited his father's talent and was soon playing for Bauru AC. When the coach noticed the youngster he immediately promoted him to the A team. Edson was just fourteen, but Bauru won the city championship with an average of 4.5 goals a match. Two seasons later, in 1956, the coach took the youngster to Santos. 'Believe me, he's the biggest talent I've ever seen,' he said.

Santos's club director wasn't particularly curious. The club had just won the latest Campeonato Paulista and had the two Brazil internationals Pepe and Zito in the team. The president didn't think the team needed any extra support. Only when the Bauru coach suggested that it 'might be good to have a striker in development' did the president change his mind. To begin with, Edson was forced to swallow his pride and play in the junior team. But he was soon promoted to the A team, and started scoring in nearly every match.

The football association rang and invited the sixteen-year-old to play two internationals against arch-rivals Argentina. Two of Brazil's three goals were scored by Santos's new acquisition, and there was no longer any doubt: the boy was one of the country's greatest football talents. The only thing missing was a stage name. Edson wasn't popular with anyone, and 'Gasolina', as he was called by his team mates, was too weird. Something easier was needed, something with a good rhythm, so it would make an impact in a country where many people could neither read nor write. Someone found out that he'd had a simple nickname at Bauru. Although Edson didn't like his nickname, he became known to everyone as 'Pelé'.

A year later he was selected for the team that travelled to Sweden to play in the 1958 World Cup. In the final, Pelé scored the most beautiful goal of the championships when he lobbed the ball over Julle Gustavsson before volleying in the goal that made the score 3-1. In the last minute he scored with a header to make the final score 5-2. When the team lined up to receive their gold medals, Pelé wept in keeper Gilmar's arms, and asked, sobbing, whether the news had reached Brazil. 'I have to tell Dad about this. I have to tell Dad about this,' Pelé repeated. Upon his return, there was no doubt about whether the message had got through. In the square in Bauru, the mayor had built a stage and praised the young man who just a few years before had been shining shoes outside the train station.

Seventeen-year-old Pelé was dubbed '*Rei Pelé*', King Pelé, by the press. He took part in four World Cups and won three of them. With Pelé, Santos became the first Brazilian club to win the Libertadores, and with Pelé the team from the coffee-trading port became the world's best club: in 1962, Santos beat Benfica in the Intercontinental Cup, and in 1963 this feat was repeated against Milan.

Everyone wanted to see Pelé in action, but as televisions were still relatively rare, there were few who were able to. Instead, Santos toured Europe with their technical, rhythmic playing style, which the Brazilian press called '*futebol arte*', samba football. During the first European tour, Santos played twenty-six matches in twelve countries over six weeks. Inter Milan and Juventus offered record sums for the Santos striker, but the club's president declined. He knew that without King Pelé in the team, the club wouldn't be able to charge so much for their show.

With every year that passed, Pelé was given a better contract. The problem was that he'd barely gone to school and had no idea how to manage a fortune. A charismatic Spanish businessman, who ran the Santos builders' merchants Pelé had a stake in, offered to manage his money. Pelé was twenty-one and bought a large villa in Santos, which his parents, siblings, uncle and grandmother moved into. Soon, he married a white woman from the port city's middle classes.

Three years later, just before the 1966 World Cup in England, it emerged that four years' match bonuses were missing. The Spaniard had cheated him and borrowed millions of dollars with the builders' merchants as collateral, which the bank was threatening to call in. To avoid personal bankruptcy, Pelé negotiated with Santos for them to take on his debts. Their condition was the indefinite extension of his contract.

In 1969, Santos went on tour in Africa, and played in the People's Republic of Congo, the Democratic Republic of Congo, Nigeria, Benin, Ghana and Algeria. The fact that some of the countries were at war with one another and that others were plagued by civil war wasn't enough to stop the world's most popular football show. When Santos came to cross the River Congo, the opposing armies in the Congo crisis laid down their weapons so that Pelé could cross the river without getting shot at. The ceasefire lasted several days and, three days later, the scenario was repeated when Santos landed in Nigeria. The two fronts in the Biafran War stopped shooting at each other for forty-eight hours so that the soldiers would have the opportunity to enjoy one of the world's first global superstars. 'We saw a whole load of armed guards and starving people, but what I remember most is all the people walking to the matches with chairs on their heads. The stadiums were big, but still way too small. Most people sat outside on their chairs,' Lima, one of Pelé's team-mates, has said.

After being the only player in the world to have bagged a third World Cup victory, in Mexico in 1970, as well as being voted best player in the tournament, Pelé decided to stop playing for

A Seleção, despite being only thirty years old. Pelé's first son had been born, and he wanted to fulfil another dream: studying at high school in order to apply to university. He passed the entrance exam and started studying at the sports high school in Santos.

An epoch was drawing to a close. Over the previous ten years, Santos had won the Campeonato Paulista eight times, six other championship titles, the Libertadores twice and two Club World Cups. The Brazilian press called the club '*Os Santásticos*', the Fantastic Santos Players, and declared Santos South America's best team of all time. Pelé tried to leave several times, but Santos wanted the show to go on, whatever the cost.

In his life story, *Pelé: The Autobiography*, Pelé describes what finally happened, during a home match at Vila Belmiro in 1974: 'After 20 minutes I was in the midfield and the ball was lofted over to me. Rather than chest it or controlling it any other way, I caught it with my hands. It was a spontaneous decision. The idea just came to me there and then. The other players stopped and stared.'

Pelé went into the dressing room, unlaced his boots and opened the locker that had been his for eighteen years. He showered, changed and locked the cupboard for the last time.

It's Sunday morning in Santos's neighbouring borough São Vicente. Heavy rain is falling on the families pouring towards the newly renovated Baptist church. Although most of the congregation are on low incomes – they live on a few hundred dollars a month – they gratefully take the collection envelopes they are handed at the entrance. On stage, a pop group is warming up with a singalong. The lyrics tell of God's unconditional love and about five hundred Baptists are swaying along with eyes closed in the pews.

As the Baptist pastor jumps up on the stage with a tiny microphone taped to his cheek, he brings to mind an old rock star making his comeback.

'God loves you. You know that? God loves you! Let me hear it: do you know God loves you?'

'YEEEEAAAAAAAAHHHH,' cry the congregation.

Behind me, five smartly dressed teenage boys each have a bible on their laps. Three of them have cut their hair into mohicans à la Neymar. Pastor Newton readies himself.

'I didn't hear you. Do you know that God loves you?'

'YYYEEEEEEEAAAAAAAAAHHHHH,' yell the boys.

Neymar was eight when the talent scout and youth trainer Betinho took him to the Baptist church. The talent scout, who also discovered Robinho, lives nearby and has long been one of the congregation's most faithful members. He knew it took more than just training to become a professional. With very few exceptions, the players in *A Seleção* come from the poorest 10 per cent of the population. Home life is often chaotic. In order to develop, the players need stability.

When Neymar went to his first service, he was living in a cramped room in his grandmother's house, along with his mother, father and younger sister. His father, whose name was also Neymar, had a failed professional career behind him, just like Pelé's father, and was unable to support his family. Neymar Junior grew up with his father's excuses around the dinner table: he just needed that one last little chance and he would hit the big time. He should have given up earlier – the only title he won was as a thirty-year-old in the state of Mato Grosso – but he didn't hang up his boots until he was thirty-two.

Their financial circumstances strained relations within the family. Like so many other Brazilian children, Neymar avoided the rows by playing ball in the street. When Betinho took him to the Baptist church, he found the peace he needed. Pastor Newton's sermons increased his self-belief and gave him hope that life would one day improve.

Neymar was so captivated by the congregation that he took along his mother and sister. To begin with, his mother was ashamed that her contribution, a tenth of the household income, was so meagre. She could rarely give more than six or seven dollars a week.

Pastor Newton drops his voice:

'Wonderful Sunday! You know that this is the first day of the week. Not Monday, as so many people think. The new week begins today. On Sunday! Let us pray.'

A baby is carried up on to the podium by its grandmother. The young parents stand behind them. Pastor Newton puts his hand on the top of the baby's head and improvises a prayer. The congregation repeats it after him in chorus. When the blessing is over, Pastor Newton lights up.

'All right! One more *santista* in our congregation.'

The congregation cheers. The fact that São Vicente is the birthplace of both Robinho and Neymar makes it easy to choose a club in this town. The teenagers behind me yell:

'*Força Santos!*'

'God is with Neymar!'

After the service I ask Pastor Newton how often Brazil's most sought-after player joins the congregation.

'His mother is here nearly every Sunday. Neymar comes as often as he can. Mostly on Thursdays. He almost always has a match on Sundays.'

I ask whether Neymar's mother still contributes a tenth of the household income, which would amount to over a hundred thousand dollars a month.

'They are very happy to give what they can,' the pastor answers evasively.

I raise my eyes to the sixteen brand spanking new air-con units under the roof.

'Yes, they helped us renovate. God bless them.'

On my way out of the newly renovated church I meet one of the pastor's students. He converted and was baptised along with Neymar a few years ago.

'It was incredibly beautiful. We were baptised on the beach with over a thousand other baptists,' the student says.

I ask when he last saw Neymar in church.

'Over a month ago. He rarely comes these days.'

The student tells me Pastor Newton booked in a special meeting with Neymar when the congregation found out that the star footballer had got a seventeen-year-old girl pregnant. The pastor informed him that God doesn't want people having sex before marriage, but the punishment stopped at a reprimand. Instead, the congregation prayed that Neymar would make a good father.

I ask the student what he makes of Neymar's chances of becoming a new Pelé.

'No one can be like Pelé, it's just not possible, but it's obvious he's the new Ronaldo. Or maybe even better. Neymar has one advantage. He doesn't drink.'

Neymar's definitive breakthrough came against Flamengo in the Brasileirão, the top Brazilian league, on 27 July 2011 at Vila Belmiro. He took the ball on the left wing and cut into the penalty area. Flamengo's defenders closed all the gaps, but instead of turning around or passing, he ran right towards the byline with the ball at his feet. With a two-footed dribble he left four opponents standing, and came out towards the goalkeeper. He tucked his shot into the left side of the net: 3-0 to Santos after twenty-five minutes against Brazil's biggest club. The commentators were going berserk: the Brazilian league hadn't seen a goal like it in years. Two minutes later Ronaldinho responded to make it 3-1. By the end of the first half, Flamengo had equalised. Vila Belmiro was on fire. The match, which had been hyped as a duel between the returning star Ronaldinho and the up-and-coming Neymar, had already served up more football than all the season's other matches put together. Neymar opened the second half by making it 4-3 after five minutes. Ronaldinho, Brazil's biggest star during the 2000s, came up trumps and equalised to make it 4-4. The match was struggling to make up its mind. Who would win the duel between the old and the new generation? In the seventy-fifth minute, Ronaldinho showed that the oldies still had it, and completed his hat-trick.

The experts were all agreed: Brazilian football had been reborn and had shown its true self. 'We can have matches like this every weekend if we stop selling our players to Europe,' wrote one columnist. Financial journalists stoked the fire, suggesting that the reason the Brasileirão could deliver a match of this quality with nine goals was that the currency had stabilised and increased in value: Flamengo could afford to pay Ronaldinho US $800,000 a month, which meant that he went straight to Brazil from Milan without ending his career in smaller European clubs. For Neymar, the 4-5 match meant he was invited to go to the Kongresshaus in Zurich and attend the annual FIFA gala. There his dream goal was hailed the best goal of the year, further increasing his market value.

At the age of twenty-one, Neymar had already earned more than Pelé had during his whole career at Santos. Pelé only realised his own value when he was rounding off his career at New York

Cosmos. That was where he met John Lennon, Steven Spielberg and Jimmy Carter, signed major contracts with Pepsi and Warner, and founded his own coffee brand, Café Pelé, which was the market leader in Russia for many years. But today, everything happens much faster.

When Santos's club TV channel screened an episode in which viewers got to enter Santos's legendary dressing room and saw Neymar gyrating to 'Ai se eu te pego!', the song immediately became a national craze. Real Madrid's Marcelo, one of Neymar's mates in the national team, took the song across the Atlantic and convinced Cristiano Ronaldo to celebrate one of his goals in the Spanish league with Neymar's dance. After that, 'Ai se eu te pego!' became a global hit. Thanks to the two biggest footballers in the Portuguese-speaking world, pop singer Michel Teló was turned from a mediocre singer in Brazil to a global celebrity. The YouTube video in which Neymar dances in front of his locker has been viewed over twenty million times. Michel Teló's official video has been watched over half a billion times.

On Monday morning I head for Santos FC's ground once again. The sun is rising and glints off the façades of the houses that line the Atlantic. Outside the harbour, a few dozen container ships are waiting to dock. Others are being piloted out of the port.

Santos is not much bigger than Southampton, but it still has the largest port in Latin America. The majority of the world's coffee exports are shipped from here; container ship after container ship is filled with cotton and cars, soya beans and sugar, mahogany and filet mignon. Since the beginning of this century, footballers have also been one of Brazil's biggest exports. Tens of thousands of young men have landed at Europe's biggest clubs, as well as in the Arab world, Japan, Norway and China. Brazilian professionals have even gone to East Timor, one of the world's smallest, youngest countries.

In Santos they know better than anyone that nearly everything of value disappears across the sea. The city is run down, and maritime trade is now so rationalised that the sailors don't even set foot on land. And it's not as though the wealth that doesn't float off over the horizon stays in Santos these days anyway. It rolls seventy kilometres up the sweeping motorway Rodovía dos Imigrantes, the Immigrants' Highway, to the megacity São Paulo. That's where, among the twenty million residents, you'll find the billionaires, the jobs and the high life.

The tourists on the cruise ships that continue to lay anchor in Santos harbour normally visit the coffee exchange in the old town, one of the few buildings in the centre that's been renovated. The other attraction is the football museum in Vila Belmiro, which tells the tale of the only treasure the city never sold. A man who didn't disappear off to sea; who managed to spread the name of Santos across the world, and showed that the city could keep hold of something the rich, powerful men in Europe really, really wanted to have. At the entrance to the museum stands his statue. A truck driver, who's been offloading soya beans at the harbour, poses in front of the Pelé statue and wonders if I can take a picture.

The truck driver grins, baring his rotten teeth. When he sees how his picture with Pelé turned out, his eyes shine like a child's.

'I'm going to put this up in my cab!'

I wander off into a modern annex built along with the stadium. On the third floor is the office of the man who wants to show the world that Pelé was no one-off. Here sits the man who has sent away several hungry European clubs, with the words 'Sorry, we don't sell our raw materials. We refine them.'

In the reception there's a life-size reproduction of Brazil's most popular saint, Nossa Senhora Aparecida, which guests tend to bow to before entering the office of club president, Luis Álvaro de Oliveira Ribeiro. The saint, who is depicted in a blue cape, was the Brazilian team's mascot during the 1958 World Cup, and is said to have played a role in their success, because *A Seleção* played the final in blue. The fact that *santos* also means saints in Portuguese has led many to believe that the club was blessed from the start.

I step into Ribeiro's office and am met by an empty hardwood conference table, with fourteen black leather chairs. One wall is filled with a row of framed photos of important figures in the club's history. One of the portraits is of Ribeiro's grandfather. He was the one who bought the plot of land the stadium now stands on.

When his grandson was elected club president at the end of 2009, his campaign slogan was '*O Santos pode mais*', Santos can do more, and just a few months later, when Santos won the Campeonato Paulista, the club showed that the president's promise wasn't just empty words. Seventeen-year-old Neymar, who had gone straight into the first eleven, came third in the top scorers' league and got the fans talking about Pelé and *Os Santásticos* again. Even the country's football journalists were charmed, and tried to persuade the Brazil manager Dunga to include Neymar in the 2010 World Cup squad. They wanted him to think like Carlos Alberto Parreira when he took the seventeen-year-old Ronaldo to the 1994 World Cup – Parreira's argument was that it was not important whether his new star actually got to play or not, but rather that he was exposed to the pressure Brazilian players are placed under at the World Cup. But Dunga didn't listen. Not even when a satirical TV show invaded his home with a poster of Neymar did he change his mind. Dunga rang the police, and selected the waning star striker Grafite.

A month later, Santos won the Brazilian cup and Neymar took home the top scorer's title with eleven goals in ten matches. The media ridiculed Dunga, saying that if the Santos striker had been in the national side, the quarter-final against Holland would have finished differently – and Dunga might have been able to keep his job.

The new Brazil manager Mano Menezes turned out to be significantly more interested in trying out the new generation, and selected Neymar for his first squad. This intensified the chatter at the big European clubs that Santos had found another extraordinary new star. The first club that managed to book a meeting was Chelsea. They wanted to meet Ribeiro in New York ahead of Neymar's first international match for Brazil in August 2010.

Luis Álvaro de Oliveira Ribeiro spools back in his memory as he leans back in his desk chair, which creaks alarmingly. He weighs over 100 kilos. Ribeiro has a bushy grey beard and friendly blue eyes. He looks like a cuddly bear but has spent his whole life in the tough world of finance.

'We'd arranged a meeting in the bar of the Hilton in Manhattan. It was me, Neymar's father, that Israeli agent Plini, Pino, or whatever they call him, and Chelsea's director of football. I understood straight away that they'd charmed Neymar's father. He was all enthusiasm, ready to sign up immediately.'

Chelsea had put together a package that would suit the whole family, with language classes in English for everyone, jobs for Neymar's mother and father and private school for his little sister. The club were also offering $25 million and a dream home in the middle of Chelsea.

'I tried to tell his father that it wasn't the right time. Neymar was eighteen. He wouldn't have been able to cope. Look at Robinho, who was twenty-one when he moved to Europe. He got so depressed we had to fly him home.'

Ribeiro leans forward:

'I said no.'

When the player's agent Pini Zahavi left the hotel bar, Neymar's father took hold of Ribeiro and pleaded: 'Please, this is my son's chance. You saw how serious their offer was. They're thinking of all of us.'

'I said to him: "I know you're angry with me now, but in the future you'll thank me. Give me a week, and I'll give you my offer."'

When Ribeiro landed after the Brazil game in the USA, he knew he didn't have much time. Neymar had scored his first goal in *A Seleção* after only twenty-seven minutes, and multi-millionaire Roman Abramovich's team Chelsea would definitely have a new, better offer. On the other hand, Ribeiro had been the Latin America head of the world's biggest real estate firm, the director of the state bank Banespa, the chancellor of the finance ministry in Brasília and one of the directors of the Brazilian central bank. His career and his body shape might have given him four heart attacks, but they'd also resulted in an unbeatable network of contacts among bank directors and business leaders in Brazil.

Ribeiro rang his friend, the vice-CEO of the Brazilian arm of Santander, and asked whether he could borrow their boardroom on the top floor of the bank's newly built skyscraper in São Paulo's financial district. Then he rang Neymar's father and invited him to a meeting on the thirty-fourth floor.

When Neymar's father arrived, there were already five men

sitting around the table. Aside from Ribeiro, there was the head of Citibank in Brazil, one of the directors of Brazil's biggest privately owned bank Itaú, the boss of the industrial giant Votorantim, Ribeiro's friend from Banco Santander and the owner of the cosmetics group Natura. These five directors are among the wealthiest men in Brazil, and they have another thing in common – they are all *santistas*.

Ribeiro switched off the light and started his presentation by painting a picture of 'Brazil undergoing a historic shift'.

Ten years ago, Brazil was on the receiving end of aid and was one of the world's most indebted, violent countries. In the favelas of the big cities, international aid organisations worked to make it possible for children to attend school, for rubbish to be collected, to deliver healthcare and safety to the inhabitants. American missionaries donated clothes and the EU financed further education for the country's civil servants. Today, Brazil is one of the biggest aid-giving countries in Africa, the country's economy is bigger than the UK's and unemployment is down to 5 per cent. Murder statistics are decreasing every year, growth is stable and the country's partially state-owned oil company, Petrobras, has found the world's third largest oil field 200 kilometres off the coast near Rio. Almost half of Brazilians belong to the middle classes and extreme poverty affects only 4 per cent of the population. Furthermore, Brazil has become a major global power in terms of foreign policy and is fighting for a permanent seat on the UN Security Council. 'The only thing we're missing is someone to be a symbol for our times,' concluded Ribeiro.

Then he clicked forward to a picture of the Brazilian racing driver Ayrton Senna.

When the military dictatorship lost its grip in the middle of the 1980s, Senna became a symbol of the country's newly won freedom. Senna was F1 world champion in 1988, 1990 and 1991, becoming Brazil's biggest idol since Pelé. After his fatal crash during the San Marino Grand Prix on 1 May 1994, Brazil went through its worst ever period of national mourning. The first thing the Brazilian team did after winning the World Cup final in the USA, two and a half months later, was to unravel the banner '*Senna, aceleramos juntos*', Senna, we succeed together, in the Rose Bowl in Pasadena. When the victory cortège reached Rio a few days later, the players raised the World Cup from the open roof of the bus, together with Senna's yellow racing helmet.

The Santos club president clicked to the next image, showing a chair, and paused theatrically before turning to Neymar's father: 'This chair has been empty since Ayrton Senna died. If your son accepts our offer and stays at Santos, I will see to it that this place becomes his.'

The next slide was a financial calculation showing that the sponsors around the table were prepared to give Neymar an annual salary of $6 million if he stayed at Santos. Although the salary would be a new record in Brazilian football, Neymar's father shook his head. The Russian oil millions and the dream home in Chelsea were more attractive.

An hour and a half into the meeting, the discussion was inter-rupted by Deodato's funk version of 'Also Sprach Zarathustra' bleeping out into the boardroom. It was Ribeiro's mobile ringtone. 'Oh hi, Pelé! How's it going? Oh, you want to speak to Neymar's father. What a coincidence. He's sitting right here next to me,' said Ribeiro, passing the handset. Pelé explained how important staying in Santos had been for his career. Moving to another continent, another language, when he was eighteen would have stunted his growth. Pelé mentioned Robinho, who had had real low periods and wanted to move home from Europe because he was unhappy. He suggested that there was no need to repeat the same mistake. 'Your son can earn just as much money playing in Brazil.' 'How do you mean?' Neymar's father asked. Pelé told him what he'd learned in New York about building a brand and promised to share his knowledge with Neymar. 'We can turn your son into Brazil's new idol,' said Pelé. Fifteen minutes later, Neymar's father relented.

'We had agreed that he would ring me at 11.20. My presentation was meant to have finished then. At 11.15 I turned on my phone, and at 11.23 he rang. Without Pelé it wouldn't have worked. I knew I had to impress his father,' admits Ribeiro.

He was rewarded for his efforts the very next year. Season 2011 was Santos's best since their golden year, 1963. The club won the Campeonato Paulista for the second year in a row and became South American champions when they triumphed over Peñarol in the Copa Libertadores. The fact that the final was a reprise of the 1962 encounter convinced the whole of Brazil that Pelé really had been reborn as a slender teenager with a mohican. Proof of the player's progress came as Neymar became the first Brazilian player to be shortlisted for the Ballon d'Or without having played in Europe.

Neymar embodies the Brazilian ideal of a dribbling player who not only scores goals, but does so with style. When Neymar scores a *golaço*, the Brazilian word for a supergoal, the nation forgets everyday troubles for a moment. The next day, when the goal spreads to every corner of the globe via YouTube, Neymar instils pride in a football nation that would like to forget that *A Seleção* has been in free fall in FIFA's rankings. Neymar's decision not to head for Europe at the earliest opportunity has also contributed to his popularity.

'Even other clubs' supporters like him. That hasn't happened since Pelé's time,' remarks Ribeiro, who for the last few years has been working full time to fulfil his promise to Neymar's father.

'The majority of players have a best-before date. But there are exceptions: Pelé, Beckenbauer, Maradona and Platini. We're going to make Neymar one of them.'

When Ribeiro was working at Brazil's central bank, he travelled with the country's former president Luiz Inácio 'Lula' da Silva to the north of Brazil to open a new iron ore port. In his opening speech, the president said: 'The day we are also exporting fridges, trucks and excavators will be the day we've succeeded.'

'That's how Santos should be thinking,' Ribeiro says. 'We should be selling refined products. We're good at finding talent. Lightning has struck three times at Vila Belmiro, giving birth to Pelé, Robinho and Neymar. We are Brazil's player factory. And it was here football was refined and turned into an art form. Of course we have to earn something from that too. We have to shake off this third-world mentality of selling as soon as anyone wants to buy.'

The president locks eyes with me.

'Why doesn't the Berlin Symphony Orchestra sell its musicians, or Cirque du Soleil its performers? It's because they are the performance. Without them there'd be no show. It's the same thing with Santos. Without our players we've got nothing to charge for.'

Santos have worked hard on a number of levels over the past few years to make this development possible. In order to avoid the financial meltdown Pelé faced during his career, the former bank director has laid on courses for Neymar's whole family. He has taught them about the difference between long-term and short-term investments, the potential risks and the safest things to invest in. The idea is that Neymar will be the first Brazilian superstar to have their financial affairs in order from the very start. Aside from Neymar's contract with Nike which takes him up to 2022, he has ten personal sponsors, including Volkswagen, Panasonic, Red Bull and Unilever. Together with his player's salary, these carefully selected brands provide Neymar with an income of over $1.5 million a month. That's on the same level as the best players in Europe.

'If Neymar wants to live the high life in Europe, he can book himself a first-class ticket to Paris, be picked up by a limo on the runway, drive to the Ritz Hotel and order the best vintage champagne from room service. In the evenings, he can go to the coolest clubs and snog Europe's hottest girls. He doesn't need to play there, and be forced to put up with the racism and the weather, just to get all that.'

Ribeiro has contracted a staff of sixteen people to shape Neymar's future. It consists of a press manager, a press secretary, a psychologist, a hairdresser, a stylist, a nutritional adviser, an English teacher, a Spanish teacher and a gang of lawyers and agents. Neymar's father is one of the brand managers and convinced his son to use 'Neymar Jr' on his shirts, in order to avoid his career being mixed up with his father's. The other brand manager is the press manager Duda, and the manager of the whole team is Ribeiro. Together, the trio carefully choose the brands that will be behind their very own brand.

'I want it to be like with the Queen in England. We select the best sponsors and grant them a warrant to supply Neymar's court.'

I tell him about an announcement I saw in the previous day's paper. The Brazilian car battery manufacturer Heliar had become Neymar's eleventh official sponsor.

'OK, that's Neymar's father. He's a short-term thinker. Car batteries? If it had been Ayrton Senna I would have understood, but Neymar? I'll have to hold a new course for him.'

Santos's president is also the first to run a Brazilian club like a modern company, and has never been late in paying players' salaries – something that's unusual in Brazilian football. He employs staff on the basis of competence, rather than which family clan they represent, and he works long term with sponsors and other collaborations. This has built a solid financial base for Santos. When Ribeiro took over, the club sold four thousand shirts a year, made around $3.5 million in sponsorship and had a turnover of around $40 million. Three years later, shirt sales had increased by 600 per cent, sponsorship by 500 per cent and the total annual turnover had tripled.

Santos's development has made other Brazilian clubs sit up and take notice of Ribeiro's approach to management. Brazil's most powerful club, Corinthians, is on the same track, and has an annual turnover of over a hundred million dollars. Admittedly, this is still only a quarter of Real Madrid's annual turnover, but income is increasing rapidly ever since Corinthians beat Champions League winner Chelsea in the 2012 Club World Cup. Internacional from Porto Alegre in southern Brazil has 120,000 members – more than Real Madrid, and in 2012 they were able to buy Diego Forlán from the Italian team Inter Milan. When Internacional get a modern management, they have the potential to overtake Corinthians and become Brazil's richest club.

The only thing that concerns Ribeiro is the fact that Santos are still not good enough to beat the best clubs in Europe. The match against Barcelona in the 2011 Club World Cup still smarts. Messi crushed Neymar 4-0.

'That was the worst thing that's ever happened to me. It will never happen again,' says Ribeiro.

In order to make his club more competitive, he wants Santos to play regularly against the best European clubs.

'I've informed the football association that we want to go out on tour again.'

The Brazilian league plays from May to December without a break. Santos's suggestion is that the league should be interrupted for two weeks in August, when half the championship has been played. This would coincide with the start of the main European leagues. If Bayern Munich, Barcelona or Benfica want to play a few warm-up games before the start of their season, Santos would be a feasible opponent. There is another thought behind this. Getting Brazil's and Europe's best clubs together would be the advertising opportunity Neymar's sponsors have been looking for.

'The football association have been skimming off the cream for a long time without paying anything in return. They've booked international friendlies around the world and cashed in while we clubs have had to foot the bill. We've nurtured players, paid their salaries and taken care of them when they've been injured. That time is over. Now we're the ones who are going to make the money.

'If the association don't alter the calendar, we'll take our A team abroad and let the B team play in the league. That's that. Brazilian society has changed. Now Brazilian football has to change, too.'

At 'King Pelé's Training Ground', the A team are training for the semi-final against their rivals São Paulo FC in the Campeonato Paulista. The coaches are standing beneath the mango trees, pointing at the players warming up on the pitch. Around the training ground there is a wall topped with rolls of barbed wire. A few school kids have been let in the back entrance and placed in a fenced-off enclosure along the touchline.

The first thing that strikes me is how skinny he is – despite all the nutritional experts' attempts to make him gain weight. The other surprising thing is how short he is. Some people have suggested that both of these things are to his advantage; that Neymar would lose his dribbling advantage if he was over 174 centimetres and 65 kilos. Personally, I think he looks like he'd be an easy opponent for a trim European full-back.

On the terrace of the press hut, a gang of female journalists are busily tapping away at their mobiles. It's unusual to see so many female journalists at a football training session in Brazil. But then Neymar is no ordinary footballer. Gossip magazines also keep a close eye on him.

'If Neymar wears his cap on the side, the next day it's the new trend. If he dances in a certain way, everyone copies him. If he wears a checked shirt, everyone wants one. Everything he touches turns to gold,' says Daniela Scatolin, producer at Rede Globo, Brazil's biggest TV company.

Neymar's heart-throb status has led the Brazilian media to task their best and most beautiful female reporters with keeping an eye on him. As women, they are not only thought to have a better chance of getting a juicy comment from him, but also to have an easier job of infiltrating the shield of male bosses surrounding the player.

'Even though we own the TV rights to all matches, we're still kept waiting. But this time it was easy. I emailed his press manager and got permission to do a five-minute interview in just a couple of weeks,' Scatolin says.

Today, she wants to get Neymar to give her the perfect

one-liner for TV Globo to use as a vignette for their international broadcasts from the Brazilian league.

'If we can get him to say something good, it would really open doors for us in Europe.'

After the training session, TV Globo's presenter Glenda Kozlowski gets her allotted minutes with Neymar out on the pitch while the male reporters look on jealously. Carefully, I lift the latch on the gate to the press building and walk out on to the training pitch. I walk around the corner flag and wander off along one of the touchlines. At any point someone could shout: 'Hey you! Come back!' But no one says anything. Everyone's busy studying, from a distance, how Kozlowski, a former world champion bodysurfer, is trying to get something sensible out of the usually monosyllabic Neymar.

I head towards the visitors' enclosure, where a few dozen schoolkids are hanging off the fence in white Santos shirts and Neymar hairdos. Their mothers are standing behind them with cameras. 'NEYMAR! NEYMAR! NEYMAR!' the kids yell, as their idol dribbles for the TV team's camera. Three burly security guards catch sight of me.

'Where are you off to?'

I do what I usually do when I get in a fix in Brazil. I pretend I can't understand Portuguese and hand over my press pass. The guards, who don't speak a word of English, look closely and hand my press pass back to me.

'I want see Neymar,' I say.

The guards smile.

'*Tudo bem, pode ficar aqui, mas não faz perguntas.*' OK, you can stay here, but no questions.

When Kozlowski's five minutes are over, Neymar walks over to the visitors' enclosure. The guards unlock the gate and let the kids run out up to the crush barriers that line the touchline. When Neymar arrives, he high-fives the kids and signs autographs. His shyness during the interview has vanished. Patiently, he freezes a smile as a young mother puts her arm around him and takes a picture. A father lifts his six-month-old son over the barrier. Neymar tickles the baby, who is dressed in a white Santos babygro, and signs his name across the chest. Then he holds the baby so that the father can take a photo. The scene is almost religious. Neymar, who is himself father to a one-year-old, holds the baby as though he were a proud cousin.

'My son will have this picture all his life,' says the father, touched.

When Kozlowski appears by the crush barriers, a few of the dads shout: 'GLENDA! GLENDA! GLENDA!' Charmed, she waves back. Two of the mothers agree that the dads are right: the thirty-eight-year-old mother of two lives up to the European beauty ideal peddled by Brazilian fashion magazines. I still have my eye squarely on Neymar. If I'm going to manage to ask any questions, I need to take my chance now.

I walk around the crush barrier, coming out on the same side as Neymar. For a year or so he's been learning English and Spanish, to prepare himself for games in Europe. I decide to test his language skills. If his English is good, it means Chelsea has the best chance of catching him. If his English is bad, it means the nationalists have got it right: Neymar will stay at Santos until the 2014 World Cup. If he answers in Spanish, though, it will mean rumours of a preliminary contract with Barcelona hold water. I walk up to him.

'*Hello, how are you doing?*'

Neymar grins. I try again in Spanish.

'*Hola, qué tal?*'

No answer. I try again in English.

'*Isn't it time for you to go to Europe soon?*' I ask.

Neymar stops signing autographs.

'*No, no. Not yet,*' he replies with a strong Portuguese accent.

'*Why not?*'

Neymar wiggles his finger in front of my face. It's still a secret.

The next day, a motorcade winds across the mangrove swamp that surrounds Santos and climbs through the rainforest-clad mountain range that provides oxygen for the entire region. This was the way impoverished Europeans hiked one hundred years ago. Now, the four-lane Immigrants' Highway runs over the mountains and valley like a tropical version of the Brenner Pass.

Out in front ride the motorcycle police, their blue lights flashing. Then come the Santos fans, Torcida Jovem, in seven hired coaches. The supporters take the opportunity to wave their flags out of the window – they know they'll have to close the windows and draw the curtains as soon as they get into São Paulo. After the coaches come the police minibuses, which are there to hinder any pre-arranged meetings with Torcida Independente, São Paulo FC's supporters' club. At the previous San–São derby, the riot police were forced to use rubber bullets and tear gas to keep the supporters apart.

As the buses approach Morumbi, it's easy to understand why FIFA didn't approve São Paulo FC's ground as one of the World Cup stadiums. The ground might be the biggest in São Paulo, but it is located in the heart of an upper-class district with no public transport. In order to get down the one-way mansion-lined streets you need a car, but there are no parking spaces. Five blocks from the stadium, the streets are tightly packed with parked cars and my taxi can get no further. I have to walk the last stretch.

The São Paulo supporters are running around with bare chests, looking for *Santistas* to beat up. In order to avoid losing any of my possessions I wear my rucksack across my front. By the entrance to the stadium, mounted police keep the supporters apart. Thousands of *São-paulinos* are shouting '*Filhos da puta! Filhos da puta!*', sons of whores, as the coach carrying the Santos players rolls through the gates.

The dull chime of a church bell rings out over the stadium while the players run into Morumbi in front of a roaring crowd of 47,771 people. I recognise the sound, but I can't place it. Then comes the riff. São Paulo's first eleven enter to the strains of 'Hell's Bells', at the request of their legendary thirty-nine-year-old goalkeeper Rogério Ceni. If Santos start touring again, they should have AC/DC as their entrance music, too, I think. Then I remember the video clip of Neymar dancing to 'Ai se eu te pego!' by his locker. It occurs to me that there'll be no rock'n'roll as long as Neymar is setting the pace at Santos.

After three minutes, the referee blows for a penalty. Neymar steps up. Four thousand Santos supporters, crammed into a slice of seats in the curve, let off the day's first smoke bomb. The crowd stand and fall silent. If the ball hits the back of the net it will be Neymar's hundredth goal since his debut in the Santos A team at the age of seventeen.

'*GOOOOOOOOOOOOOOOOOOOOOOOL!!!*'

Neymar sticks his thumb in his mouth, dedicating his hundredth goal to his son. His team-mates catch up with him and let rip a pre-rehearsed dance routine by the touchline in front of the Santos supporters.

Half an hour later, Neymar takes a perfect through pass and

gains speed, heading towards the penalty area. The defender who gave away the penalty doesn't dare tackle. Neymar shoots towards the left post.

'*GOOOOOOOOOOOOOOOOOOOOOL!!!*'

This time, Neymar runs down to the corner flag and swings round it a few times. Juary, one of Santos's major players from the seventies, used to celebrate his goals the same way. The gesture is a way of flirting with the older generation of supporters, who feel that Neymar is more interested in advertising hoardings than honouring Santos's history.

Five minutes later, Neymar shows everyone why he is Brazil's biggest hope coming up to the 2014 World Cup. He beats the right-back once, twice, and a third time. Then he does a Garrincha: stops short, jogs a few steps while looking the defender in the eye – and carries on dribbling. When he's pulled a fourth and a fifth dummy, the São Paulo player knocks him to the ground. The result: a yellow card and a free-kick from a good position. No goal comes from it, but the defender is subbed in the second half.

With a quarter of an hour left, Neymar gets the ball on the left flank. He dribbles past the replacement defender and enters the penalty area. He tricks another defender and smashes a pile-driver towards the top right-hand corner that the goalkeeper tries to stop with his palms, but the ball twists up and flies in just below the crossbar.

'*GOOOOOOOOOOOOOOOOOOOOOL!!!*'

For the third year in a row, the little club from the coffee-trading port have kicked their big brother São Paulo out of the semi-final of the Campeonato Paulista. Neymar hasn't just scored his hundredth goal, he's scored a hat-trick in one of the season's most important matches. The *santistas* in the away section drown out the whole of Morumbi when Neymar, on request, starts gyrating to 'Ai se eu te pego!'. For the fans, it's clear once again that the trinity has come together in their club. Pelé is the Father, Neymar the Son and Santos the Holy Spirit.

Two weeks later, Santos win the final, and become Paulista champions for the third time in a row. This hasn't happened since Pelé's time.

2

'If you bring up the World Cup final I'm off!'
The man who took the blame for a Brazilian trauma

Quiosque 79. That's where my search takes me as I follow the tracks of Brazil's most maligned footballer of all time. It's there, by the seventy-ninth kiosk on the long promenade in Praia Grande, an eastern bloc-style resort that was built for industrial workers in São Paulo in the 1970s, that I finally find Tereza Borba. She has long black hair that curls in tight, oily locks. Her skin is the shade of milk chocolate, her eyes are blue and her nose is straight and pronounced – she is the product of what Brazilians call *as três raças*, the three races: European, African and Indian (meaning the indigenous peoples of Brazil).

When Tereza and her husband ran Quiosque 79 at the end of the 1990s, the beach bar had the more imaginative name *Raios de Luar*, Moonrays. From *Raios de Luar*, Tereza and her husband watched people stroll by. In the summer the flow was rapid and constant – close to a million visitors flocked to Praia Grande, but during the low season the numbers dropped to around a quarter of that. Tereza and her husband knew or recognised most of those who made a habit of strolling along the shore.

One day, Tereza's husband caught sight of an older man he'd never seen before, but was sure he recognised.

'My husband, who's crazy about Vasco, went up and asked him if he really was Barbosa. "Yes," he answered. "But if you bring up the World Cup final I'm off!" "No, no, no," my husband said. "I'm a *vascaíno*. You're our biggest idol of all time."'

Barbosa grinned from ear to ear.

'He had no teeth left and was renting a little room in an outhouse. He was more or less done for. After that Barbosa started coming to us every evening. My husband gave him free beer and we talked,' Tereza Borba tells me.

She pulls out an album full of well-thumbed photos. She wants to tell me the story of a childless, unhappy goalkeeper who suddenly found a daughter, and of an adopted woman who suddenly found a father figure. She wants to tell me about their fight for restitution.

But before Tereza's tale can start, there's another story to tell.

A hundred years after Brazil gained independence from Portugal in 1822, the working class club Vasco da Gama won the second division in the Carioca, the Rio de Janeiro state championships. It was around thirty years after the end of slavery, and, for the first time, a club with players descended from slaves had qualified to play in the highest league. Flamengo, Fluminense and Botafogo, the football clubs of the white elite, didn't like the new company, and froze Vasco out. The working-class club responded by winning the Campeonato Carioca at the first attempt. To avoid contact with the black players, Flamengo, Fluminense and Botafogo left the league the following season and formed their own league for amateur clubs. Vasco weren't allowed in, because their players sometimes received a few beef offcuts, a chicken, or some eggs in payment and were therefore considered professional sportsmen. The new rules also required that each club had its own stadium, which Vasco did not, and the players had to be able to read and write, which excluded those descended from slaves, who had no access to education.

The breakaway league therefore became the preserve of the white elite. This wound up Vasco's club director so much that, on 7 April 1924, he wrote a letter to the three clubs that is today known as *A Resposta Histórica*, The Historic Reply. The letter was the beginning of the end for racial discrimination in Brazilian football. Vasco's class struggle democratised and popularised football, and turned it into Brazil's primary springboard for slave descendants who wanted to make something of themselves in society. In 1927, Vasco had scraped together enough money to silence the elite clubs – the members built São Januário, Rio's largest ground, with room for 40,000 spectators. Two years later, the New York stock market crashed, and the plantation owners who'd sponsored the elite clubs with their coffee export fortunes could no longer support the amateur ideal. In 1933, Brazilian football was professionalised, and after that people descended from slaves could play for whichever clubs they liked.

At the same time, the country's former finance minister assumed power with the help of the generals. Getúlio Vargas broke with the influential plantation owners, seeking to industrialise and modernise the country. He encouraged rural populations to move into urban areas and started the country's first workers' unions. When he realised that football had taken a hold, and that it was equally popular in all social classes, he began to use it to overcome the country's ethnic, social and regional divisions. From 1935 onwards, Vargas gave his speeches at Vasco's home ground, São Januário, where he exhorted the working classes to claim their place in society through football.

For the 1938 World Cup in France, the Brazilian football association had a first eleven that consisted of ten Afro-Brazilians and one white working-class player. The star of the team was Leônidas da Silva, who had made the bicycle kick his trademark, and had earned the name 'l'homme de caoutchouc', the rubber man, in the French media. Brazil took their first step as an international footballing nation, coming third after beating Sweden 4-2. 'The rubber man' was voted the championship's best player, but the representatives of the Brazilian football association were still unhappy. They threatened to leave FIFA because the championship in France only used European referees. The Afro-Brazilian players had been given more yellow cards than anyone else and had more free-kicks awarded against them. The team felt they'd lost the semi-final against Italy, the reigning World Cup holders, as a result of a racist referee from Switzerland awarding Italy a cheap penalty.

When the anger had subsided, the Brazilian football association put in an application to host the 1942 World Cup. Soon, however, German troops had marched into almost every country in Europe, following the outbreak of the Second World War. FIFA's president was forced to hide the World Cup in a shoe box under his bed, and, instead of hosting the World Cup, Brazil sent soldiers to help defeat Italy with weapons. By the time the Axis powers surrendered, FIFA was one of the few functioning international organisations remaining. FIFA's chairman, the Frenchman Jules Rimet, was eager to get the World Cup up and running as soon as possible, and presented a proposal for a World Cup to be held in 1948. This was voted down in light of the fact that London would be hosting the Olympics that summer. The World Cup was postponed until 1949.

Europe lay in ruins, and it was suggested that a South American country should host the tournament. The choice was between Argentina and Brazil. The Brazilian football association dusted off their 1942 application, and FIFA thought it was the right time to hold the World Cup in a country where a multicultural society was seen as a positive thing. White Argentina, which had only joined on the side of the Allies a month before the end of the war, was not even allowed to present its proposal.

The only thing Brazil lacked was a stadium worthy of a World Cup final. The country's largest stadium, the majestic Pacaembu, only held 42,000 spectators, and, what was more, it was in São Paulo. The football association wanted the final to be played in Rio de Janeiro, which was still Brazil's capital at that time. But Vasco's charming stadium was too small.

During Getúlio Vargas's fifteen years in power, interest in football had dramatically increased, and the home stadiums of Rio's two biggest clubs, Flamengo and Fluminense, had become too small. The capital needed a new football stadium. Mario Filho, editor-in-chief and owner of *Jornal dos Sports*, the capital's daily football paper, wanted the nation to think big. Why not build the world's biggest football stadium, bigger than Glasgow's Hampden Park? The editor-in-chief thought it was time to show the world what Brazil was capable of.

In order to avoid the stadium being subject to the caprices of a particular club director, Mario Filho thought it should be paid for and owned by the local authority. He also wanted the stadium to lie in the geographical heart of the city, to bridge the gulf that had opened between Rio's rich southern areas and the working-class Zona Norte. The editor-in-chief pointed out a racetrack that the city's jockey club had abandoned due to the nearby river's tendency to flood, turning the track into a boggy mire. The local council opposition disagreed with the proposal, saying that the stadium should be funded and run privately. They suggested an area of marshland in Jacarepaguá, on the other side of the mountains, where land was cheaper as a result of frequent malaria outbreaks.

The state statistics office conducted an opinion poll among the city's football fans. Eighty per cent agreed that Rio needed a shared, municipal stadium, 85 per cent wanted the stadium to be located in the geographical centre of the city and 77 per cent were happy to sacrifice something to make the project happen. The mayor ruled that Rio's first municipal stadium, Estádio Municipal, should be built on the site of the old racetrack. 'To believe in the new stadium is to believe in Brazil,' Mario Filho wrote.

At the same time, FIFA sent word that they had postponed the World Cup until 1950. This gave Brazil welcome respite. An architectural competition was launched, and several proposals were received, including one from Oscar Niemeyer, who had made Brazilian modernism world famous with his sensuous concrete curves. Niemeyer wanted to sink the stadium eleven metres into the ground, but the decision-makers realised this might result in supporters being drowned – frequent heavy rainfall could easily have turned Niemeyer's arena into a giant swimming pool. The mayor settled instead for an ellipse-shaped stadium, like the Colosseum in Rome, with 120,000 seats and 30,000 standing places. The architect's ambition was to build something spectacular.

The other tourist attractions in Rio had either been natural phenomena – the Sugarloaf Mountain, Corcovado and Copacabana – or built by Europeans – the Christ the Redeemer statue and the trams of Santa Teresa. The municipal football stadium could be the first tourist attraction to have been created by Brazilians.

The only thing missing was the cash. Brazil's economy hadn't suffered from the Second World War – in fact, the opposite was true – but the state wasn't good at collecting taxes. The mayor challenged the local authority's finance department to come up with a creative financial model.

The finance department put forth the daring idea of letting the public pay for the stadium. His plan was that the most enthusiastic supporters would buy a subscription that would secure them seats in the new stadium. The cards would give the holder the right to see all Flamengo and Fluminense home games for five seasons. Additionally, the offer was topped off with an unbeatable bonus: entry to each of the eight World Cup matches, including the final, that were scheduled for Rio. The five-year card was a hit, and the idea was taken further: for the equivalent of $10,000, fans could buy life-long subscriptions, *cadeiras perpétuas*. Despite the high price, over a hundred seats were sold on the first day. Soon, 20,000 *flamenguistas* and *tricolores* had bought either a five-year season ticket or a lifelong ticket. That gave the local authority enough money to see the stadium project through. For the first and only time in the history of football, the supporters of two rival clubs joined forces to finance the construction of a stadium that would be owned by the taxpayer. The people in power, the fans and the general public were all driven by the same vision and desire: they wanted to show the world that Brazil could execute a monumental project and win its first World Cup on home turf.

In January 1948, two weeks after the foundation stone had been laid, Vasco represented the Brazilian colours at the first game of the world's first continental club tour nament. By getting through the Campeonato Carioca unbeaten the previous year, the working-class team had qualified for the South American club championships in Chile. Vasco, who were coached by Brazil manager Flávio Costa, had seven Brazil players in their first eleven. Perhaps the most important of these was the goalkeeper Moacir Barbosa. He played brilliantly against the best clubs from Ecuador, Peru, Bolivia, Uruguay and Chile, and was pitched, in the final match, against the famous strikers of the favourites, River Plate from Argentina. Despite several good chances on goal, neither Alfredo Di Stéfano nor anyone else managed to overcome the Brazilians. Vasco da Gama became the first South American club champions.

When work on the world's biggest football stadium was halfway to being finished, the pink-paper tabloid *Jornal dos Sports* got the hots for the 1,500 construction workers: 'Here we have these strong men who are giving Brazil a new soul, awakening our giant body from a slumber induced by lack of discipline,' Mario Filho wrote. A few months later, FIFA's chairman visited the construction site. Jules Rimet was taken aback by the sight of the enormous, elliptical concrete ring that was held aloft on robust columns. The massive ramps, one in the north end and one in the south, looked like something from a flying saucer. 'Even today, the Colosseum is a symbol of the Roman Empire's greatness. Without exaggerating, we can compare Rio's majestic masterpiece with that arena,' Rimet said, and was met with cheers from the workers.

Three months later, in November 1949, Malmö FF landed in Brazil. The club had won the Swedish league in the spring, had been unbeaten for six months, and were the first Swedish club to be invited to spend a month in Brazil playing against the country's top clubs. For the Brazilians, the intention was to get a taste of good European competition ahead of the World

Cup: Sweden's Olympic gold from the previous year hadn't gone unnoticed. However, for the first week, the whole Malmö team lay knocked out with diarrhoea in São Paulo. Palmeiras beat them 5-0 and São Paulo FC 6-0. The following week, the first eleven had perked up and managed a 4-4 draw against Corinthians. Then, when MFF arrived in Rio, they were put in touch with the director of the Brazilian arm of the Swedish calculator manufacturer Facit. Gunnar Göransson, who had played with IFK Norrköping before becoming a businessman in South America, made sure the players were given different food, and MFF drew 4-4 against Flamengo at their home ground in Gávea.

When the Swedish preparations for the World Cup started a few months later, the Swedish football association contacted Malmö FF to find out how the climate affected the players and which hotels and training grounds were best. The association had also heard about the 'Malmö boots' – which a shoe factory had been manufacturing in Malmö, after a Brazilian model. Sweden's managers ordered some of the shoes and also asked to borrow the Brazilian balls MFF had bought on their trip – the football association wanted the national team to get used to them during the training camp at Bosön, on the outskirts of Stockholm. The association also contracted Göransson, the Facit director, whose task it was to ensure that the team would get food suited to Swedish stomachs. The final World Cup squad included six Malmö players who were accustomed to Brazil. But Gunnar Gren, Gunnar Nordahl and Nisse Liedholm, who had been the big success story when Sweden became Olympic Champions in London in 1948, were notable for their absence. Seventeen years after Brazil had professionalised their football, the Swedish football association still clung to its amateur ideals. The national team was forced to make do without 'Grenoli', who were all professionals in Italy.

Sven Jerring, a reporter for Sweden's national radio, met the squad at Stockholm's Bromma airport before their departure, and asked whether Sweden had it in them to make it past the group stage. 'Perhaps the chances aren't that good, bearing in mind the major losses we've had to Italian professional football, but we will do everything in our power,' team captain Putte Kock replied. The radio station didn't fancy Sweden's chances of going through either, and decided not to send a reporter.

Twelve days before the World Cup, on 16 June 1950, the Swedish team landed in Rio. It was the same day as the world's largest football stadium was opened. In the mayor's ceremonial speech, he praised Mario Filho, who had initially suggested the idea for the stadium and helped to sell around 20,000 subscriptions, and, on the pitch, a match was played between the best players from São Paulo and Rio de Janeiro. On the way out of the stadium the mayor noticed something strange. Although he'd named the stadium Estádio Municipal, the public were calling it something completely different. They were using the name of the River Maracanã, which runs past the stadium.

In order to get some peace and quiet ahead of the World Cup opener, *A Seleção* travelled to the state of Minas Gerais, where Flávio Costa fine-tuned a first eleven based on Vasco's five best players: goalkeeper Barbosa, captain and right-back Augusto, and the trio of strikers, Chico, Friaça and Ademir. The regional football association in São Paulo didn't like the selection and complained that Costa had chosen Rio players almost exclusively.

The first World Cup match, against Mexico in front of 81,649 paying spectators at the Maracanã, proved that Brazil's manager had made the right decision. Brazil won 4-0. The next match was to be against Switzerland at Pacaembu, and to placate the state's football association, Costa selected three players from the biggest São Paulo clubs. Still, the crowd felt the match offered little in the way of entertainment. Switzerland employed the defensive 'catenaccio tactic', where a sweeper watched over a five-defender back line, and the spectators started booing the host team. The frustration spread to the players. Two minutes before full-time, Switzerland equalised, making it 2-2, meaning that Brazil would need a victory in the last group round match in order to go through. *Jornal dos Sports* encouraged the crowd in Rio not to behave like the supporters in São Paulo, and a record 142,000 spectators helped *A Seleção* beat Yugoslavia 2–0.

Brazil had been banking on getting revenge for their loss in the semi-finals of the last World Cup. The reigning champions, Italy, were feared opponents, but they were already weak when they arrived in Brazil, after an extremely long sea voyage from Genoa – they'd been reluctant to fly over the Atlantic because AC Torino's A team had all died in a plane crash the previous year. In the Italians' first match they played a fully rested Swedish team, who were on top form – three days before the match, FIFA had announced that the 1958 World Cup would be held in Sweden. The problem for the Swedes was the crowd. Almost a third of the population of São Paulo had Italian heritage. They flooded into Pacaembu to see Italy beat Sweden. Over 50,000 spectators, more than when the home team faced Switzerland, packed into the stadium, and nearly all of them were Italians. But they left Pacaembu disappointed after Sweden delivered the first upset of the tournament, winning 3-2.

That was why Sweden were pitched against Brazil in the first match of the final round, in which four teams competed for the title in a mini-league. Interest in the tournament exploded in Sweden, and the general public demanded to be able to follow the matches live. Sweden's national broadcaster regretted not having sent Sven Jerring to Brazil, and searched desperately for someone to commentate on the match. An emergency solution came in the form of the Rio-based Facit director. Gunnar Göransson was called in to commentate on Sweden's match against Brazil at Maracanã.

In the first half, Sweden were already 3-0 behind, and first-time radio presenter Gunnar Göransson couldn't remember the names of the Brazilian players who were running rings around the Swedish players. Instead, he used the players' jersey numbers. At home, hundreds of thousands of Swedes sat in front of their radios, trying to understand what was going on in the match. '*Number eight is playing with Gärd. Oh, oh, oh, he's really playing. Number nine is outside the penalty area. Number eight, but then . . . Uh-oh, oh. Oh! Goal! Uh-oh. Number eleven. Seven-one . . . Number nine passed to number eleven, who ran up and took a shot straight away. It's a goal. Oh, uh-oh. Seven-one. Kick off again.*' In front of 138,000 spectators, Sweden had their biggest ever defeat in the World Cup, but the keeper Kalle Svensson, who had played his worst ever World Cup match, was still praised as 'Rio-Kalle' when he came home. The Facit director, on the other hand, came to be known as 'Uh-oh' Göransson by the whole of Sweden.

The great atmosphere and the fine result at the Maracanã persuaded the Brazilian football association to move the next match from Pacaembu. The fans in Rio thanked them by setting a new attendance record: 152,000 came to watch *A Seleção*'s encounter with Spain. Brazilian ball possession was so dominant that the crowd came up with a way of insulting their opponents.

Every time the Brazilians passed, the audience yelled '*Olé!*'. By the end, Brazil had crushed Spain 6-1. There was no doubt. Brazil were on their way to winning a World Cup on home turf.

During the championship, the Brazilian team had been staying at a remote villa in the Atlantic Forest on the outskirts of Rio. Very few people knew where the villa was and the players were able to prepare for the matches in the peace and quiet of the natural surroundings. The day after the Spain match, however, an order came to move the squad to Vasco's stadium São Januário. Because there were so many people who wanted to wish the team luck, the association thought it would be better if the players were centrally located.

With three days to go before the decisive match, residents of the football-crazy capital flooded to catch a glimpse of the players. Vasco's club members and their families had unlimited access to the training ground, and the media were given plenty of opportunities to document the historic days before World Cup victory. Many of the country's politicians came by to bathe in the glow. The presidential elections, in which the former ruler Getúlio Vargas intended to stand, were to take place in the autumn, and it was important to get a good spot.

Presidential candidate or plebeian – almost everyone saw the final match against Uruguay as no more than a formality. The star striker Ademir was top scorer with nine goals in five matches, and the previous year Brazil had trounced Uruguay, winning 5-1 in the South American championship. Furthermore, the teams Uruguay had had problems with earlier in the World Cup (3-2 against Sweden and 2-2 against Spain) had been steam-rollered by Brazil with a margin of six and five goals respectively. Last but not least: the final game of the round-robin tournament was set to be played at the Maracanã, and for Brazil a draw would be enough to win the World Cup.

The day before the final, the football association invited the players and their wives to lunch in the entertainment suite at São Januário. The married couples were then allowed an evening off. Flamengo defender Juvenal moaned that he wanted to see his girlfriend as well. Despite the fact that he wasn't married, the manager gave him the all-clear, and soon Juvenal and his girlfriend were on their way to one of Rio's nightclubs. When the crowd realised the Brazil defender was at the bar, they immediately started buying him drinks. The next morning he was sick. Flávio Costa went crazy, and asked the team's doctor to examine Juvenal. The doctor concluded the player had too much alcohol in his blood to play a football match. Flávio Costa yelled at his defender so much that Juvenal started to pack his bags. But Nena, the reserve, was injured and there were only six hours before the match was to begin. The manager was forced to pull himself together and channel his energies into getting Juvenal to stay and sober up.

At eleven o'clock, the team were to have lunch. When the players sat down to eat, the social democratic party's presidential candidate came to visit. The players stood outside the dining room and listened to his speech, which started, 'Here you stand, only a step away from giving our nation an immortal trophy.' The players had barely sat down before the governor of São Paulo state came to wish them luck. When he had left, it was the education minister's turn. Because the sports budget fell within the education department, the players were forced to greet him, too. When the squad finally gathered in the entrance to board the players' bus, many of them hadn't finished their meals. A street vendor rushed up with a bag full of photos of the team with the words 'World Champions' written across them. He wanted the team to sign them so he could sell them straight after the match. 'We haven't actually won yet,' the manager said, and threw him out.

On the way to the Maracanã, the bus drove towards the beautiful Quinta da Boa Vista park, where the Portuguese emperor had once had his residence. The manager told the story of the secret trysts between Emperor Dom Pedro I and his mistress, the Marquesa dos Santos. For a moment, the players forgot they were on their way to the country's first World Cup final. Even the bus driver lost concentration and rammed the bus into the park gate, causing the players to fall forward. The bullish team captain Augusto, whose kick had done for Pelé's father's knee ten years before, hit his head so hard on the seat in front he had to have it bandaged. For five minutes, the bus stopped while the driver checked the damage to the vehicle. On the radio, the players heard that the local authority had released a further 15,000 tickets: 165,000 spectators were expected at the Maracanã. When the players arrived at the stadium, they went down into the underground dressing room. There were two and a half hours left before kick-off and they wanted somewhere to rest. The manager found some mattresses, which the players laid out on the floor. Some of them complained of hunger. The manager vanished once again, and came back with a batch of cheese sandwiches. Then he turned off the lights.

Uruguay's team had got up early to prepare. The thirty-three-year-old captain Obdulio Varela walked along Flamengo beach before breakfast to get some fresh air and reduce the tension in his body. On the way back to the Paysandú Hotel he passed a kiosk where the owner was lining up the day's newspapers. One of the papers bore the headline: '*ESTES SÃO OS CAMPEÕES DO MUNDO*', Here Are The World Champions, with a large picture of the Brazilian team. The Uruguayan captain bought all twenty copies and ran back to the hotel. He showed the newspapers to the team manager, who thought the self-satisfied atmosphere that had been whipped up in Brazil was an insult to the proud Uruguayan team, who'd not only won Olympic gold in 1924 and 1928, but had also hosted and won the first football World Cup in 1930. The management decided to use this disrespectful treatment to motivate their team. They went into all the toilets on the upper two floors, where the squad were staying, and spread out the papers on the tiled floors. On the walls, the captain scrawled 'Trample these papers! Piss on them!' By breakfast, the team was in a good mood. To reduce tension even further, one of the Uruguayan delegation's bigwigs spoke to the players just before the final: 'You've already done more than necessary for Uruguay. Nothing more is needed.'

Although the Maracanã had been built for 150,000 paying spectators, 173,850 had been admitted. It was the largest football crowd the world had ever seen. The mayor gave a speech before kick-off, and turned to *A Seleção*: 'I kept my promise to give you a stadium. Now I hope you will keep yours and give Brazil its first World Cup victory.' When the whole audience bellowed along to Brazil's national anthem, the Uruguayan midfielder Julio Pérez pissed himself. 'It just ran down my leg,' he said later.

As expected, Brazil dominated possession, but Uruguay countered with lightning speed and had the best chance in the first half. At half-time, several thousand more spectators found their way on to the terraces, and the roar that went up ninety seconds into the second half could be heard all over Rio: Friaça had scored.

It was 1–0 to Brazil, and the staff at the gates couldn't keep people out any more – everyone wanted to be part of the party of the century. The crowd in the stadium was approaching 200,000, a tenth of the population of Rio, and Brazil were on their way to winning their first World Cup.

Obdulio Varela shouted to the other players in the team not to let their marking slip, and complained about the English referee, who he thought was favouring the home team. In the sixty-sixth minute, Ghiggia got the ball on the right flank and Uruguay's sharpest striker, Schiaffino, dashed towards the goal. He got the ball just as he was entering the penalty area. Barbosa threw himself in the right direction, but couldn't stop the shot: 1-1.

Flávio Costa called to his players to cover the left wing. The message didn't get through. Play became edgy. The nervousness spread to the stands, where the singing and dancing broke off. Of course, Brazil would win the championship even with a draw, but the game didn't feel safe. The hungover centre-back Juvenal wasn't covering the field in front of Barbosa, and neither Chico nor Jair came down to help on their flanks. In the seventy-ninth minute, Varela passed once again to Ghiggia, who sprinted up the right side. Neither Juvenal nor the left-back, Bigode, kept up. A few metres before the corner flag, Ghiggia turned in towards goal. Schiaffino feinted, just as he had with the last goal, and bolted for the penalty area. In order to avoid a repeat of the first goal, Barbosa took a step forward to intercept the pass. But the pass to Schiaffino never came. Instead, Ghiggia toe-poked the ball, sending it bouncing towards goal. Barbosa saw what was happening, and threw himself sideways with all his strength. It was too late. The ball missed Barbosa's fingers by a hand's width and rolled into the goal.

Silence fell over the Maracanã. There were eleven minutes

remaining and the players were struggling to keep it together. Finally, in the eighty-seventh minute, Brazil managed a concerted move that went all the way to super-striker Ademir, but his shot was wide. In the last minute he shot again. Wide.

The party was cancelled. The unimaginable had happened. Slowly, the Maracanã discharged its disappointed, record-breaking crowd. The only ones making any noise were a gang of teenagers who had climbed up on the granite plinth outside the main entrance, where the mayor had immortalised himself with a bust in bronze. They kicked off the head, rolled it across the street and kicked it down into the river. The following day, the newspapers reported that 169 people had been injured following the final; a sergeant had shot himself in the temple with his service pistol; a retired reserve officer had died of a heart attack by his radio. On the back of one of the papers, a family had put in an advert: 'Must go: three five-year season tickets in section 28.'

The defeat against Uruguay provoked a wave of self-contempt, accusation and grumbling among the once proud Brazilians. Nelson Rodrigues was one of those trying to understand what had gone wrong. He was the younger brother of Mario Filho, the editor-in-chief at *Jornal dos Sports*, and wrote a column in the football magazine *Manchete Sportiva* during the 1950s. Nelson was better than anyone else at getting into the Brazilian psyche and analysing football's role in society. Ahead of the team's departure to the 1958 World Cup in Sweden, he wrote a column in which he spelled out something few had dared to mention. Rodrigues had noticed that the defeat at the Maracanã had created an inferiority complex which had made the Brazilians believe they weren't made of the right stuff. Although the founding father of modern Brazil, Getúlio Vargas, had praised Brazilians for being just the right blend of European, African and Indian, large sections of the population looked up to a white Europe which had refrained from mixing its population. The fact that their South American neighbours Uruguay and Argentina had followed the European example was seen as the reason those countries had developed more quickly.

The fact that Uruguay, whose population was fifty times smaller than Brazil's, had thrashed their neighbours at the Maracanã was seen as evidence by many Brazilians that Europe was right. It was white Uruguay who had won, and mixed Brazil, with seven Afro-Brazilians in the team, who had lost. Nelson Rodrigues wrote that the Brazilians saw themselves as inferior because they were mixed, and he called this inferiority complex '*complexo de vira-lata*', the mongrel complex. In the hunt for scapegoats after the Maracanã defeat, the pattern seemed clear to everyone. The white officials in the football association, who had moved the team from their remote villa by the coast, to the lion's den of São Januário, walked free. Even the politicians who had disrupted the preparations before the match with their speeches went without criticism. Nor was the mass psychosis that had led so many Brazilians to celebrate victory in advance criticised.

Instead the nation's glares were focused on a single man.

Despite the fact that Barbosa had done the logical thing and gone out to intercept a pass, Ghiggia's goal was presented as the result of a goalkeeper's gaffe. Because few had access to the TV footage that offered proof to the contrary, people's image of the goal was founded upon urban myth and hearsay. The fact that Barbosa was black meant that it was much easier to lay the blame – he became the personification of the 'mongrel'. It made no difference that the international press had nominated him goalkeeper of the tournament. Barbosa got the blame for the defeat and was forced to quit the national side. It would be another forty-nine years before an Afro-Brazilian goalkeeper was trusted with guarding Brazil's goal.

The only people who supported Barbosa during that time were *os vascaínos*, Vasco supporters. Barbosa continued to play for the club until 1960 and helped the team to a further two victories in the Campeonato Carioca. When he retired from football at the age of forty-one, he was celebrated as the club's best goalkeeper of all time. With the money he'd saved, he opened an angling shop, as well as getting a job as a lifeguard at the public swimming baths by the Maracanã. One day, the football stadium's caretaker came over and told Barbosa they were going to be replacing the goalposts. He wondered whether Barbosa wanted to have the old ones as a keepsake, and suggested, half joking, half in earnest, that Barbosa could burn them to break his curse. Barbosa took the posts home and invited his friends and former team-mates to a *churrasco*, a Brazilian barbecue. The meat and sausages were barbecued over the coal from the Maracanã's goalposts, but the curse remained.

Twenty years after the World Cup, the angling shop had gone bust and Barbosa was moonlighting as a sales assistant when a woman came in to do some shopping. When the woman saw that Barbosa was going to serve her, she turned on her heel, fetched her ten-year-old son, came back into the shop and pointed at Barbosa: 'This is the man who made the whole of Brazil cry.' When Barbosa related the story in a TV interview, he was unable to hold back his tears. 'That one event made me sadder than anything else in my life,' he said. The Brazil manager tried to clear his name. 'It was the centre-back Juvenal who ruined everything.' He hadn't been marking Schiaffino, meaning that Barbosa was forced to leave the near post. Even TV Globo's sports director tried to exonerate Barbosa: 'No Brazilian player has ever been treated so unfairly. He was a great goalkeeper who made some miraculous saves. That goal in the 1950 World Cup hung over him like a curse. The more times I see the sequence, the surer I become that he was innocent. We'd lost that final before we even stepped on to the pitch.'

Other people thought differently. Ahead of the final, deciding qualifying match of the 1994 World Cup, Barbosa travelled to the football association's training ground in Teresópolis to wish goalkeeper Taffarel good luck. When the superstitious manager Zagallo heard that Barbosa had turned up, he told Taffarel not to go near his seventy-two-year-old predecessor – he might bring bad luck. 'In Brazil, the maximum sentence for a crime is thirty years. I've served forty-three years for a crime I never even committed,' Barbosa complained.

Around this time, Barbosa's mother-in-law became ill, and he and his wife decided to leave Rio and move in with her in Praia Grande. A short time after Brazil's scapegoat moved into his mother-in-law's apartment, his wife found out she had bone cancer. Barbosa did what he could to take care of her, but it was impossible to stop the disease advancing. When his wife died in 1996, and his mother-in-law went into an old people's home, Barbosa was left alone. Soon he had nowhere to live either, and he had no more than a pension of around $130 a month to live on.

It was at this point that Tereza Borba, the owner of the beach kiosk Moonrays, saw Barbosa wandering along the beach in torn clothing. Tereza and her husband took his cause on. After a while, they began to look into how one of the country's best ever goalkeepers could have such a meagre pension. Tereza rang the authorities responsible for pensions, who told her that Vasco's club management had never paid any social security contributions for him during the fifteen years he had been their supporters' idol. The only thing that had given Barbosa any right to a pension was his employment as a lifeguard in the swimming pool alongside the Maracanã, but as it was only a part-time position it meant his pension was almost negligible. Tereza informed the authorities that they were making deductions that were no longer justified, and succeeded in getting Barbosa's pension increased to about $180 a month. But not even in Praia Grande, where rents were cheap, could you rent an apartment for that kind of money. When someone broke into the room Barbosa had been renting in someone's backyard, stealing everything of value – a Vasco pennant, his Brazil goalkeeper's shirt and a chocolate box – Tereza decided enough was enough. She asked her husband if it would be OK if Barbosa moved in with them. The couple's two teenagers had to share a room so that Brazil's most hated goalkeeper could have a room to himself.

'It was great to have him stay with us, but he always felt he was in the way. I said it wasn't a problem, but he didn't want to be any trouble,' explains Tereza.

One of the men managing Vasco at that time was Eurico Miranda. He personifies the caricature of a Brazilian *cartola*, a football bigwig. He arrives at press conferences with sweat on his brow and red eyes, in a suit that won't do up. He's generally puffing away on a fat cigar, with a statue of the Catholic patron saint Nossa Senhora Aparecida on the table in front of him – hoping the saint will protect him from vicious questions. Despite the fact that his career has been beset by court cases related to corruption, abuse of power and assault, he has never been convicted and was elected to Congress in 1995.

When Tereza rang Eurico Miranda, he had been a congressman

for two years. She told him she had found Barbosa alone on a beach, that his wife had died, that he had no relatives and that he was currently living at her house. It didn't take long for Eurico to understand the situation.

'He asked me to find a good one-bedroom apartment in Praia Grande and send over the tenancy agreement. He would handle it,' Tereza tells me.

Eurico Miranda also sent money for furniture and ensured that Barbosa was on Vasco's payroll. Each month, the club paid him $600 for food and clothing. Together with his pension, Barbosa now had over $750 a month to play with, and his rent was paid. That was enough for a relatively good life in Praia Grande.

'It was so great to see him. Every day his face shone. Sometimes he would even speak about the World Cup final with the customers in the beach bar,' says Tereza, opening her photo album – she wants to show me some pictures from a trip she and Barbosa took at the end of the 1990s.

'I said to him: "We're going to turn this match on its head once and for all. You were one of Brazil's best goalkeepers of all time, and you're going to be remembered for it." I got in touch with the mayor of Rio and asked whether he wanted to help reinstate Barbosa's honour. He liked the idea and offered to make him an honorary citizen of Rio.'

In 1999, a ceremony was held at the Maracanã. The mayor had invited all the players from the 1950 team who were still alive, and apologised on behalf of the Brazilian nation for the way Barbosa had been treated.

'It was a big deal for him to finally get recognition at the Maracanã. But he probably got the most fun out of seeing his old team-mates again. They hadn't seen each other for a long time.'

The following day, Tereza went up to the Christ statue with Barbosa. In spite of having lived in Rio for most of his life, he had never been there. She flicks through the photo album.

'Isn't that sweet?'

Tereza and Barbosa are hugging one another like father and daughter at the feet of the Christ the Redeemer statue.

'He was like a father to me,' says Tereza, who was adopted and grew up with a single mother.

The same year Barbosa became an honorary citizen of Rio, Dida became a permanent fixture on the national team, and, with that, the first Afro-Brazilian goalkeeper to have been entrusted with the position since the 1950 World Cup final. Brazil's most popular talk show invited Barbosa in to talk about his life, and the elite São Paulo university USP booked him to give a talk. Almost fifty years after the tragedy at the Maracanã, it seemed that Brazil had finally moved on from the defeat.

As Barbosa was approaching his seventy-ninth birthday, he'd been ailing for some time. His unbalanced diet had given him anaemia, and his habit of drinking a few glasses of whisky in the evenings had damaged his liver. Tereza decided to throw a big birthday party at the beach kiosk to cheer him up.

She points to a photo in the album.

Barbosa has a cardboard party hat on his head. He is smiling his toothless smile. His friends stand behind, with their arms around him. During the party, he came up to Tereza and said, 'If I die tomorrow I'll die a happy man.' A few days later, Barbosa went into hospital. His liver couldn't filter his blood any more. On 7 April 2000, ten days after his birthday party, Moacir Barbosa died.

When the news was beamed out across Brazil, Vasco supporters couldn't believe their ears: the player who had suffered more than any other as a result of racism within Brazilian football died on 7 April, on the anniversary of *A Resposta Histórica*. 'This can't be a coincidence,' wrote supporters on Vasco's website. Although Barbosa had managed to turn around his history as Brazil's scapegoat in the last three years before he died, the obituaries remembered him for the goal he'd let in in the World Cup final. The *Guardian* wrote about him as '*the goalkeeper who made a mistake his nation never forgave or forgot*'.

For Tereza it was like losing a family member.

'I think he saw me as the daughter he never had. He always called me "my little girl",' she says, tears welling up in her eyes.

But Tereza's Moacir Barbosa story doesn't end there.

Ten years after the funeral, she received a letter from the local council. The authorities explained that Barbosa's bones were to be dug up and cremated. A dengue fever epidemic had claimed many lives in Praia Grande and the surrounding areas, and the churchyard needed space to bury them. The council also informed Tereza that no one had paid the past three years' churchyard fees. Tereza told them the beach kiosk had gone bust after she had become ill. She was unemployed and couldn't afford to pay the fees. Tereza appealed to the authorities to let Barbosa's bones stay in the ground: 'Why dig up a man who has already been crucified all his life. Let him rest in peace,' she said, and explained that this was one of Brazil's greatest goalkeepers, buried in this town. 'One day, tourists will travel here to visit his grave.' But it made no difference what she thought. The churchyard management gave her three days to pay the debt; otherwise the bones would be exhumed.

Tereza and I get up from the seating area in the beach bar that she ran in the 1990s and stop a taxi on the deserted promenade. We pass the complex where the children of the members of the industrial workers' association have their annual summer camp. A dozen tower blocks, with hundreds of identical apartments, rear up into the sky. The taxi drives up on to the highway and turns off towards the churchyard. The concrete blocks holding the coffins of the dead form long rows. Each block is five graves high and seventy long. The graves of the poor have the dead person's name, date of birth and date of death engraved in the concrete, the middle classes have a marble plaque for the engraving of the deceased's name, and the upper classes have gone all out on decorations in the form of images of Catholic saints.

Moacir lies in a middle-class grave. His marble plaque is black with a silver plate in the corner of which is a football. Under his name and date of death, the Brazilian Academy of Letters member Carlos Heitor Cony has written: 'Here rests an ever-smiling, admirable man. A good man God could only create in His best moments.'

Tereza explains:

'I became desperate when they wanted to destroy the grave, and I rang Santos's biggest paper. Suddenly the message travelled all over Brazil and when Eurico Miranda saw it he rang me. He paid the debt and made sure no one else would dare touch the grave.'

When the church caretaker walks past, I ask what they did with the bones of the deceased who had been dug up to make space for the dengue fever victims. He points towards a white-painted storage area on the edge of the graveyard. A dove guards the door, which is locked with a chain and padlock. Tereza takes a step back and holds her nose. She thinks it smells. I don't. The insects have had many years to strip the bones clean.

'Come on, let's go,' she says, waving away the flies.

I stay a moment and check with the caretaker that it really is the bone storage area we've found. He nods. I ask whether he has the key to the padlock.

'If we open the doors, the bones will all fall out. We have to wait until the truck comes,' he says.

The last time the truck from the crematorium in São Paulo came to the graveyard in Praia Grande was five years ago. Since then, the storage area has been filled to the roof. I peer through the gap in the door. Sunlight from one of the air vents exposes hundreds of pale blue plastic sacks that have been thrown in at random. The sacks are tied with steel wire and marked with paper tags on which the names and dates of death are written. Some of the tags have fallen off the sacks and are lying on the floor together with a few bones. It seems hard to tell whose bones are whose.

'It's the poorest people in the district who end up here. Their relatives aren't as fussy. Everything is burned together,' the care-taker says.

Tereza, who has been keeping her distance, waves to me. She wants to leave this place. We wander over to the planted areas of the graveyard and sit down on one of the benches. The sun is shining on a palm frond, giving us shade. Despite Tereza's large sunglasses, you can see that she's crying.

'Was that where he would have ended up? They're crazy! That's typical Brazil. They thought they could cremate away the World Cup final,' Tereza says, wiping a tear from her cheek. 'I'll make sure they don't succeed.' Tereza wants to erect a statue of Barbosa in Praia Grande. She's already talked to the council, who like the proposal, but so far no politicians have cared to raise the issue. It's time for Brazil to host a new World Cup, and the final is going to be played in a newly renovated Maracanã. Tereza sighs:

'They think a statue will bring bad luck if they put it up now. They want to wait until the World Cup is over.'

3

'Come on, we're actually on our way to
the World Cup now!'
Brazil's best-loved footballer

During the international film festival in Rio in 2003, there was
a sneak preview of the long-awaited film on Garrincha's rise
to fame. The film, which was called *Estrela Solitária*, Solitary
Star, wasn't yet fully edited, but the director was eager to test
it on an audience. He invited Garrincha's daughters to the
sold-out screening and informed them that the world premiere
of the film was to take place on Garrincha's seventieth birthday,
in his home town of Pau Grande. 'We're going to be showing
it in the middle of the village square,' said the director. I scrib-
bled down the date and convinced an American photographer
to come with me on the day. It was to be our first story
together.

Five weeks later, we jumped into one of Rio's yellow taxis to
make the seventy-kilometre journey to Pau Grande. A tropical
rainstorm took us by surprise, and clouds covered the green-clad
mountain range that forms a stunning backdrop to the village
that produced Brazil's most mythologised player. After a while,
we started to worry we'd taken the wrong road, and stopped

beside a man who was pushing a bike along the roadside. I rolled down the window and rain splashed into the back seat while I asked if he knew where Pau Grande was.

'*Pau Grande*? I don't understand. Do you mean here?' said the man, grabbing his crotch.

The taxi driver burst out laughing.

'You can't ask that!' he said to me.

I tried again.

'Pau Grande? Is it here somewhere?'

The man at the side of the road was in stitches. How funny could it be? A gringo in a yellow taxi asks for Pau Grande. Not before the taxi driver took over the discussion did the man give us any sensible directions. We weren't far from our destination. After just a few kilometres we would see a sign on the right-hand side with the words '*Terra de Garrincha*', Garrincha country. When the taxi had picked up speed again, I asked the driver what had been so funny. He told me that Pau Grande is not just the name of the village where the world's best right-winger grew up. It's also Brazilian slang for 'big cock'.

When the taxi arrived in Pau Grande, the eyes of the village residents followed us as we drove around the square again and again trying to find the place where the film was to be shown. We couldn't find it. 'Maybe the screening has been cancelled because of the rain,' said my American photographer friend.

At a bus stop we found a few schoolkids. We asked whether they know where the seventieth birthday party was to be held.

'*Que?*'

'Garrincha's seventieth birthday celebration. Do you know where it is?'

'What celebration?'

The fact that students from the Garrincha High School,

named after the man who'd put Pau Grande on the map, didn't know anything about it didn't bode well.

'Ask the lady in the fast-food stall,' the teenagers suggested.

She hadn't heard about any celebration either, but pointed us in the direction of Garrincha's cousin, who lived further up the hill.

'If anybody's arranged something it'll be him. He likes to party,' she said.

The tyres spun in the clay as the taxi struggled up the gravel road. In the end, the driver gave up and parked the car on the verge. The blazing sun was peeping through the clouds, so we smothered our necks with sun cream and walked up the last bit. The house was large and was built together with a *birosca*, a kiosk selling biscuits, beer and cachaça (a Brazilian sugar-cane spirit). The fan whirred drowsily on the ceiling and it was obvious that the taxi's stubborn attempts to climb the hill had awoken the girl behind the counter. She yawned as she explained that Garrincha's cousin was probably taking a siesta at the moment, but that we were free to knock on the adjacent door. It took five minutes before the cousin managed to pull on a pair of shorts and a vest. He bore no resemblance to Garrincha, and explained that he belonged to the unofficial family tree that Garrincha's alcoholic father had spread across the village. In order to avoid getting into the precise details of his relationship to the two-time World Cup winner, he simply called himself '*O primo de Garrincha*', Garrincha's cousin.

'He must have more "cousins" here. Things like that aren't important out here in the country,' the man said, inviting us in.

On an enormous terrace with a view out over the whole village, the cousin had installed a disco. About thirty beer crates were stacked in a corner, and behind the bar there were several rows of half-drunk bottles.

'We have the best parties in Pau Grande here,' the cousin said.

I asked whether there were any plans to hold a party there this evening. The cousin scratched his chest and gave me a quizzical look. Was he missing something? 'Yeah,' I said, 'today's your cousin's seventieth birthday.'

'Oh! Is it today? You want me to sort out a party now? I can fix this place up in no time.'

We said we'd already accepted that our plan had gone to pot. Our plan with the story was to describe how the world premiere of the film would finally bring Garrincha recognition, but by now we'd realised that not even in his home village, where he had invested his money in everything and everyone, was there anyone who intended to celebrate him. The whole trip felt really . . . Garrincha.

'But we had a good laugh on the way here in any case,' my colleague said, explaining about the misunderstanding with Pau Grande. The cousin smiled and wandered off to look for something. When he came back, he had a black folder under his arm with large press photos in plastic sleeves that he'd been given by a photographer who followed the Campeonato Carioca during the 1960s. The cousin flicked through the black and white football photos until he came to a picture taken in Botafogo's shower room. Garrincha stands naked and smiles at the photographer while he lathers shampoo in his hair.

'You can see for yourselves what a huge piece he had. At least twenty-five centimetres! You bet he got recognition. The whole village is named after him,' said the cousin, and laughed.

*

The first person to notice that Garrincha's legs weren't normal was the midwife. He was bow-legged in his left leg and knock-kneed with his right. If there had been a hospital in Pau Grande in the thirties, an orthopaedic surgeon would easily have been able to fix the crooked legs, but the only medical facility in the village at that time was a small clinic belonging to the British textile factory. That's where Garrincha's father worked. He was descended from Indians, and had fled the famine in the north-east to get a job on the outskirts of Rio. He'd married a black woman who was the first in her family to have been born free. Garrincha was, just like Jimi Hendrix, a *cafuzo*, a mixture of African and Indian. His shortness led his big sister to call him '*Garrincha*', after a small bird with a puffed-up chest and skinny legs.

School wasn't much of a success for Garrincha; he preferred to go down to the river to fish. Life seemed so predictable in Pau Grande: when the students finished compulsory schooling at fourteen, they got a job in the British textile factory. It was exactly the same for Garrincha. He started working in the cotton depart-ment and was moved to the thread department when he was fifteen. But his habit of pulling a sickie once a week and sleeping on the bundles of cotton during working hours annoyed the management. When he was caught napping three days in a row, he was given the boot. When his father got wind of this, he kicked Garrincha out.

Football was Garrincha's saviour. According to the regulations of the textile factory's football club, all players had to be employed at the factory, and, as the football team had become dependent on Garrincha's dribbling skills, the coach absolutely wanted him back. The football club's chairman, who was also foreman at the factory, persuaded the company management to reinstate Garrincha and promised that the fifteen-year-old would behave. And while there was no significant improvement in his work, Garrincha certainly woke up when he was on the football pitch.

In 1952, Garrincha was nineteen, and the textile workers were to meet the bank clerks' amateur team. The chairman of the banks' union was a close friend of Araty, a popular Botafogo right-winger, and invited him out to referee the match. Araty normally refused such invitations when he was off work, but since it was the godfather of one of his children who had asked him, he took the train out from Rio. After thirty minutes' play and three goals from the textile workers' nineteen-year-old, Botafogo's right-winger said: 'this boy is a hundred times better than many of us.' When the match finished, he approached Garrincha, left his card and said: 'You should come to Rio and play for Botafogo. No one there is better than you.'

Hearing something like that from an established professional, who, moreover, played in the same position, would have most teenagers screaming 'AT LAST!', and running to pack their bags. But Garrincha preferred to sit under his cork tree in Pau Grande, fishing with his friends. When Araty told his team-mates about the nineteen-year-old with the crooked legs, they dismissed his story, thinking it reminded them of the legend among indigenous people, about the '*Curupira*', a creature with backwards facing feet that crept around the rainforest, leading children astray. The only one who believed Araty was a devoted *botafoguense* who spent more time on football than on his job as a shipbroker. He went to Pau Grande to see with his own eyes the player with the crooked legs. Just to be on the safe side, he watched two matches: both ended 5-0 to Pau Grande. There was no doubt the legend was both true, and living.

The following year, the textile workers played against one of the city teams in Rio, and the shipbroker went along to convince Garrincha to go with him to Botafogo. Garrincha still wasn't particularly interested. When he had visited Vasco and Fluminense it hadn't even led to a trial. The shipbroker promised he wouldn't be treated in the same way at Botafogo and shoved 100 cruzeiros into his hand. That was more than a week's pay at the textile factory.

Two days later, Garrincha turned up at the clubhouse in Botafogo. 'Aha, so you're the player Araty mentioned,' said the coach, and waved to the fitness coach: 'Put him against Nílton Santos!' After thirty minutes, Nílton Santos, at that time Brazil's best wing-back, walked off the pitch and said to the trainer: 'Sign him! It's better we have him with us than against us.'

From the press box, the city's sports reporters had followed the duel between the left-back and the right-winger. Botafogo's club management realised that within twenty-four hours the whole of Rio would know about the crooked-legged talent, and they called the board into the clubhouse the very same evening. But the board members couldn't agree on how the contract should be formulated and what salary the club should pay. Botafogo's club director took a gamble and asked Garrincha if he'd sign a blank sheet of paper, which the club could fill in later. Garrincha signed. Botafogo paid the lowest fee ever recorded in Brazilian football, the equivalent of around $25, and gave him a monthly salary of just $100 more than he had earned at the textile factory. The accommodation he was offered was the same as that of the junior coaches – a mattress under the concrete terraces at the club's stadium.

At the medical examination, the doctor was shocked. Garrincha was 1.69metres tall, weighed 67 kilos and had one kneecap twisted inwards and one twisted outwards. What's more, his left leg was six centimetres shorter than his right. But his handicap soon turned out to be an advantage. During the 1953 Campeonato Carioca, Garrincha scored twenty goals in twenty-six matches, and for the first time in several years the title seemed within Botafogo's reach. There was just one thing that worried the management: Garrincha was totally in love with the ball. He seldom passed, preferring to dribble it down the wing. In one match, he made his way through the whole defence, dummied the keeper and then turned to dribble past yet another player instead of shooting at the open goal. The audience loved the play-acting and gave him a new nickname: '*Mané Garrincha*', Gawky Garrincha.

Two years later, in 1955, Garrincha made his debut for Brazil, and in the run-up to the 1958 World Cup he was heavily tipped for the first team. Brazil's management were unsure whether he was made of the right stuff, and were determined to avoid embarrassing themselves the way they'd done in previous World Cup tournaments: just before the 1938 World Cup in France, the football associations of the rival states Rio and São Paulo had an argument over which players should be selected; during the 1950 World Cup on home turf megalomania had taken over; and in the 1954 World Cup two Brazilian players were sent off when the Hungarian Sándor Kocsis knocked Brazil out in the quarter-final.

In order to overcome the problems ahead of the 1958 World Cup, better organisation and a new chairman were required. The football association elected João Havelange, who had played in the Brazilian water polo team at the Helsinki Olympics in 1952, and led the Brazilian delegation at the 1956 Olympics in Melbourne. Havelange came up with the winning formula of letting the association in São Paulo take charge of the organisation, and the players in Rio the content. He also realised that the football association had to do something to counter the effects of the social background shared by most of *A Seleção*: almost all of the national players came from slums created when the emancipated slaves found their ways into Brazil's big cities in the early twentieth century. Because the authorities cared little about the families who had built their homes on unclaimed land, they were rarely offered education or healthcare.

As a sportsman, João Havelange knew that the body healed more slowly if your teeth were full of cavities – the same thing had happened in the 1938 World Cup, when 'rubber man' Leônidas da Silvas was unable to play in the semi-final against Italy because a simple strain was refusing to heal. Havelange employed a dentist to fix the players' teeth. When the dentist was through with the team, he had filled 470 holes and removed thirty-two teeth. Garrincha had to be given a general anaesthetic while the dentist removed all the teeth in the left half of his top jaw.

The next stage was to prepare the players mentally. The trauma of the 1950 World Cup final lived on, and the management honestly believed that the defeat was a result of an inferiority complex among the black players in the team. They were seen to be psychologically weaker than the white players, and Havelange hired a psychologist from São Paulo's public transport company. He was asked to check the players' psychiatric condition, carry out an IQ test and then write a report stating which players he thought would be most capable of dealing with a World Cup final, should Brazil get through. Right from the start, Garrincha had problems. He made a spelling mistake in the box in which he was supposed to write his occupation. He meant to write '*atleta*', athlete, but instead misspelled it as 'atreta'. The IQ test didn't go too well either. He scored just thirty-eight out of a possible 123 points. That wasn't even enough to be a bus driver. During the one-to-one conversations afterwards, the psychologist noticed something strange: Garrincha didn't show a hint of aggression. How would a player like that react if the team were losing? Would he have the motivation to deliver? Or would he act like Disney's Ferdinand the Bull and shy away?

On the way to Sweden, the Brazilian team stopped in Italy to put the final touches to the line-up. The manager Vicente Feola, who had been assistant coach during the 1950 World Cup, was unsure whether to play Garrincha on the right wing or use the reliable Joel from Flamengo. The manager knew Garrincha was unpredictable, and that he sometimes ignored the coach's instructions, but he was also well aware that Garrincha would deliver that unexpected touch that could turn the match. The decisive test came against Fiorentina, whose line-up contained half the Italian first eleven.

Garrincha did his job on the right wing, and in the second half Brazil were leading 3-0. In the eightieth minute, Garrincha once again collected the ball along his wing and dribbled past a defender. He dummied the next player, too, and then took on a third opponent. He couldn't slow down the right-winger either, and Garrincha turned in on goal. The centre-back failed to stop him, and when the goalkeeper rushed out to cover the goal Garrincha dummied him, too. Fiorentina's goal lay open. But instead of putting the ball in the net, Garrincha waited for another opponent. When even that Italian had been dispensed with, Garrincha walked the ball into the net, kicked it up into his arms, and strolled back to the centre spot. The stadium was completely silent, apart from the voice of the captain, Bellini, shouting, 'Come on, we're actually on our way to the World Cup now!'

Garrincha had just scored one of the most famous goals of his career, but for the manager it was all that he needed to make up his mind. In the next match, against Inter Milan, Joel played. That match also ended 4-0, and Garrincha lost his place in the first eleven.

When the squad landed in Gothenburg, they were met by the Facit director from Rio. 'Uh-oh' Göransson had got to know Brazil's football bigwigs during the 1950 World Cup, and had taken Flamengo on their first tour of Sweden in 1951. He'd been employed to arrange all the practical details of Brazil's World Cup stay.

Since Brazil's group stage matches were to be played in Gothenburg and Uddevalla, the Swedish director had selected a picturesque hotel in the small town of Hindås as their World Cup base. Göransson had also, on the instructions of the Brazilian team's manager, ensured that the hotel management replaced all female cleaners, waitresses and receptionists with men. The only thing Göransson had missed was the fact that the favourites, the Soviet Union, who were in the same group as Brazil, had also chosen Hindås. From their facilities, they could look out over the football pitch that lay between the Brazilians' hotel and the nearby lake. The Brazil boss asked Göransson to find a pitch that was more sheltered, and the Swede duly found a grassy pitch five kilometres into the forest.

Brazil won their first World Cup match against Austria 3-0 without being particularly convincing. Their next match, against England, finished 0-0. Brazil were at risk of going out at the group stage if they didn't win the last match against the Soviet

Union, who had taken Olympic gold in Melbourne two years previously, and had the world's best keeper, Lev Yashin, on their team. Botafogo's captain, the thirty-three-year-old Nílton Santos, understood that *A Seleção* would have to change their line-up to be in with a chance. He called in the Brazil captain, Bellini, and told him he thought having Joel on the right wing wasn't working. Nílton Santos wanted to bring back the guy who had made a fool of him at that first trial for Botafogo five years earlier. 'Garrincha's unpredictability will put the Soviets' technical play out of joint,' Nílton said, also asking the team's manager to give Santos's seventeen-year-old superstar a chance. The next day, Feola held a press conference in which he surprised the international press by putting out an invitation to an open training session, the day before the match, on the pitch by the hotel. The Soviets noted the time, Friday 3 p.m., and went back to their hotel. What they hadn't understood was that Brazil's press invitation was a smokescreen for what was planned to take place in the morning, five kilometres into the forest. The reserves Garrincha and Pelé swapped jerseys with the first-team players and went into the first eleven. When the advertised training was scheduled to take place, the Soviets were left standing on the empty pitch in Hindås wondering where the Brazilian team had gone.

What happened in the match is often described as the best three minutes in Brazilian football. Straight from the kick-off against the Soviet Union, the ball found its way to the feet of Garrincha, who belted up his wing like Ferdinand the Bull after he'd been stung by a bee. Kuznetsov countered him. Garrincha veered to the left, then the right. Kuznetsov fell and Garrincha rushed on towards the penalty area. He dribbled past Krizhevsky and Voynov and got a good shooting angle. The shot hit the left-hand post and the spectators at the Nya Ullevi stadium got to their feet. Thirty-four seconds into the match, and still no Soviet player had had a touch of the ball. Yashin took a goal kick, and Botafogo's other star, the midfielder Didi, hunted the ball down and hit it long towards Pelé. The seventeen-year-old dribbled his way through the defence and hit a howitzer of a shot that made the crossbar sing. Fifty-five seconds had passed, and the crowd at the Nya Ullevi applauded. After just two minutes, Vasco's new star striker Vavá got the ball and dashed towards the penalty area. Just before the two centre-backs closed him down, he fired in a shot that Yashin couldn't stop: 1-0.

The Soviet Union never got a look-in, and lost 2-0. Brazil had qualified for their fourth World Cup quarter-final in a row. But more than anything, A Seleção had discovered a weapon that it was impossible to defend against – Pelé and Garrincha on the pitch at the same time.

In the quarter-final against Wales, Brazil won 1-0 and in the semi-final, the new first eleven smashed France 5-2. After the match, the French striker Just Fontaine, who was top scorer with nine goals, was asked what it was that made Brazil so unstoppable. 'They're tricky bastards, basically. If you mark Pelé, Garrincha takes the ball. And vice versa. And if you mark both, then up pops Vavá.'

On Midsummer's Eve, Sweden beat West Germany 3–1 in a tough semi-final. Despite the meticulous planning, the Brazilian management hadn't imagined that they would have to face the host nation, the only other team who played in yellow, and they hadn't taken an away kit with them. FIFA's solution was to offer to draw lots on who would get to play in yellow. The Brazil manager didn't like that idea, saying that if Sweden won the draw 'it would be good form to offer the away team the choice of shirts'. FIFA had never heard of any such rule, and held the draw without Brazil's involvement. Sweden won, and chose to play in their normal strip at the national stadium at Råsunda. This meant that Brazil's players had no shirts, with just a few days to go to the final. In fact, they didn't even know what the away kit was supposed to look like.

After the 1950 World Cup final defeat, one of Rio's daily papers had launched a competition to design a new kit. The white jerseys were seen to lack 'moral symbolism', and the newspaper, with the support of the national football association, challenged the country's designers to use the other colours in the Brazilian flag – yellow, green and blue. A nineteen-year-old illustrator won the competition, but never designed an away kit. Vicente Feola, who had spent the 1950 World Cup final on the sidelines, wasn't superstitious, and thought the team should play in white, but the players were having none of it. They saw how their colleagues' reputations had been dragged through the mud, and their lives had been destroyed after playing in white. Green wasn't too appealing either. The manager, who had worn the same brown suit every day since Brazil had beaten Fiorentina, was the most superstitious of them all, and suggested blue. His reasoning was that Brazil's patron saint, Nossa Senhora Aparecida, wore a blue cape, and that she had brought the team luck in the past. The fact that both Italy and Uruguay, who together had won four of the World Cup's five finals, had done so wearing blue was the argument that convinced the players. 'Uh-oh' Göransson recommended a shop in Hötorget, Stockholm, and the team's dentist and cash administrator headed off to buy eleven blue t-shirts. When they got back to the training camp at Bosön, the kitman cut the badges off the original shirts and sewed them on to the blue ones.

The fact that Sweden, who had won Olympic gold in 1948 and bronze in 1952, had knocked out the reigning World Cup holders West Germany in the semi-final meant that many thought the Swedish team had a good chance of winning the final. And, sure enough, after only four minutes, thirty-six-year-old Nils Liedholm made it 1-0 and suddenly millions of Brazilians glued to their radios had the 1950 World Cup on their minds. To show that the team intended to behave differently this time, the captain Bellini picked the ball out of the net, and gave it to Didi, who marched determinedly back to the centre spot. Shortly afterwards, 'Nacka' Skoglund hit a beautiful volley that curled towards the goal's top right-hand corner. The Brazilian keeper missed the ball, which sailed towards the net, only for left-winger Zagallo to appear and head it off the line.

In the next attack, Garrincha collected a pass and marauded in characteristic style down the wing. He dribbled past Sigge Parling and Sven Axbom and headed for the corner flag. He toyed with Orvar Bergmark before delivering a perfect pass to Vavá, who knocked in the equaliser. Twenty minutes later, Garrincha did the same again, passing three defenders before once again making the perfect pass to Vavá who made it 2-1. When Pelé made it 3-1 and Zagallo increased the lead to 4-1 in the second half, there was no longer any doubt. Brazil won 5-2, and the initiative Getúlio Vargas had started during the 1930s had born fruit. Brazil had laid to rest the ghost of 1950 – they had overcome the mongrel complex – and won the World Cup with a team that reflected the country's Indian, European and African heritage. In a column following the World Cup win, Nelson Rodrigues made peace with the country's past, writing that Brazil was no longer 'a withered bouquet of the three races'.

Happiest of all was Brazil's president Juscelino Kubitschek, himself a *botafoguense* who had watched the quarter-final against Wales at the presidential palace with Garrincha's father. Ahead of the final, Kubitschek boarded the presidential plane. He landed in the spot where, the previous year, he had initiated Brazil's boldest, craziest and most fantastical project, the construction of a new capital city on the unpopulated savannah in the centre of the country. The new capital was to be built to a modernist blueprint. By the time the final was played at Råsunda, Brasília had already taken shape. Sixty thousand construction workers had installed the electricity, water and sewage infrastructure, and the president's residence was ready. Brazil's most famous architect, Oscar Niemeyer, had designed an elegant, low building with a glass façade, which was given the name 'Palácio da Alvorada', Palace of Dawn. A new dawn was indeed breaking for Brazil, and as soon as the final whistle had been blown at Råsunda, Kubitschek sent a telegram to the team in Stockholm: 'The new Brazil has won its first victories. Brasília's Brazil, planted in the heart of our fatherland, has created a new spirit to show us the way.'

For Kubitschek, the World Cup victory came as final confirmation that a new epoque had begun. The next year, João Gilberto released the first bossa nova album, *Chega de Saudade*, the carnival drama *Orfeu Negro* won the Palme d'Or in Cannes and the oil corporation Petrobras, which had been founded by Getúlio Vargas, discovered oil in the Amazon. Outside São Paulo, Volkswagen had set up Brazil's first car factory, and Scania had built South America's first HGV factory. It seemed as though Brazil was about to repeat the USA's cultural and economic success and become one of the world's influential powerhouses.

The year after Brazil's World Cup win, Botafogo, who had four World Cup final players in their team, were invited to tour Europe. The first match was to be against Sweden's AIK at the Råsunda, the stadium where the final had been held. Botafogo's international stars lost 1-0, and two days later the team travelled to Umeå, in northern Sweden, to play Gimonäs CK. Garrincha captivated the eight thousand spectators at Gimonäs's ground, and scored one of the goals in the match which ended 3-1 to Botafogo. Afterwards, the hosts arranged a party at a hotel in town, where the players were also staying. Twenty-five-year-old Garrincha was enjoying the northern Swedish hospitality, and asked a girl the same age as him, a hairdresser, to dance. The couple hit it off, and Garrincha asked his room-mate Nílton Santos to stay in the bar an extra hour or so. The following day, two police officers came to the hotel looking for Garrincha. He got scared, hid under the bed and thought he was being accused of rape. The police had actually come to do a blood test. The hairdresser he'd been with the previous evening had become worried – if she got pregnant, she wanted to be sure who the father was. Garrincha agreed to the blood test, and then continued on the fifty-five-day-long tour of Europe.

Nine months later, a representative of the Swedish embassy in Rio turned up in Botafogo's clubhouse with a document that he wanted Garrincha to sign. The document, which was translated into both English and Portuguese, stated that Garrincha was the father of a boy who'd been born at Umeå hospital on 10 February 1960.

Garrincha couldn't be contacted: he was with Botafogo on tour in Mexico.

Seventeen years later, in the winter of 1977, the British sports writer Ian Wooldridge was in South America to report on the two Grand Prix in Buenos Aires and São Paulo. The previous year, British driver James Hunt had won the Formula 1 title, and Wooldridge was there to write about his compatriot's attempt to retain the title. It was summer in the southern hemisphere, and with thirteen days between races the journalist flew to Rio for a few days' holiday. His bosses on the *Daily Mail* thought he might as well file some football pieces, seeing as he was in Brazil. They wanted him to interview Pelé – but the world's most famous footballer was in New York. Instead, the paper's local contact suggested Garrincha.

When Wooldridge checked into one of the hotels along the promenade in Copacabana, it had been six years since Garrincha had played his last professional match, and the Englishman was keen to meet the master of dribbling, who he'd been fascinated by since the beginning of his journalistic career. Wooldridge's first World Cup as a reporter had been the 1958 World Cup in Sweden, and he had also reported from the 1962 World Cup in Chile, where Garrincha was voted player of the tournament after almost single-handedly making Brazil *bicampeão*, double World Cup winners. Wooldridge encountered a star who'd put on weight, had become an alcoholic and who suffered from severe osteoarthritis in both knees. Garrincha had left his wife and eight daughters behind in Pau Grande, and had just had his first child, a son, with the queen of bossa nova, Elza Soares. During the interview, the boy, who was not yet a year old, climbed up on to Garrincha's knee, and Wooldridge asked, through his interpreter, how it felt to father a son after eight daughters. 'No, you're wrong there,' Garrincha answered. 'I already have a son. He lives in Sweden.'

An experienced tabloid journalist, Wooldridge got to work and rang the news desk in London. They in turn contacted the *Expressen* newspaper in Stockholm, and asked for their help in finding the son. Instead of searching through the register of births, *Expressen* took the direct route. The next day, the paper ran the headline 'Garrincha has a son in Sweden', and encouraged readers to get in touch if they knew anything.

'My uncle saw the headline, and rang us in Halmstad. They talked to Mum and wanted me to give them an interview. Dad wasn't happy about it. "It will only make things hard for you," he said. But I thought it sounded exciting. So my uncle rang *Expressen* and gave them our number,' Ulf Lindberg tells me, thirty-five years on.

The journalist who rang was the legendary reporter Sten Berglind.

'He wanted to know whether I'd met my biological father. I told it like it was: that I'd been left in a children's home after my birth and adopted nine months later by a family from Skellefteå. Then we moved to Halmstad. When I was seven my adoptive parents told me who my real father was and we decided not to make a fuss about it. Only a few of my closest friends knew.'

After Ulf Lindberg agreed to an interview, *Expressen* contacted a freelance photographer in Halmstad, who visited Ulf at home.

'He dragged me along to Örjans Vall, the local stadium, to take some pictures of me mucking around with the ball. It was winter and there was a lot of snow. At the side of the pitch, a bunch of HBK players were hanging around, and asked who was kicking the ball about in the middle of the pitch. It wasn't until afterwards that the photographer told them who he'd been photographing. They rang me and asked if I wanted to come in for a trial.'

Ulf Lindberg was seventeen and had a trial the following week for Halmstads BK.

'It went well for the first fifteen minutes. I mean, I'd played a bit before. But then the pain started. First in my knees, then in my hips. I wanted to play. But it was impossible.'

Ulf had inherited his father's osteoarthritis and limped off the pitch.

The Brazilian gossip magazine *Fatos e Fotos* was the first in Brazil to feature the Swedish son, who was the spitting image of his father – the same thick lips, big nose and brown eyes. The following year the World Cup took place in Argentina, and a Brazilian TV channel hired Garrincha as a studio guest. The Swedish newspaper *Aftonbladet* saw its chance to get a scoop, and offered to send Ulf out to Buenos Aires and arrange for father and son to meet for the first time.

'I was 100 per cent up for it. But everything took so long. We never got a reply from Garrincha. In the end my trip was cancelled. It was a shame. Imagine how brilliant it would have been to meet him there.'

What the son didn't know was that his father was a serious alcoholic and never even turned up in Argentina. Drink had taken over, and a month after the 1978 World Cup final Elza Soares left the marriage after she was beaten up by Garrincha. The twice World Cup winner was making a living by lending his name to a football school that had been set up by the social services in Rio to catch teenagers who were getting into bad habits. The head of social services saw how badly things were going for '*a Alegria do Povo*', the Joy of the People, as the spectators at the Maracanã called him, and paid a private doctor to take Garrincha to a clinic every Wednesday. But there was no halting his decline. On 20 January 1983, Garrincha died aged forty-nine. His best friend and long-serving team-mate at Botafogo and for Brazil, Nílton Santos, persuaded the local authorities to open the gates of the Maracanã, and, for the first and only time, place a coffin on the pitch. It was an ordinary Thursday and it rained nonstop. Still, thousands of fans turned up, from every club in the city, to pay their last respects to the player who embodied Brazil's most coveted talent – the ability to dribble. The day after, the wake continued in Pau Grande, where the residents hung a banner over the entrance to the textile factory: '*Garrincha, você fez o mundo sorrir, agora o faz chorar*', you made the world smile, now you're making it cry.

It wasn't until 2005 that Ulf Lindberg found his way to Brazil, when Swedish writer Fredrik Ekelund and filmmaker Lars Westman filmed the documentary *Garrincha och röda pölser*, Garrincha and Hot Dogs. Ekelund, who has organised football trips to Brazil ever since he wrote the book *Sambafotboll*, Samba Football, before the 2002 World Cup, invited Ulf and his football-playing son Martin on one of his trips – and as soon as they touched down in Rio there was a commotion. Every one of Brazil's TV channels had sent someone to the airport to interview Ulf Lindberg. To prove kinship, *O Globo*, Rio's biggest daily paper, took Ulf up the Sugarloaf Mountain, where the photographer asked him to roll up his shorts. The next day, the sports section's front page compared an image of Garrincha in action at the Maracanã with a picture of Ulf baring his knees. To show that the legs had been passed down all the way to the grandchildren, sixteen-year-old Martin came along too. Afterwards, Ulf travelled to Pau Grande to meet his sisters. When the old men in the town square caught sight of him, they burst into tears.

'I thought it was disgusting,' says Ulf. 'They're the same ones who, year after year, helped my dad drink himself to death. Gone along to every party he invited them to and drunk every glass at his expense. And they were sitting there blubbing. Well, I just felt like going up and saying: "Sorry, boys, it's too late. He's dead now. You should have thought of that before."'

Later that week, Botafogo organised a *churrasco* and invited the eighty-year-old Nílton Santos. When he caught sight of Ulf, he couldn't believe his eyes, and hugged the man who had been conceived in the hotel room Nílton Santos had shared with Garrincha in Umeå: 'It's totally insane. You look just like your father.'

I was also invited to the restaurant that day and saw how Nílton Santos, a man known in Brazil as 'the encyclopaedia of football', took a few steps back and stared at Ulf while tears ran down his cheeks. His wife put her arm around him and drew him away from the flashing cameras of the photographers. When we sat down to eat, Nílton Santos was still noticeably moved. I had the seat opposite him, and tried to liven things up with some anecdotes I'd heard about the 1958 World Cup final at Råsunda. It made no difference; Nílton Santos was just sitting on the merry-go-round of his memories, occasionally wiping his eyes with the napkins his wife passed to him.

'He looks so much like Mané, he looks so much like Mané. They even move in the same way,' he repeated.

When the waiters and the other guests realised who the visitor was, chaos broke out in the restaurant and Nílton Santos was left in peace. Everyone wanted to hug Garrincha's son.

When football enthusiasts around the world are asked to name the world's greatest player, there tends to be a fight. Those who vote with the head generally choose Pelé and rattle off his stats, which no other player has ever even come close to. According to Pelé himself, he scored 1,238 goals in 1,367 professional matches. What's certain is that he took part in four World Cup tournaments and won three. That lob over the head of Julle Gustavsson followed by a volley in the 1958 World Cup final is still seen as one of the greatest World Cup goals, and he was named Athlete of the Century by the International Olympic Committee – even though he never took part in the Olympics.

Those who vote with the heart, or belong to a younger generation, tend instead to view Diego Maradona as the best footballer of all time. The squat Argentinian, who has a religion named after him, is still an idol for new football lovers, who think his life story makes him more human and easier to identify with.

A similar debate occurs when Brazilians try to decide who is the country's best player. Although Pelé tops the statistics, most people choose Garrincha. Of the sixty international games Garrincha played, Brazil won fifty-two, drew seven and lost only one – the last, when Hungary beat Brazil in the group stage at the 1966 World Cup in England. Pelé played far more international games, and, what's more, he scored more goals, but he's thought to be *too* good. He married a white middle-class woman, attended high school during the time he played for Santos and went to university. He taught himself English and market economics and exploited his own brand. But he denied paternity of two of his seven children, charged for interviews and referred to himself in the third person. Garrincha married a black woman, a rape victim from one of Rio's poorest favelas, acknowledged paternity for all his children and let everyone rip him off.

Because a large proportion of Brazilians are exploited in a society that still hasn't cut itself loose from its roots in nineteenth-century slavery – even now, in the twenty-first century, Brazilian buildings are built with two lift systems, one for the nobles and one for the servants – most see more of themselves in Garrincha than in Pelé. The fact that Garrincha had fourteen children with five different women means that he represented the old sexual ideal that some Brazilian men still try to live up to – the more women you conquer, the more manly you are. When Garrincha's daughters sued the author of the Garrincha biography *Estrela Solitária* because he had described their father as a sex machine, the court in São Paulo acquitted the author: 'To state that someone has genitals measuring twenty-five centimetres in length does not constitute grounds for defamation; on the contrary it is a compliment. It is manly, and in our country at least, it is something to be proud of,' said the judge.

The fact that Garrincha is bigger that Pelé in Brazil, and that his reputation can even seduce the country's judiciary, came as a complete surprise to Ulf during his stay.

'Of course I knew he was big. I understood that much from the number of Brazilian journalists who'd come to Halmstad and interviewed me. But I had no idea he was so big.'

When Ulf turned fifty, he was invited by a samba school to join the parade in the carnival in Rio. And when *A Seleção* played against Sweden in Råsunda's last international match, in summer 2012, he was invited to Stockholm by the Brazilian foreign ministry. The ambassador wanted him to represent his father and meet the other legends from the 1958 World Cup final before the stadium was rased to the ground. For the first time, Garrincha's son was going to meet Pelé.

'I'd been promised that we would get a bit of time to talk. You know, I wanted to know more about Dad, but Pelé didn't have time. He was off to a dinner at the royal palace and had to go.'

Garrincha's son is now fifty-three, has four children and is only able to work part-time because of the osteoarthritis in his knees. For the last eight years he's been earning money selling hot dogs from a fast-food van that he rolls into the main square in Halmstad. Since *Garrincha och röda pölser* was shown on Swedish national television in the spring of 2006, not a day has passed without someone mentioning his dad.

'It's mostly immigrants who are curious. Yugoslavia and Hungary were big footballing countries in Garrincha's days. But in the evenings, when the Swedes get a bit more lubricated, even they dare to ask questions', Ulf says, laughing.

The thing Ulf regrets most is that he never met his biological father. The only contact they had with one another was two letters Garrincha got a friend to write for him in English and sent to Halmstad. In them, Garrincha encouraged his son to become a professional footballer. No other letters came. Garrincha's last interview was done by an Argentinian sports reporter who met him in the summer of 1981, a few months before he went into hospital. 'I asked if he had a picture of his son in Sweden and almost regretted it. "Mané", who had been very calm, became nervous when he couldn't find the photo. He started shouting, asking his wife for help. It wasn't until he found the picture in his wardrobe that he calmed down. He proudly showed his son off and asked to be photographed, holding the picture up by his face,' the Argentinian reporter told ESPN. The picture Garrincha held up is the one in which Ulf is mucking around with a ball at his local football ground.

'I'm glad that he knew about me and was proud, in any case,' Ulf says.

Before the 1966 World Cup in England, there was a moment when father and son could have met. Gunnar Göransson had become the chairman and director of football for Flamengo, and convinced João Havelange to set up the Brazilian training camp at Kopparvallen stadium in Åtvidaberg. For a week, Garrincha, Pelé and the rest of the international stars were in Sweden, where, among other things, they played a friendly against Sweden at a packed Nya Ullevi.

'I was six and a half then. He could have got in touch. He could have done that, you know? Maybe he tried, but Mum didn't want to. I don't know.'

Ulf's adoptive mother is seventy-seven, and after three clots on the brain she can't say much about what went on during Ulf's childhood. Ulf has never been in contact with his biological mother either.

'I just think that if she wanted to get in touch, she'd get in touch.'

The same evening the documentary *Garrincha och röda pölser* was aired, Ulf's mobile rang. He saw that it was a number starting with 090, the local code for Umeå, and got nervous.

'I thought "Oh bloody hell, it's her calling."' But it wasn't. It was a younger sister he'd never known he had. Through his sister, who was also given up for adoption, Ulf found out that his biological mother had recently died of cancer.

'It was a shame I never got to meet her either, but I get by all right. Last week they called from Brazil again, wanting to invite me to a football conference in Rio. And I've been promised tickets for the World Cup in 2014. I really want to travel there again.'

Ulf falls silent on the telephone before continuing.

'Sometimes I can think of nothing but Rio. Just imagine

buggering off there every winter in October and coming back at the end of April. And escaping this bloody weather. Wouldn't that be perfect? I could have taken the van and set it up by the beach in Copacabana. You know? Who could resist buying hot dogs from Garrincha's son?'

4

'That's enough, Pelé, it's you and ten others!'
At home with a four-time World Cup winner

The Barra da Tijuca district was built in the 1980s for the fright-
ened middle classes who felt life had become too crowded and
violent in Rio. An area of marshland was filled with sand, and
hundreds of skyscrapers were built in rows along the Atlantic.
Because mortgages were more or less impossible to get at the time,
the flats were bought by those with access to easy money: corrupt
officials, drug lords, the gambling mafia, private doctors and
construction entrepreneurs. People from another walk of life were
buying the flats, too: the country's professional footballers. In the
flashiest, most gated communities, Ronaldo and Ronaldinho have
their mansions; in the more ordinary luxury villas live the national
stars. Because the borough was laid out by the same urban planners
who created the futuristic Brasília, walking is a rarity here. Barra
da Tijuca is built for cars, and life circulates between the home,
the beach and the ever multiplying shopping malls. If I can, I
generally avoid coming out here. Those of us who live in 'real' Rio
tend to refer to the borough as 'Brazil's Miami'.

In the middle of the promenade lives the most successful man
in Brazilian football. He has won two World Cups as a player and

two as a coach. He's also been in a fifth World Cup final, and won Olympic bronze and a multitude of national titles, both as a player and a coach. But after the 2006 World Cup in Germany, where he was assistant coach, he retired. Today, Mário Lobo Zagallo is eighty-one years old. He recently became a widower, after his wife Alcina's sudden death.

In order to be allowed into the residential complex Parque Atlântico Sul, I have to show ID and have my photo taken in a bullet-proof booth with armed guards. The kidnapping paranoia that spread throughout Brazil in the 1990s still has the country's wealthy in its grip. The concierge rings up to Zagallo's maid to double-check before I am let into the complex, which has its own roads, tennis courts and play areas. Zagallo lives in one of the complex's twenty-two-floor buildings.

He meets me at Reception, in a pink Ralph Lauren shirt and his favourite washed-out black jeans. He's slimmer than when we met a few months ago. It's evident that being alone after almost sixty years of marriage has taken its toll. We take the lift up to a communal area on the second floor of the skyscraper. The white leather sofas, flower arrangements and pleasant lighting create the feel of a hotel reception.

He sits easily in the white armchair, as is his custom when he has visitors. We're going to talk about the 1970 World Cup in Mexico, and what came to be known as the greatest football team of all time. But before we get into that story, there's some background to cover. We need to take a look at one of Brazilian football's biggest legends. The man whose statue greets you at the entrance to the Maracanã's museum.

When Fidel Castro toppled the Batista regime in Cuba on New Year's Day 1959, a wave of self-confidence flooded South America.

The Cuban revolution demonstrated that it was possible to remove US-supported dictators. The CIA picked up the signals and instructed their ambassadors on the continent to be on their guard.

One of those who celebrated Castro's revolution was Brazil's vice-president João Goulart. In 1961, he invited Che Guevara to the newly inaugurated capital, Brasília, and awarded him the country's highest medal. Two weeks later, Brazil's president died and Goulart succeeded him. The US immediately pricked up its ears. It was one thing for Cuba, a mid-sized island in the Caribbean, to shift to the left; another thing altogether for Brazil, the biggest country in the southern hemisphere, to do so. The CIA immediately set up a working group to establish which political direction João Goulart was intending to take.

The first thing the group found out was that the new president intended to implement agricultural reform. Goulart also wanted to address illiteracy and introduce universal suffrage. Previously, only educated people were entitled to vote, which excluded large sections of the black population. The educational reform was to be paid for with taxes and by increasing the role of the state in the business world. Goulart also wanted to impose a ceiling for the profits that foreign firms could take out of the country. For the CIA there could be no doubt – Brazil was turning to communism.

The working group presented a plan of how the USA could stop Brazil becoming a socialist state. President John F. Kennedy approved the plan, which, among other things, involved supporting elements of the Brazilian media willing to produce negative news items on João Goulart. The president also tasked the US ambassador with scoping the terrain among the Brazilian right wing: was there any interest in deposing the new president? The leaders of the Brazilian right-wing party, which was run by land-owners and business leaders, were receptive, as were parts of the military. The difficult thing for the CIA was finding out which military personnel were against Goulart's policies and which were for them. It wasn't until two years later, after Kennedy had been assassinated, that the military figures interested in staging a coup had been identified. Now, though, all that was needed was to name a date and get the green light from the White House.

On Friday 13 March 1964, the Brazilian trade union confederation arranged a political rally with João Goulart in the park opposite the defence ministry. Never before had such numbers, more than 150,000 people, gathered to listen to a president in Brazil. João Goulart was riding an unprecedented wave of popularity, and took the opportunity to introduce two new laws: the assets of foreign oil companies were to be nationalised and taken over by Petrobras, and a government department was to be created to manage the agricultural reforms. The political shindig was rounded off with a concert by Garrincha's partner, the queen of bossa nova, Elza Soares.

Several followers of the banned communist party had also sneaked into the crowd. They were waving red flags and holding up banners demanding the ban be repealed. When TV footage reached the USA, the CIA demanded an immediate meeting with Kennedy's successor, Lyndon B. Johnson, and suggested their plan should be implemented. The president authorised the CIA operation, which had the codename 'Brother Sam'. Four American ships were loaded with weapons, ammunition and diesel, and headed off to offer support in case the coup encountered any patrols. The convoy, escorted by six destroyers from the Caribbean fleet, also included a battleship and an aircraft carrier with twenty-five fighter planes. When it arrived off the coast of Rio de Janeiro, the Brazilian generals were ready to take over. On 31 March, the 4th Military Region rolled into Rio, and João Goulart fled to his farm in southern Brazil. The next day, one of the generals declared himself president and the USA became the first country to acknowledge the Brazilian military regime. The twenty years of working towards a democracy since the Vargas dictatorship had gone up in smoke. The military took over the ministries and hounded Goulart's supporters. Two and a half months after the coup, the security services knocked on the door of Elza Soares's and Garrincha's home. They wanted to know why she had performed at Goulart's political demonstration. When Elza refused to reply, they pushed her up against the wall.

'For God's sake, don't hurt my angel,' Garrincha said.

The policemen cared little about what the country's best-loved footballer said, and turned the house upside down in search of left-wing propaganda. Before they left the celebrity couple, one of the policemen stuck his hand into Garrincha's bird cage and took out his pet canary. The agent broke the bird's neck and threw it on the floor.

The chaos that followed the military's seizure of power even infected football. As reigning champions, Brazil automatically qualified for the next World Cup, and their only chance to test their team ahead of the World Cup in England in 1966 was in their training matches. The management couldn't decide on a strategy and so ended up selecting forty-four players for the tournament. It was also unclear who was in charge. The manager Feola, who had led the team to World Cup victory in 1958, was back, but his poor health meant the fitness coach tried to take control. The lack of structure became evident as the Brazilian team assembled in Sweden ahead of the World Cup. Not once at the training camp at Åtvidaberg did Brazil play the same eleven twice. When the team landed in Liverpool with the aim of winning their third World Cup in a row, the management ratcheted up the discipline and refused to let the Beatles meet Garrincha and Pelé. The management, which included several members of the military, were of the opinion that a meeting with the long-haired musicians would ruin the players' concentration. Their decision didn't help. After losing the second match of the group stage 1-3 against Hungary, seven of the players were replaced. In the last group stage match against Eusébio's Portugal, the reigning world champions were knocked out of the World Cup, once again losing 1-3.

For the first time since the 1930 World Cup in Uruguay, Brazil had failed to get further than the group stage. The media back home, which suffered censorship where politics were concerned, could write whatever they liked about football and took their frustration out on their team. The chairman of the football association João Havelange was intensely criticised and searched feverishly for a manager who could calm things down. In an outburst of bravery, he chose João Saldanha.

At the end of the 1950s, when João Saldanha was director of football at Botafogo, he'd jumped into the role of A-team coach and won the 1957 Campeonato Carioca without any prior coaching experience at all. Saldanha was also present in Umeå in 1959, when Garrincha met the hairdresser, and continued to coach Botafogo until 1960. After that, he worked as a sports journalist for one of Brazil's biggest daily papers, and was a frequent guest on the country's top football programme, Grande Resenha Esportiva Facit. Viewers loved João Saldanha, who was a popular figure in Rio's bars. There was just one thing wrong with him: he was a member of the banned communist party, PCB.

Saldanha had joined Partido Comunista Brasileiro in 1945, and taken part in international party conferences in Beijing, Pyongyang and Warsaw. He'd been in prison in Brazil, been shot at a political rally and been forced into exile in Paris for a while. Saldanha was a thorn in the side of the military regime, but for João Havelange he was perfect: most of the country's journalists idolised him.

The first thing Saldanha did as manager was list his ten commandments:

1. I want eleven animals who can fight for ninety minutes.
2. We will be afraid of no one.
3. But we will be humble.
4. I will give everyone freedom in a system that allows freedom for everyone.
5. No backlines of more than four defenders.
6. We mark when the ball is theirs, and stop marking when the ball is ours.
7. We will not go along with anyone's game-sabotaging system.
8. It is more important to become three-time world champions than to earn money.
9. Everyone takes part in the game, just like in basketball.
10. The only thing that is unforgivable is getting into a situation that leads to a sending off.

Saldanha knew which players he wanted to use and built up a first eleven from Santos and Botafogo players. He also rejected the old idea that Pelé and the new star striker Tostão couldn't be on the pitch at the same time – previously they'd been thought to step on each other's toes. The result was Brazil's most lethal attack ever. The new team won their qualifying group for the 1970 World Cup in Mexico with a 23-2 goal difference. The only uncertainty was who would act as reserves for Pelé and Tostão. For Saldanha, such a problem was a luxury. He had four strikers to choose from and planned to select the ones who were on form when the time came to register the players for the World Cup.

Brazil's new dictator, Emílio Médici, was of a different opinion. After enacting a coup within a coup, he had gathered all power around himself, unleashing mass arrests, torture and murder on the opposition. Aside from fascism, his biggest passion was football. Ahead of the match against Argentina, three months before the World Cup, the dictator called in the media and told them his favourite player at Atlético Mineiro, Dadá Maravilha, ought to be selected as a reserve striker: 'He's an excellent striker who will be able to resist the tough Europeans. What Brazil needs is players who run on the wings. As I see it, no goals are going to come from the middle. We'll only be able to score headers from free-kicks,' Médici explained. Saldanha lost his cool when he heard what the dictator, who had forced many of his friends into exile, was saying about the team he'd put together. The following day, the manager responded to the dictator in a TV interview: 'You choose the ministers for your government, I'll choose the players for my team.'

Saldanha not only declared war on Brazil's most powerful man, he also turned against his own team's most important player. The manager was irritated that Pelé was intending to use the 1970 World Cup to earn the money he owed the bank after being tricked by the Spanish businessman. Pelé wanted to sign an individual contract with the football association that would give him a fatter match bonus than all the other players put together. But Saldanha was a communist and didn't want the player earning more than anyone else. When he criticised Pelé's goal drought with the national side, implying Santos had been overplaying him with seventy-eight matches in a year, he made his first enemies in the press. A short time after that, the national team's doctor announced that Pelé was short-sighted, and rumours began to circulate that Saldanha planned to give him the boot. When someone broke into the team's clinic, stealing the doctor's notes, Saldanha accused the media of being behind the break-in. Flamengo's coach Dorival Yustrich, who sympathised with the generals, exploited the situation, calling Saldanha 'an incompetent fool' in a radio interview.

When the manager heard what Yustrich had said about him, he asked the football association's driver to give him a lift to Flamengo's team residence, where they were staying in preparation for that Sunday's match. 'Why've you got a pistol stuffed in your trousers?' the driver asked. 'I'm going to settle a matter of honour,' Saldanha replied. It was almost ten in the evening when the football association's white camper van pulled up outside Flamengo's house in São Conrado. Saldanha shoved the security guard out of the way and went into the hall with his revolver drawn. On the ground floor he found only Flamengo's cook. The Brazil manager walked up the stairs, where he ran into Flamengo's goalkeeper. 'I don't know who you are, but if you come near me, I'll shoot,' Saldanha said, pointing his Colt .38 at him. Then he searched each room. Yustrich wasn't there. Disappointed, the manager went out to the van which was waiting with the headlights off but the engine running.

The next day, the football association called a crisis meeting. Flamengo's chairman wanted to report Saldanha to the police, but João Havelange convinced him to let it go. Management figures also defended Saldanha, saying that this was the third time Yustrich had launched a personal attack on their manager. Even the media showed some understanding. They knew that Flamengo's coach had deliberately provoked Saldanha in order to knock him off balance, thereby increasing his own chances of taking the reins with the national side. But the football association's administrative head threatened to resign unless Saldanha was sacked. Later that evening, Flamengo's chairman changed his mind and reported the matter to the police.

Saldanha had selected the players, chosen the formation and over-seen Brazil's best ever qualification round. He'd also planned the tournament in Mexico down to the last detail and had found an appropriate place to stay, even going so far as to tell the hotel's owner to freshen up the hotel's football pitch at the Brazilians' expense. But the stress of the championship had worn him out, and it was deemed that the risk of him having another outburst if someone criticised him was too great. For João Havelange, it was a tough decision to make. Four days after Saldanha had forced his way into Flamengo's villa, Havelange called him into the football association's head office and fired him. With six weeks to go before their departure to Mexico, Brazil's best ever team found themselves without a manager.

Mário Zagallo has almost no hair left on his head, his thin arms are covered in blotches and his belt is fastened tightly round his narrow waist. He looks more like a pensioner in an old people's home than the most decorated man in world football. Almost throughout the interview he reclines in the white armchair, but when I mention Saldanha Zagallo's eyes flash. He throws his body forward and locks eyes with me.

'Saldanha was crazy! It wasn't just that he invaded Flamengo's villa with a drawn revolver. He didn't look after *A Seleção*. Once he forgot to go down into the dressing room at half-time and tell them who was being substituted. Instead he was in the press box, firing up the journalists. He was always courting controversy.

'The result was that the team came back on to the pitch with twelve players for the second half. You can't do that if you're on your way to the World Cup!'

Zagallo was thirty-nine in 1970, and coached Botafogo, who he'd turned into Brazilian champions the previous year. One day in April, when he was taking the team's afternoon training session, he saw a car draw up alongside the pitch. The fitness coach went to see who it was, and ran back: 'It's the football association. They've fired Saldanha. They want you to be the new manager!' Zagallo went over to the car, and the director of the Brazilian team opened the rear door.

'He asked me to jump in the back seat and then they drove me home to get a change of clothes. Then we went directly to the team meeting. There was never a doubt in my mind. It was written in the stars that I should take over that team. After all, most of the players were my boys from Botafogo.'

Zagallo leans back again.

'I didn't like Saldanha's 4-2-4 game. We needed something else.'

Zagallo takes my square-ruled A4 pad, and rests it on his knee. With a shaky hand, he draws the team formation that came to define a style.

'I kept Tostão up front and put Pelé just behind and to the right. In left midfield, I brought Rivelino into the first team, and on the right wing I put Jairzinho. In the centre I had defensive midfielders Gérson and Clodoaldo. The backline was more or less the same as Saldanha's. Everaldo on the left, centre-backs Piazza and Brito, and the right-back Carlos Alberto,' Zagallo says, drawing a long arrow showing that Carlos Alberto had the freedom to join the attack.

'And then I replaced the goalkeeper. You can't go to the World Cup with a nervous twenty-two-year-old. A World Cup keeper needs experience.'

He chose thirty-two-year-old Félix from Fluminense.

Zagallo draws circles to show how the players should move around in his ground-breaking 4-3-3 formation:

'We would attack with seven men and defend with nine. And as soon as we lost the ball we would withdraw to the centre circle.'

On 1 May 1970, a month before the World Cup was due to start, the squad went to Mexico. Saldanha had chosen the pleasant cultural city of Guanajuato, which lies on a plateau between Mexico City and Guadalajara, as his base. His plan was that the players would have time to acclimatise to the lack of oxygen in the high altitude, in case the team reached the final – which was to be played at the Azteca Stadium, 2,241 metres above sea level in Mexico City. The fact that the team had a month's preparation time in situ before the World Cup kicked off also gave Pelé time to recuperate.

'During a training session, Pelé came up to me. We'd been good friends ever since we won the World Cup together in 1958 and 1962. You could see that he'd been affected by the way Saldanha had treated him. He said: "Zagallo, do what you want. Put me on the bench, kick me out, but be fair. If you think I can play, I want to play." I said to him: "That's enough, Pelé, it's you and ten others. There is no one else."' What Saldanha had done to him was bullying, plain and simple.

The players and press corps complained about the hotel and the city Saldanha had chosen. There was no beach, no nightlife and the Mexican girls were much less interested in the world-famous players than the Swedish girls had been in 1958. Zagallo, however, was not complaining.

'For me it was perfect. We hadn't come to have a party. In Sweden things were totally different,' Zagallo says, lighting up.

'The Swedish girls would go up and stick their fingers into a player's hair just to see what an Afro felt like. They loved our black kids. And I'll never forget the time we were with Botafogo in Umeå. The sun refused to set. It could be the middle of the night, and still the sun was shining. We just didn't get it . . . That evening it wasn't just Garrincha who had his fun. Even we white players had a good time.'

In Guanajuato, the players followed a strict training schedule to maximise their physical fitness and settle them into the new 4-3-3 formation. Carlos Alberto Parreira was the fitness coach and worked with the players until the other countries in their group arrived. Then he was given the task of spying on the opposition. The evening before each match, he and Zagallo held tactical slide shows for the squad.

The first match was played against Czechoslovakia at the boiling Jalisco stadium in Guadalajara. After only twelve minutes, the Czechs took the lead. Saldanha, who'd been hired as a pundit for TV Globo, let his *schadenfreude* get the better of him – he blamed the goal on Zagallo abandoning his 4-2-4. Twelve minutes later, Pelé took a tumble just outside the penalty area, and the referee blew for a free-kick. Rivelino and Pelé stood either side of the ball, and the Czech wall was unsure how to position itself. Rivelino took advantage of their uncertainty and curled the ball around the wall and into the net. In the second half, Brazil found their feet and Pelé was so happy when he scored that he stopped, jumped and punched the air with his fist – an uncommonly lively goal celebration for that time. The classic image of Pelé was taken, and the star had put his former manager in his place. Two minutes later, Botafogo's Jairzinho made it 3-1, and when he made it 4-1 at the end of the match Brazil could relax and start preparing for the next match in the group stage – which had already been presented as the real final of the tournament.

It was the reigning champions against the double World Cup winners. The ones who invented football against the ones who took it to a new level. The team who didn't let any goals in against the team who scored the most. It was Europe vs South America. England vs Brazil. Bobby Moore vs Pelé.

'It was like playing chess. Incredibly even, and yet open. Either team could have won,' Zagallo says.

In the first half, Pelé received a perfect ball in front of goal, which he headed like a missile towards the base of the post. He drew breath to cry '*GOOOOOOL!*', but at the last minute Gordon Banks got his hand to the ball and managed to sweep it out. That save is still said to be one of the best of all time. After that, Francis Lee rocketed forward and headed into the arms of Félix. The ball rebounded off the Brazilian goalkeeper, who only managed to stop it just before Lee reached it. In the second half, Tostão crossed the ball to Pelé in the penalty area; he rolled it on to Jairzinho. It was a textbook example of how a trio of attackers should work together to break through a solid backline. Bobby Moore was beaten and Jairzinho made it 1-0. The score stayed that way for the rest of the match. Then Romania were beaten 3-2, and Peru went out 4-2 in the quarter-final. In the semi-final, Brazil faced the worst imaginable opponents: the ghost of Maracanã 1950.

'My players were young, you know: they'd hardly been born when *Maracanazo* took place. But our damn journalists did everything they could to put the wind up them. They told one horror story after another, and the evening before the semi-final I had to calm them down during practice. There was absolutely nothing to be afraid of. The team we were going to play were a totally different Uruguay from the one that won in 1950.'

But it made no difference what Zagallo said. That Brazilian

finesse had vanished and during the first fifteen minutes Uruguay had two dangerous chances on goal. In the nineteenth minute, Carlos Alberto gave an unnecessary backpass to the centre-back Brito, who got nervous and accidentally passed to an opponent. The ball quickly went to Cubilla who took it on his thigh and shot. Félix should have come out to cover, but for some reason he stayed by the post, not even trying to stop the ball. 1-0 Uruguay. The ghost of the Maracanã hovered over the packed Jalisco stadium. It wasn't until a minute before half-time that Clodoaldo managed to equalise.

Zagallo leans his slight frame forward again.

'I shouted at them in half-time: "What the hell are you doing?! Are you insane? How the hell can you let them score a goal against us! We are twenty times better than this team. Now go out and win this match! I don't intend to accept defeat."'

In the second half, it was a transformed Brazil that walked out on to the pitch. Jairzinho scored his sixth goal in five matches, and when Rivelino made it 3–1 in the closing minutes Zagallo rushed on to the pitch and threw himself on the heap of players. Despite only two months in charge, he'd made it to his third World Cup final.

There they were to face Italy, whose players had excelled themselves during the semi-final against West Germany – which, after its dramatic extra time, is still known as 'the game of the century'. Because Italy had also won two World Cups, the 1970 final had become a battle to determine which team would get to call themselves the best footballing nation in world history – as well as carrying home Jules Rimet's cup for good.

There was never any doubt. Saldanha's tactic of setting up base in the mountains had the desired effect. The Brazilian team coped well with the high altitude in Mexico City and won 4-1. The last goal was a *golaço*. Pelé got the ball just outside the penalty arc and knocked it nonchalantly to the right without looking. He knew that the right-back from Botafogo, Carlos Alberto Torres, would come up. And he did. The thumping shot, which was given extra speed by the thin air resistance, became a World Cup classic, and football lovers around the world took the Brazilian team to their hearts. In England, the Brazilians were given the name 'the Beautiful Team', and the Brazilian style of playing signalled the birth of modern football.

'We were good – no doubt about it,' Mário Zagallo says. 'But everyone was good in 1970. Just look at England – they've not had a team like that since. Or the Germans with Beckenbauer. Even Romania and Peru had great teams. For me, 1970 was the greatest World Cup ever.'

I ask whether Saldanha came down from the TV booth to congratulate him on his success.

'Him! We weren't even on speaking terms. He thought I was the dictatorship's lackey because I put Dadá Maravilha in the squad. It was so ridiculous. Dadá Maravilha wasn't even on the bench. If I'd wanted to toady up to Médici I would have played his favourite player, right? The only time I had anything to do with Médici was a welcome ceremony in Brasília when we got home. We talked about football for forty minutes. That was all. You have to learn to distinguish between football and politics.'

The rivalry between Zagallo and Saldanha continued to flare up over the years, and when the World Cup in Italy came around, twenty years later, the hatchet still hadn't been buried. Saldanha suffered lung problems caused by his smoking, and could only breathe with the help of oxygen. When he found out Zagallo was going to be a studio guest for the TV channel he usually worked for, he was beside himself. Saldanha went against his doctor's orders and flew to Italy to be an expert for 'his' channel. He was on his last legs, but he livened up on screen when criticising *A Seleção*, who he thought had become Europeanised and lost their character.

'We stayed in the same hotel in Rome, and he rolled around in his wheelchair in the foyer. It was horrible to see. He should have been at home in his sickbed,' Zagallo says.

After Brazil had been knocked out by Argentina in the last sixteen, Saldanha's health declined, and four days after the 1990 World Cup he died in hospital in Rome. The official cause of death was chronic obstructive pulmonary disease (COPD), but Brazilian reporters ascribed a different reason. In the obituaries, they wrote that João Saldanha died from his passion for football.

After his death, the football association in Rio commissioned a bronze statue of him to be placed by the entrance to the Maracanã's museum. The statue captures Saldanha in a typical pose. He is pointing his left index finger towards his forehead, as if to say: 'How dumb are you anyway?!' The gesture is not only typical of him, but of all Brazilians who are temporarily transformed into managers ahead of each World Cup.

Another character trait Brazil managers and supporters share is superstition. For the fans, it's important to see the match in the right company, in the right clothes and with the right routines.

When I moved to Rio de Janeiro, Brazil had just become World Cup winners for the fifth time. The streamers still hung from the lampposts, and the green and yellow flags still fluttered on the balconies. Around the town, supporters had sprayed the words '*Todo mundo tenta, mas só o Brasil é penta*', the whole world's tried, but only Brazil's won five. I was jealous when I heard about the gold party in Copacabana, and counted down the days until 2006, when I would finally be able to experience my first World Cup in Brazil. I knew it was something exceptional, and that it wasn't just a case of ringing round and deciding at whose place you were going to watch the match. Match companions had long since been decided, and consisted of the people with whom you'd most recently watched Brazil win the World Cup. Nothing could be changed. It might bring bad luck.

As the World Cup in Germany got going I accepted these cultural norms and watched the matches in town, or together with my partner and our two-year-old daughter. It went fine. Brazil won their group stage matches and pulverised Ghana 3-0 in the last sixteen. Before the quarter-final against France, one of our friends got cocky and invited us to his place: 'Bring your wife and baby. We're watching the match at home. The whole gang's coming.' More than twenty people crammed themselves in front of the shiny new plasma screen our friend had bought on credit. Most of them had seen the 2002 World Cup final together; many of them were even wearing the same clothes. 'I haven't washed this shirt since the gold party,' an acquaintance boasted as he wandered around smelling like a wrestling mat. At a free-kick in the second half, Roberto Carlos was straightening his socks, and lost his man, Thierry Henry, who made it 1-0 to France. I felt the stares burning into the back of my neck. When the final whistle blew, no one was speaking to me any more. I got the blame for the defeat. My presence had brought bad luck.

The same thing happened when I saw Botafogo lose in their debut in the second division against Vila Nova, a little club from the state of Goiás. After the match, one of my friend's football mates came over to him: 'You said this Swede would bring us good luck. So far it seems he's mostly brought us bad luck.'

Another time, when I was in a more or less full to capacity Maracanã, Botafogo made a spectacular comeback to 4-4 against Vasco. As a result, the team went through to the Taça Rio, in the Campeonato Carioca, and my friends wanted me to postpone a trip so I could be there for the final. My presence would bring good luck.

A few years ago, when Botafogo had led the Brazilian league up until the eighteenth game then started losing, Cuca – one of Brazil's most superstitious coaches – wanted to shake the team up. On the way to a match, he stopped at a butcher's and bought a large, bloody ox heart, which he hung up in the dressing room. 'The team wasn't working any more, it had become cold. More blood was needed. To begin with, the players avoided the heart, but at the end of the warm-up, they were all boxing it. The heart was what we needed. We went and played a super-match,' Cuca explained afterwards.

Their rivals Flamengo also turn to higher powers for help. The club has hijacked the Catholic saint Judas de Tadeu and made him their own patron saint. In Rio, people pray to him in a church in the borough of Cosme Velho, just opposite the station where the cog train goes up Corcovado Mountain. In 1953, when Brazil's biggest club hadn't won a title for over ten years, the club's president drove to the newly opened St Thaddeus church to pick up the minister, Father Goés, who he knew to be a devout *flamenguista*. The president wanted Father Goés to hold a mass for the players in the club's own chapel. 'In the name of the holy apostle Thaddeus, I guarantee Flamengo will be this year's champions,' Father Goés said. The next day, the players went to St Thaddeus church, each lighting a candle in thanks for the priest's blessing.

When Flamengo became Carioca champions that year, their

rivals Fluminense, whose clubhouse and training ground are adjacent to the St Thaddeus parish, couldn't let it lie. The supporters demanded that the minister stop using the Catholic patron saint's power exclusively for Flamengo. Father Goés didn't appreciate the rival team's complaints, and replied: 'I'll make sure we win next year, too.' The patron saint took Flamengo's side once again. The Fluminense supporters were incensed, and implored the archbishop to stop Father Goés. It couldn't be done. For the third year in a row, Flamengo won the Campeonato Carioca, and, ever since, all *flamenguistas* pray to the saint whenever the club needs help.

Before important matches at the Maracanã, the players' bus still occasionally drives past the church, to provide extra strength. And when Flamengo are at risk of relegation from the Brasileirão, the whole team lines the pews. In 2010, Flamengo found themselves, for the fourth time in ten years needing a win in the last match of the season in order to keep themselves in the top division. Despite the fact that it had worked three times before, the club's then president, Patrícia Amorim, delayed the visit to St Thaddeus church. She's Jewish and didn't believe that a Catholic patron saint would be able to save such a hopeless situation. It wasn't until the board of the club forced her that she went along to the church, taking five of the club's most important players with her. One of those to receive a blessing was Paulo Victor. Today, a portrait of the goalkeeper hangs outside the mountain shrine behind the church. In the thirty-third minute, he made the save that kept Flamengo in the Brasileirão.

The St Thaddeus church lies fifteen minutes away from my house, and one Sunday I cycled up there to attend the Sunday mass which is generally held in English in the hope of tempting in tourists standing on the other side of the road, waiting for the train up to the Christ the Redeemer statue. First I went over to the shrine behind the church, where believers light candles. The greasy soot from the thousands of candles that burn in the mountain shrine every week lay like a film over the worn granite path. It was very slippery, and a sign encouraged elderly people to support one another, to stop the patron saint causing any accidents. Around the walls of the shrine, hundreds of other signs were hung: 'Thank you, Thaddeus, for curing my cancer', 'Thank you, Thaddeus, for making our child well again', 'Thank you, Thaddeus, for freeing our daughter from alcohol', 'Thank you, Thaddeus, for helping our son get into medical school'. One family offered thanks for being able to buy their dream flat by the beach; one man expressed joy about getting the job he wanted. The thank-you signs are shaped like Brazilian street signs and can be ordered from the church office. A small one costs ten dollars, a large one fifteen.

'As soon as Flamengo are on the rocks, their supporters come here. If they live far away they hire a bus. If their prayers are heard, they come back, light a candle or buy a thank-you sign as a souvenir,' the man at the church's sales counter tells me.

'They either put the signs up in the shrine, or they hang them at home, in their private Flamengo shrines. Before each match, they light a candle, pray for three points and touch the sign.'

Every year on 28 October, Judas Thaddeus Day is celebrated. Flamengo players generally take part in the mass, and, outside the church, hundreds of supporters gather and try to force their way into the packed church to catch a glimpse of their idols. Traffic comes to a standstill and for a few hours there's no way to get to the Statue of Christ as the train station is blocked solid.

When Father Goés conducted these ceremonial masses in the 1950s, he did so with a Flamengo shirt under his sleeveless mass vestments. The tradition has been observed by his successors. The last minister, Father Benedito, not only wore his Flamengo shirt on St Thaddeus Day, but also every Sunday there was a Fla–Flu, the classic Rio derby between Flamengo and Fluminense. When Father Benedito died in the summer of 2012, many were worried about who would take over. The new minister, Father Diegues, isn't interested in football, and the second priest, Father Valdir, has a secret.

After the English language mass, I wanted to interview Father Valdir. He invited me into the vestry. On the wall hung a depiction of the old Pope and the Virgin Mary, and Father Valdir pulled out a chair for me by the vestry's dressing table. He laid his hand over my wrist and asked me what I thought of Rio's beaches.

'It's so boring going to the beach on your own. Would you like to join me some time?' he asked.

I gave him a friendly smile and got straight to the point. I asked whether the rumours were true. Father Valdir blushed.

'OK, if you write that we'll lose our whole congregation. You can't do that. We need more people. The Pentecostal churches have been taking far too many lately.'

So it was true. Father Valdir was a *vascaíno*. He supports Vasco, Flamengo's worst rivals.

'If the *flamenguistas* find out about this, it's over. I hope you understand that,' he said, and had no more time to answer my questions.

Brazilian superstition isn't limited to religion. Numerology is also involved. The high priest of the Brazilian belief in the significance of certain numbers doesn't look like your average expert on these matters. He looks more like the pensioner feeding pigeons in the park. Eighty-one-year-old Mário Lobo Zagallo went so far as to change his name from Zagalo to Zagallo so that it would contain seven letters, a lucky number in many cultures. In the lift on the way to the ground floor of his skyscraper after my interview, I mention the subject.

'For everyone else, thirteen equals bad luck, but for me it's always brought good luck,' he says.

It started with him and Alcina getting married on 13 January. Then it turned out that the slogan 'Brasil campeão', which means 'Champion Brazil', contained thirteen letters. When Zagallo also realised that 5+8 and 9+4 equalled 13, he was convinced. In 1958 he won his first World Cup, and in 1994 he won his last World Cup.

A few years ago, Zagallo signed a new mobile phone contract and was given several numbers to choose from. Most mobile numbers in Rio start with 82, which many numerologists see as a celebration of the 1982 World Cup team, the most popular team Brazil has had since 1970. When Zagallo saw the rest of the numbers he was sold. His new number includes 82 58 94 13.

'Once, when I was checking in my baggage at the airport in São Paulo, the guy on the check-in desk said: "No way, Zagallo, not here too. Your bag weighs thirteen kilos!"'

The 2014 World Cup final will be played on 13 July. This has persuaded many Brazilians that Zagallo should be on the coaching staff. They think his connection to the number thirteen will contribute to Brazil winning their sixth World Cup. When the football association called in Carlos Alberto Parreira, whom Zagallo has been working with ever since the 1970 World Cup, as assistant coach for the new Brazilian team, Zagallo thought they would call on him, too. But no.

'It hurts, actually. I've won more World Cups than anyone in the whole world. And I saw Brazil lose at the Maracanã in 1950. I can help the new players exorcise that ghost if they reach that final.'

Zagallo wanted to be assistant coordinator for the team, but, instead, the football association asked him to be 'ambassador' in the run-up to the 2014 World Cup, together with Carlos Alberto, Ronaldo and the star of the Brazilian women's football team, Marta.

'What they don't understand is that I have to be there on the bench. I can't sit anywhere else, because the date will bring me luck. I have to be down with the players on the pitch,' says Zagallo, shaking my hand and turning into the lift.

The last I see of him is his finger on the lift button marked '13'.

5

'Democracy came to be associated with winning'
Sócrates and the football movement
that overturned a dictatorship

For a year, Corinthians' supporters' club, Gaviões da Fiel, the
Faithful Hawks, have been preparing for carnival in São Paulo.
They've chosen a theme for the parade, composed a samba and
decorated their carnival floats with the supporters' club's main
symbol – a hawk with an angry glare. In order to get over the
previous year's fiasco, when the Hawks' samba school ended
up in ninth place, they've contracted one of Rio's best *carnavale-
scos*. He has decided how the carnival floats should be decorated,
what carnival costumes the participants will be dressed in, and
how few clothes the dancers will wear. Thousands of supporters
have also been busy in the carpentry workshop, the kitchen,
the dance studio, the planning meetings and everywhere else,
pouring their souls into their work to make this evening as
colourful as possible.

When the Hawks' carnival procession, which consists of over
three thousand dancers and a samba orchestra with three hundred
drummers, bangs its way into the parade arena, Sambódromo do
Anhembi, thousands of *corinthianos* roar their enthusiasm. Once

again, the Hawks show that they, with 96,000 paying members, are far and away Brazil's biggest, strongest and wildest supporters' club. Although they're banned, rockets and flares have been smuggled in and let off all over the stands.

'*Bando de loucos! Bando de loucos!*', crazy gang, crazy gang, the fans yell, jumping around the concrete terraces in time to the beat.

The chanting and the smoke make the samba party feel just as much like a derby at Pacaembu as a carnival. For a few minutes I catch only brief glimpses of the enormous golden hawk which is leading the parade, looking ready for battle with its mechanical wings.

High up on the last float, in front of yet another golden hawk with a gaping beak, comes the surprise. The two-metre-tall star goalkeeper Cássio waves to the audience. It was his calm confidence that secured Corinthians' win over the club's counterpart in Argentina, Boca Juniors, enabling them to take home the 2012 Copa Libertadores. It was also Cássio who stopped Champions League winners Chelsea scoring when Corinthians beat them in the FIFA Club World Cup in Japan. This evening he's wearing the black shirt of the Hawks' members, and is celebrating his club's official crowning as the best football team in the world.

Beside Cássio dances an older man with grey, slicked back hair. The man is wearing a cream suit, white shirt, black tie and black sunglasses. He doesn't look as if he has much to do with either football or samba. He looks more like a tropical version of the Blues Brothers. Although I can still only see him from a distance, I realise it must be Washington Olivetto, Brazil's most successful advertising guru, who has won a total of fifty-three Golden Lions at the international advertising festival in

Cannes. Olivetto is one of Corinthians' most famous supporters and it is he who built up the club's best-known brand: the revolutionary football movement Democracia Corinthiana. This year, it is Olivetto and his advertising world that are the Hawks' carnival theme.

In addition to providing one of São Paulo's most spectacular carnival parades every year, the Hawks also arrange training for teenagers, pay for trips to away matches for poorer fans and hold a free samba party every Saturday in their enormous club building. Many people are impressed by the Hawks' unity and see the supporters' club as a contributing factor to Brazil managing to cut its ties with the generals' military dictatorship in the 1980s. At the same time, there are those who hate the Hawks, whose history is shot through with violence. In 2012, two Palmeiras supporters died after a fight at a derby, and, in the aftermath of this carnival, a fourteen-year-old Bolivian dies when Corinthians fans fire a flare into the home stands during an away match in Bolivia.

I've spoken to police who feel that the Hawks' operations have created a city within a city, a mafia that operates outside the law. Others think the Hawks' history is a heart-warming tale of marginalised people creating something together. Corinthians' supporters' union is neither black nor white, winner nor loser, heaven nor hell. It's everything at once.

Olivetto's golden float rolls through the sambadrome and one of the world's foremost advertising men sings along to the chorus.

'I am a Hawk. We're really crazy. This is true love.'

Corinthians are one of the few clubs who have managed to combine Brazil's two biggest passions – samba and football. The club was also the first to be established by working-class people.

In 1910, two painters, a cobbler, a truck driver and a construction worker met and founded Sport Club Corinthians Paulista. They took their name from the London team Corinthian Football Club, who had recently been on tour in Brazil.

The club's intention was to be close to the people and only have working-class players. Only four years after it was founded, the club demonstrated that it also had something the upper-class clubs lacked – genuine motivation. Corinthians won their first title in the Campeonato Paulista and soon became São Paulo's most popular club. In 1918, the club – which, for the first few years, had been playing home matches on a patch of waste ground – built its own stadium, with the help of its fans. There, the team went almost unbeaten for a decade, until the stands became too small. At the end of the 1930s and the beginning of the 1940s, Corinthians won the Campeonato Paulista four times out of five, and could draw over 70,000 spectators to the publicly owned stadium, Pacaembu, despite the fact that it only held 42,000.

In the mid-1950s, when São Paulo replaced Rio as Brazil's largest city, the competition increased and Corinthians stopped winning titles. The club started to lose top spot and was increasingly poorly managed. When Brazil became a military dictatorship in 1964, the cracks widened further as Corinthians' president sympathised with the dictatorship and joined the generals' party.

With the World Cup victory in Mexico in 1970, football was transformed into an instrument of propaganda for the regime, and when João Havelange became FIFA's new president he was replaced as chairman of the Brazilian football association by an army captain. The other posts in the association were taken by majors, admirals and lieutenants – the only civilian team managers who travelled to the 1974 World Cup in West Germany were the manager, Mário Zagallo, and the fitness coach, Carlos Alberto Parreira. The military propaganda machine wrote sambas and slogans. A sticker, featuring a motif of Pelé's bicycle kick, bore the motto: '*Brasil, ame-o ou deixe-o!*' Brazil, love it or leave it!

In order to stop the workers' movement attracting large crowds to the annual 1 May demonstrations, the military regime followed Franco's lead in Spain: they forced the football association to organise derbies in all the major cities. In Porto Alegro, arch-rivals Grêmio and Internacional played each other; in Rio, Flamengo and Fluminense, Botafogo and Vasco. In Belo Horizonte, Cruzeiro played Atlético; in Salvador, Bahia faced Vitória; in Recife, Sport were pitched against Naútico; and in São Paulo, Corinthians played Palmeiras and São Paulo FC played Santos. Instead of demanding employment, freedom and fraternity on 1 May, the supporters heckled each other. Opposition to the dictatorship was broken down and the generals held on to power.

At Corinthians, a group of young, educated and radical fans met in secret to discuss the running of Brazil in general and Corinthians in particular. In 1969, they formed the supporters' club Gaviões da Fiel, which came to be a thorn in the side of the club management and the military dictatorship.

However, there was one challenge the conservative club management and the radical Hawks could agree upon: lifting a cup once more. Corinthians hadn't won a single major title since 1954. It wasn't until the 1977 Campeonato Paulista that the club had a team to reckon with. Corinthians reached the final, and when midfielder Basílio put an end to Corinthians' twenty-three year-long dry spell with a goal that made it 1-0, one of

Rádio Globo's most famous commentators broke down. Osmar Santos was so excited that he ignored the censors and unleashed an uninterrupted 282-word tirade in which he squared up to the dictatorship and urged fans to take to the streets: '*Today is truly the day of the people. The day we can sing and be happy. The day we can go out with our guitars raised high. Today, more than ever, it's the day of the people. The people's party. Basílio! With just one small step. Basílio! Thirty-seven minutes into the second half. Life's sweet mystery . . . this Corinthians . . . inexplicable Corinthians, who find joy in the depths of the people's soul . . .*'

The win gave Corinthians the money and self-confidence to sign a promising player from a club in the interior of São Paulo state. The midfielder had been nurtured in a club that called itself Botafogo-SP, though it had nothing to do with its namesake in Rio. The player's name also had a famous origin. His parents had borrowed it from the Greek philosopher Socrates and added Brasileiro as a surname, so he became 'the Brazilian Socrates'. In 1979, the new star made sure that Corinthians became Paulista champions once more.

The Hawks' supporters' club grew and the club management lost ground. Since the beginning of the 1970s, the mining magnate Vicente Matheus had been Corinthians' director, dribbling his way around the club's regulations by regularly stepping down to the post of vice-president, while continuing his authoritarian leadership of the club. Just before the 1981 election, the Hawks grew tired of his manipulation and discussed proposals for a revolution with board member Waldemar Pires. The plan was to have Pires elected as the mining magnate's puppet – but when the election was over refuse to give way to Matheus. The coup was successful, and Matheus went crazy when he realised that the new president wasn't going to let him direct the club from his vice-presidential post. The new situation led the club's director of football to resign, asking his radical son, a thirty-four-year-old anthropologist, to take over.

One evening in late 1981, the new director of football was sitting with his intellectual friends in a bar in São Paulo when he caught sight of Brazil's most celebrated advertising director. Washington Olivetto had been awarded his first Golden Lion at Cannes in 1974, and was already a rich super-celeb in the town. Everyone knew he was also a *corinthiano* through and through. The director of football got straight to the point. He asked whether Olivetto wanted to be the club's head of marketing. Olivetto declined politely, explaining that he had his hands full with his ad agency. After a few beers, he said: 'OK, I'll do it, but on two conditions. I work for you evenings and weekends. And I don't want to be paid.'

Washington Olivetto's ad agency is situated on Rua Loefgreen, in the fashionable district of Moema in São Paulo. Previously, McCann-Erickson, one of the world's biggest advertising agencies, had their offices here, but in 2010 Olivetto's legendary agency W/Brasil merged with them, creating W/McCann.

Olivetto's desk stands at the end of an open-plan office where almost a hundred advertising creatives sit hunched in front of large, thin screens. There's no glass wall between the boss and his employees. Everything Olivetto says can be snapped up by passers-by. That's how he wants things: a creative, transparent environment. Olivetto clutches a cocktail while he discusses an upcoming campaign with an Art Director. He's half an hour late as he takes me by the hand, empties his glass and orders two espressos. His eyes shine as he casts his mind back and tells me about his unpaid job as Corinthians' head of marketing.

'The first thing I did was take out a full-page advertisement in the daily papers. The headline read: "Send an idea to Washington. We hear he's in need of one." In the picture, I'm scratching my head in front of a typewriter. The message was that everyone should send in any ideas that would help the club.'

The new signals from the leadership inspired Sócrates and the other players to challenge the tradition which essentially gave the club ownership of the players. After almost thirty years of authoritarian management at Corinthians, and almost twenty years of dictatorship in Brazil, the players longed for democracy. Sócrates wanted the players to be able to take part in decisions in all areas that related to them: transfers, first-team selection, departure times for away matches and means of transport. The new president liked the initiative and convinced the coach. Universidade de São Paulo also got whisked up by the winds of change, and invited Corinthians' director of football, their head of marketing and Sócrates to give a talk about their plans to democratise the previously authoritarian club.

Juca Kfouri, then editor-in-chief of Brazil's biggest football magazine *Placar*, chaired the session. He asked if the club was in the process of introducing some kind of 'Corinthian democracy'.

'When I heard him say "Corinthian democracy", I noted down the phrase straight away. Us ad guys are always on the hunt for words and slogans. Those two words captured everything we were trying to do,' says Olivetto.

The Brazilian football association had recently given the green light for adverts on club strips, and Olivetto had an idea. He asked a colleague at his advertising agency to make a logo for 'Democracia Corinthiana'.

'I told him it had to be both political and pop.'

The result was better than he'd anticipated. '*Democracia*' was written in large, blocky letters, with '*Corinthiana*' in a loopy Coca-Cola style. To remind people of the actions of the dictatorship, his colleague had splashed blood all over the logo.

When the players ran on to the pitch with the new logo across their backs, they looked like eleven living posters, protesting against the dictatorship. The military went crazy. Lieutenant Colonel Bastos, who was on the board of the Brazilian football association, called in Corinthians' president and told him the printing of political messages on club strips was prohibited. Olivetto was forced to remove the logo.

Despite this setback, the internal struggle for democracy continued undiminished. One thing the players wanted to change was match preparation. Before most home games, the players were summoned to a hotel more than a day in advance, with no visits or excursions allowed. They were all supposed to have turned off their lights by 10 p.m. Such routines, inspired by the military, applied to the majority of Brazilian clubs.

'It was moral law, plain and simple,' Washington says. 'They wanted to stop the players going out and partying the day before the match. But it didn't work. You can't keep horny twenty-year-olds locked up. The players sneaked out and bribed the receptionists when they came back.'

Sócrates told the club managers that the players wanted to have a vote on whether the early match gatherings should be stopped or not. Everyone, from the club director and the coach, to the players and kitman, got one vote. Unsurprisingly, Corinthians became the first club in Brazil to ditch the arrangement. Instead, the team would meet at the clubhouse a few hours before the start of a match.

Early on, Sócrates became the natural leader and spokesman for the Corinthians players, partly because he belonged to the fraction of Brazilian football players who had a university degree to his name when he became a professional: he had trained as a doctor during his time at Botafogo-SP. Sócrates stuck out on the pitch, too. He was tall, over six foot three, thin as a rake, and wore size five shoes. He tripped about like a ballerina on the pitch, and rarely indulged in complicated dribbling, preferring to make use of what may be the most elegant, effective backheel in the history of football.

Sócrates debuted in *A Seleção* as a twenty-five-year-old, and was made captain three years later, when the 1982 World Cup in Spain came around. The new manager Telê Santana wanted him to lead Brazil's fight for restitution; the team had missed out on a place in the 1978 final as a result of Peru's 0-6 loss against the host nation Argentina, a match which, in Brazil, had always been viewed as rigged, and with good reason. Sócrates had an incredibly talented band of team-mates at his side, among them Zico, Júnior and Leandro from Flamengo, the best club in Brazil at that time. Other big names were Éder and Toninho Cerezo from Atlético Mineiro and Roma's intelligent midfielder Falcão, the only foreign-based player in the squad.

If 'the Beautiful Team' from the World Cup in Mexico in 1970 was a strikers' team – Pelé, Tostão, Rivelino and Jairzinho all wore number ten for their respective clubs – then Telê Santana's Brazil side was the midfielders' team. Sócrates, Zico, Falcão and Éder were all attacking midfielders for their clubs.

During the first match against the Soviet Union in Seville, the crowd was curious about '*Quadrado Mágico*', the Magic Square, as the attacking midfielders were called in Brazil. The first thing that became apparent, however, was that another part of the team wasn't working: the keeper Peres let in an easy shot from thirty yards. It wasn't until the second half that the members of the Magic Square started to find one another. The players shot thundering long-range piledrivers, dribbled and danced in ever-wilder jigs around the Soviet Union penalty area. These dazzling technical feats, along with the constantly surprising positional changes, had the fans cheering. There was something about the team's kit, too: they wore simple, bright yellow t-shirts with a dark green crew neck, and the shorts were pale blue, tight and short. When Sócrates weaved his way across the pitch with his bushy hair and lush beard, he looked like a sexy, sporty Che Guevara.

In the seventy-fifth minute, the Brazilian captain picked up the ball just outside the Soviet penalty area, and worked his way to the right until he found his angle. The shot was hard, high and unstoppable. Sócrates had scored his country's first goal in the World Cup, and stood in front of the Brazilian stand. He raised his right arm in the air and clenched his fist like a member of the Black Panthers. The goal celebration, which he always made at Corinthians, also worked in Spain, which was starting to recover from Franco's dictatorship. In the closing minutes, Brazil increased the pressure, and the right-back Leandro, who set up most attacking moves, found Falcão with a pass across the edge of the penalty area. The Soviet defenders rushed out, and the keeper waited for the shot. But instead, Falcão let the ball run through his legs and on to Éder, who ploughed in a left-footer, giving the goalkeeper Dassajev no chance at all and settling the match.

Brazil scored another eight goals in two group-round matches, but still ended up in the trickiest of four final-round groups. Brazil were to meet Italy and reigning world champions Argentina, with only the group winners going through to the semi-final.

With nine days to go until the match against Argentina in Barcelona, there was plenty of time for expectations to flourish back in Brazil. Telê Santana's system struck a chord with the Brazilian people, and made the '82 team one of the most popular of all time. The attacking game was unpredictable and surprising. It was also beautiful to watch, but hard to mark – the opposition didn't know who out of Sócrates, Zico, Falcão or Éder would make a break for goal. The atmosphere at home was hardly dampened by the fact that Júnior, Flamengo's popular left-back, lent his voice to the World Cup song, called 'Voa Canarinho', Fly Canary, after the national team's nickname. All Brazil sang along to the chorus: '*Fly canary, fly! Show me what I already know!*'

The only thing that worried Telê Santana ahead of the match against Argentina was Diego Maradona, who had scored two goals against Hungary in the group round. In order to put a stop to Boca Juniors' twenty-two-year-old, Santana chose the defensive Batista as back-up. Batista would replace Zico if Maradona became too difficult to handle. Eleven minutes in, Éder had a free-kick. He took a long run-up, and the ball took off at 183 kilometres an hour. The Argentinian keeper managed to steer the projectile on to the crossbar, but the ball bounced down and up into the air again. Zico, following up, knocked it in to make it 1-0. The Brazilian reporters dubbed the shot '*Eder-cets*', after the Exocet missiles that had been fired at British ships during the Falklands War, which had ended just one day before the World Cup began.

In the second half, Brazil made it 2-0 and then 3-0, and the world champions were humiliated just as their country had been after the Falklands War. Maradona couldn't control himself: he jumped up with his studs out and kicked Batista, who had just replaced Zico, in the stomach. The referee took out his red card and Maradona's first World Cup was over. For the Canaries, on the other hand, they needed only a draw against Italy to secure their place in the semi-finals.

'*Brasil perto do título*', Brazil close to the title, screamed the front page of the country's biggest paper at the time, *Jornal do Brasil*. The fact that the Magic Square had danced around their opponents wasn't the only thing behind the optimism; Italy's national side was their worst in years. In the group stage, Italy managed no more than a draw against Poland, Peru and Cameroon, and got through by the skin of their teeth. The Italian star Paolo Rossi was also out of shape, after a two-year ban for his part in a match-fixing scandal.

Still, Rossi made it 1-0 with a header five minutes into the match against Brazil. Seven minutes later, Zico passed to Sócrates, who dribbled into the penalty area and shot at goal. The ball went between Zoff's outstretched legs and the left-hand post. Brazil were back on track. In the twenty-fifth minute, Brazil played the ball out of their own half, and midfielder Toninho Cerezo switched the play across to the other wing. It was a lazy pass, and was snapped up by Rossi, who ran unmarked towards the goal. 2-1.

The mood among the Brazilians on the pitch and in front of their TV sets grew tense. Italy's manager had studied Santana's system and figured out how to throw the Magic Square out of kilter. In the sixty-eighth minute Roma's Falcão finally equalised. Brazil were back in the semi-final. What happened next has been analysed as many times as Ghiggia's goal in the World Cup final at the Maracanã in 1950. Toninho Cerezo headed out a ball which the linesman mistakenly judged to be over the goal line. The subsequent corner flew in towards the centre where one of Italy's players managed a shot which bounced off a Brazilian defender. The ball fell to Rossi a metre from the goal. Hat-trick.

Dribble and shoot as they might, Brazil just couldn't get an equaliser. Italy, who had been gasping for air throughout the tournament, had woken up at just the right moment. One of the world's best ever teams had been knocked out 3-2, but when the press conference at the Sarriá stadium in Barcelona was over, and Telê Santana had explained how 'fate played a trick on us today', the international press stood up and applauded.

The 1982 World Cup meant two things for Brazil's government. The players in that much-loved team became even greater heroes and role models than before. Now the generals could no longer pacify the population with yet another World Cup title. Criticism of the military regime grew, and Sócrates continued to lead the democratisation of Corinthians. In the autumn, the regime gave in to the pressure and promised to hold an election in the Senate on 15 November 1982 – the first free election in over twenty years. The problem was that the electorate didn't trust the military regime not to persecute the opposition. Many Brazilians were unsure whether they should dare to vote; they feared their names might be revealed.

Despite the fact that the generals had previously stopped Corinthians mixing football and politics, Washington Olivetto came up with a new slogan. At a match in the Campeonato Paulista four days before polling day, the players ran on to the pitch with '*Dia 15 Vote*', Vote on the 15th, printed across their backs. It wasn't political propaganda. It was a public information service. There was nothing the military could do. A month later, Corinthians became Paulista winners again, beating the generals' favourite team, São Paulo FC, 3-1.

Washington Olivetto adjusts his Blues Brothers glasses.

'It was incredibly important for us to win. Democracy came to be associated with winning. Everyone wanted a piece of us.

When Flamengo played us in São Paulo, Zico rang after the match and asked whether they could come and have dinner with us.'

The president of Corinthians was re-elected for another term, and when it was time to sign a new coach the club management asked the players who they wanted. Zé Maria, a former centre-back who'd played for Corinthians for thirteen years, got the most votes. He accepted. The Hawks, who'd given their full support to the democratisation process, also thought the choice of coach was excellent, and Corinthians consolidated their position as Brazil's second biggest club after Flamengo.

'There was nothing that couldn't be done,' says Washington Olivetto.

At the end of 1983, Corinthians won the Campeonato Paulista once more, and for the first time in over thirty years the working-class club had taken home the championship two years in a row. The lessons of Democracia Corinthiana spread like wildfire through Brazil, sowing the seeds of Latin America's biggest ever democratic movement, Diretas Já. It wasn't enough for senators to be elected in a free election; Diretas Já wanted Congress to pass a proposal for a free presidential election. To begin with, a few hundred people gathered in squares around the country to demonstrate, but, soon, the movement was organising demonstrations with several hundred thousand participants.

On 10 April 1984, more than a million demonstrators filled Avenida Presidente Vargas in Rio, and, six days later, almost one and a half million people gathered in central São Paulo. To increase the pressure, Sócrates threatened to accept an invitation from Italian club Fiorentina unless Congress voted in favour of a free presidential election.

One of the foremost leaders of Diretas Já was the union leader

Luiz Inácio 'Lula' da Silva, who, several years earlier, had founded the workers' party Partido dos Trabalhadores. He had been imprisoned for starting a strike at Scania's HGV factory in São Paulo in 1979, and was also a *corinthiano* through and through. At the biggest demonstration in the history of Brazil, Sócrates walked up on stage beside Lula da Silva, and gave a speech to the masses. The following week, 298 of the 366 congressmen voted in favour of the proposal to hold a free presidential election: Brazil was to be a democracy once more.

But the generals refused to acknowledge the resolution. Sócrates was so angry he kept his promise: after six years, 172 goals and 297 matches, he left Corinthians and moved to Italy to play for Fiorentina.

'We were completely deflated. Everything we'd fought for was lost. It was really sad,' says Washington Olivetto, who resigned as the club's head of marketing. Democracia Corinthiana was dissolved, and Vicente Matheus became club president once more.

But things had been set in motion. At the beginning of 1985, the generals gave up and announced their intention to appoint a civilian president. This historical shift coincided with Washington Olivetto's colleague in Rio, Roberto Medina, convincing some of the world's biggest rock bands to play in an area of reclaimed swampland outside Rio. It was the first time an international rock festival had been organised in South America, and almost a million South Americans flocked to Rock in Rio to see artists such as AC/DC, Iron Maiden, Ozzy Osbourne, Queen, Rod Stewart, Yes and Whitesnake. On the fifth day of the festival, 15 January 1985, Congress decided that the former governor of the state of Minas Gerais, Tancredo Neves, would be Brazil's first civilian president in twenty-one years. That night, AC/DC played. It was a historic concert that came to mark the transition from dictatorship to democracy. During the last song, 'For Those About To Rock (We Salute You)', two cannons were unveiled and fired a twenty-one-gun salute, to the delight of the crowd. Rock in Rio became South America's Woodstock, a happy ending to the democratic revolution started by Sócrates and Corinthians.

Washington Olivetto nods contentedly to himself.

'It felt a bit like "mission accomplished".'

Corinthians' home, Parque São Jorge, is named after the patron saint, St George, and lies in the centre of São Paulo, with restaurants, bars, banks, hair salons, a library, a gym, a swimming pool, a chapel, a 400-square-metre club store and the old Alfredo Schürig stadium, where the first team once trained. On the fifth floor of the complex, the new club president, Mário Gobbi, has his office. He is part of a new generation of leaders who oversaw another revolution in 2007, kicking out the businessman Alberto Dualib, who at that point had been directing the club for more than a decade. Today, Corinthians are a democratic club once more, making their accounts available online, among other things.

Gobbi, a police commissioner by day, is a large man with a double chin, who is fond of holding his guest's gaze. In the photo on the wall behind his desk, he is running, besuited, across a football pitch, yelling like a madman with outstretched arms. The picture was taken after the final whistle against Chelsea in Yokohama in December 2012. For the second time, Corinthians had won the most prized title in Brazilian football – they had beaten the Champions League winners in the final of the FIFA Club World Cup.

When I tell him the title isn't so highly prized in Europe, the police commissioner gets angry.

'Aha, the title's not valued? That's odd. Then why did the

Chelsea players start kicking our boys' legs in the second half, desperately chasing an equaliser? To me it seemed like they valued the title pretty highly,' Gobbi says, fixing his eyes on me.

The difference in the level of interest in the Club World Cup was, however, evident in the stands. A few hundred wealthy Chelsea supporters had travelled to Japan to see their team try to take a title they'd never had a shot at before. In contrast, almost 30,000 relatively poor *corinthianos* had gone halfway round the world to support their club in Yokohama.

'It was like being on the streets at home in São Paulo,' Gobbi says. 'You could hear Portuguese everywhere you went. There were more of us there than there are *A Seleção* fans at the World Cup.'

The invasion was made easier by the special relationship that São Paulo has with Japan. At the start of the twentieth century, when slavery was abolished, Japanese immigrants replaced a large proportion of the former workforce on the coffee plantations across the state of São Paulo. Hundreds of thousands of Japanese left famine in their own country to ensure that the proliferating coffee houses in Europe would continue to be supplied with coffee beans. This migration has meant that there are now over a million people of Japanese descent in the state of São Paulo. Many of them still maintain close contact with their relatives in Japan, and many of these families welcomed Corinthians fans into their homes for the match against Chelsea.

The biggest problem was getting money for flights. Most of the club's supporters live in the suburbs of São Paulo, and earn less than $700 a month, the bulk of which goes on food and rent. Hundreds of supporters chose to sell their cars.

'Being a *corinthiano* means doing crazy things,' says Mário Gobbi. 'The best thing is that none of those thirty thousand people regretted it. They were present at the party of the century.'

When the fans came home, they were treated to yet another Christmas present. After almost a year of negotiations, Corinthians finally reached an agreement with AC Milan on a transfer fee for Alexandre Pato. He cost $20 million, the highest fee ever paid in Brazilian football, and that bit of business also set another record: never before had an in-demand Brazilian player been so young when he returned home. Pato was twenty-three.

Pato is famous for his speed and technique, but also for his injuries. Another problem is that he isn't the type of player the Hawks appreciate. Typically, a Corinthians star player is a defensive midfielder who rarely scores a goal, but who never loses the ball and always hunts it down if it's anywhere near him. He's also loyal to the club and isn't ashamed of the Hawks and their vulgarity.

Pato doesn't really fit that profile. He dresses fashionably, dates Milan owner Silvio Berlusconi's daughter and doesn't know when to keep his mouth shut. In his last months at Milan, he was so disliked by the other players that they refused to pass to him during matches. The reason was that Pato had related dressing-room gossip to his girlfriend, who in turn had told her dad.

In order to avoid winding up the Hawks, who in 2011 had forced the returning player Roberto Carlos to leave the club and flee the country after he was blamed for a defeat in the Libertadores, the club director decided on a modest welcome ceremony. When Ronaldo was presented in 2008, Parque São Jorge was filled with tens of thousands of *corinthianos* welcoming the star. When Pato came home, they used the clubhouse's press room.

'What's wrong with that? How were our other acquisitions presented at the start of the season? In the press room! So Pato should be presented there, too. At Corinthians there's no special treatment,' Mário Gobbi says.

The president intends Corinthians to become Brazil's biggest club. In financial terms, the club has already succeeded. In 2003, Corinthians had a turnover equivalent to $25 million. Ten years on, the club makes almost $150 million a year. Corinthians has become Brazil's most solvent club because it has started, just like Santos, to think long-term, and has succeeded in breaking a cultural habit.

Previously, it was entirely conceivable that a major Brazilian club would get through four coaches in a season. As soon as the leadership weren't satisfied with results, the coach was fired. But in the last five years Corinthians have had only two coaches. Mano Menezes was signed in 2007 to pull the club out of the second division, and, when he became Brazil manager after the 2010 World Cup, Tite took over. The management of the club has been similarly professionalised. Club presidents used to be charismatic men who were drawn to football for the fame. Now many of the country's biggest clubs are run by competent administrators. A bank director, Luis Álvaro de Oliveira Ribeiro, runs Santos, a forty-four-year-old investment banker oversees Palmeiras, and another bank director has taken over Flamengo. The time when the football bigwigs, the so-called *cartolas*, ran clubs as their personal companies appears to be over.

'Has Brazilian football matured?' I ask.

'It depends what you mean by matured,' says Gobbi. 'We could be even better. Brazil is living in a new age now. You can't win big titles if you think short-term. What's needed is a good youth programme, well-ordered finances and stable leadership. You don't get to be a club's financial manager by being the president's cousin. You get to be a club's financial manager because you're good at finance. Football and vanity don't belong together.'

I ask Gobbi what he thinks of the combination of violence and football. The police have accused Corinthians' club management of covering up or brushing off the violent crimes the Hawks have been responsible for. The club management has always denied this. Commissioner Gobbi does, too.

In contrast, Corinthians' biggest rivals, Palmeiras, have taken a tough approach to their violent supporters' club *Mancha Verde*, the Green Blot. When a glass thrown by a supporter struck the goalkeeper's head in a confrontation after a defeat in the Libertadores, their club president denounced *Mancha Verde*. He wants the 'vandals' to stop going to matches.

On the way out of Gobbi's office, I tell him I'm thinking of joining the Hawks' outing to an away match the following day. Corinthians will face Sócrates' original club Botafogo-SP, and I ask Gobbi if he thinks it's a stupid idea: the club's press agent has advised me against going.

The club president shakes his head.

'No, no! Of course you should go! They're not as dangerous as people think. See it as a cultural experience. I'm sure you'll have something to write about in any case.'

The Hawks' clubhouse is in rundown Bom Retiro, where Corinthians' first stadium was built in 1918. The neighbourhood is known for being the first stop for all the immigrants who've made São Paulo the biggest city in the southern hemisphere. In the 1930s the Italians lived here, in the 1960s it was the Koreans, today it's the Bolivians. Most have no residence permits and work illegally for Brazilian textile manufacturers who have set up illegal sweatshops in basements and backyards.

When the taxi pulls into the cul-de-sac the Hawks have taken over and made their own, some powerful looking women are in the middle of it setting up food stalls ahead of tonight's samba training. There's a smell of barbecued ham, coriander and deep-fat frying. All eyes are immediately upon me.

According to the police, there are links between the Hawks and PCC, Brazil's biggest and most violent crime syndicate. PCC handles the sale of cocaine and marijuana in the metropolis, and has grown so big that a few years ago they were able to shut down South America's biggest city for two days, by setting fire to buses, underground trains and police stations. At the end of 2012, violence flared up once again and PCC killed ninety-four police officers in less than twenty-four hours. I smile warmly at the ladies on the food stalls, and cast my eye over the façades of the houses behind them. Have PCC graffitied their tag here?

At the end of the cul-de-sac stands the hangar that serves as the samba school's rehearsal hall. A gigantic silvery hawk has been painted on the wall. On the other wall are the words: '*LEALDADE, HUMILDADE, PROCEDIMENTO*', loyalty, humility, conduct. A few sambistas are stacking drums in front of the stage, others are filling fridges with beer, a man heaps coals on the barbecues. Under the steps, a shrine to St George has been set up. A candle burns in front of a picture of the Christian saint slaying the dragon. This is where the Hawks pray before matches.

I climb the steps in the hangar to ask the Hawks' president if there is any room on one of the buses going to the away match tomorrow. His secretary, who works barefoot, takes a drag on her cigarette and directs me to the supporters' shop by the entrance to the hangar. I'm to speak to 'Alemão', the German. He's the one who organises the away match outings.

Alemão is white, has a shaved head and looks like your average European skinhead.

'Sure, you're welcome to join us. The buses leave at one o'clock,' he says.

The next day, I arrive at the Hawks' hangar at 1 p.m. A dozen Hawks are hanging out in the supporters' shop, and Alemão tells me there won't be the usual six buses today. It's a Wednesday and the match is being played in Ribeirão Preto, 300 kilometres north of São Paulo. Due to the traffic jams, it will take at least five hours to drive to the match, which doesn't start until 10 p.m. It's unlikely that anyone will be home again before 5 a.m. That means only people who neither work, study nor look after children are able to go.

'Just the die-hards today,' grins Alemão.

In order to neutralise the effect of my presence, I speak to a few of the Hawks before the bus arrives. Many have eyebrow piercings, tattoos on their faces and black hoodies. One guy has a brace holding his smashed front teeth in place. When I go into the hangar's toilets I meet one of the die-hards in the doorway.

'Gringo,' he sneers, and walks off.

The only guy who doesn't fit the mould is a chubby high-school student with rosy cheeks. He looks more likely to be the victim of bullying than a hooligan.

Two hours after the appointed time, everyone has arrived. The bus, which looks like a tour bus someone's bought at a scrapyard, is parked outside the back of the hangar, blocking one of the lanes of São Paulo's major expressway. None of the drivers behind dare to honk their horns; instead they wait patiently for the next lane to become free so they can drive around the bus as it is being loaded up with banners, rockets and Hawks.

I introduce myself to the driver and sit down in the seat behind the front row. In front of me sits Lourdes, an eighty-year-old black woman who goes to every away match. She's called 'Tia',

Aunty, by the Hawks, and is treated with the greatest respect. The only other female passenger is a sixteen-year-old, middle-class blonde girl in a black dress featuring a skull and crossbones motif. Beside her sits one of the leaders. He is glaring at me. I feel the need to disarm the situation.

'Hi, I'm Henrique, the reporter from Sweden. I had a chat with Alemão yesterday about me hanging out with you. I'm writing a book about Brazilian football and really want to include you in it. After you beat Chelsea everyone in Europe wants to know who you are.'

My flattery isn't working.

'Alemão doesn't decide things here. If you want to come with us, you ask me, our vice-president or our president. OK? Where did you say you were from again?

'Sweden, Ibrahimović-land.'

That doesn't work either. Milan, PSG and the Swedish team are outside these guys' radar.

'OK,' he answers after a few seconds' consideration. 'But no filming or photographs.'

Silence. Then he continues:

'Do you like powder, Brazilian powder?'

I hesitate. If I reply that I don't like cocaine I might not be allowed to come along. If I say I like it, he might rip open a bag. I decide to pretend to be worldlier than I am.

'Brazilian powder is great, but Bolivian is better.'

'Hear that, boys?! We have a reporter who likes powder. Bolivian powder. Is there anyone who has a bit of Brazilian for him?'

I sense I'm on the wrong track, and try to navigate back to football.

'This evening's going to be Pato's first game. That's pretty exciting.'

The Hawk gives me an icy stare.

'And Brazilian pussy. What do you think of Brazilian pussy?'

The sixteen-year-old beside him smiles nervously, while more Hawks gather in the gangway. I know I have to act, otherwise I'll end up as the bus's whipping boy, or worse, all the way to Ribeirão Preto.

'Brazilian beaver's good, but Swedish isn't all that bad either,' I reply with a pasted-on smile.

My idiotic comment makes the Hawks' eyes light up. Despite the fact that Brazilian beauty is praised all over the world, a blonde with blue eyes is still seen as the best trophy a Brazilian man can win. The mood lightens and the guys ask if I can 'send over a few Swedish girls' to them.

'They'll all be here for the 2014 World Cup. Swedish girls love to party,' I say.

The Hawks' imaginations are now running wild, and I lean back in the tatty seat.

On the way out of the mega-city, the bus stops at a petrol station to wait for yet another Hawk. The president has been held up, and the vice-president is replacing him. Half the bus gets off to buy sweets. The other half spark up their joints. They don't stop passing the joints from seat to seat when a police car pulls into the petrol station to fill up. They don't even shut the windows; they just let the marijuana smoke mix with the smell of petrol outside. The Hawks know that the police are afraid to get involved, for fear that the PCC will retaliate.

In the end, the vice-president shows up. He is bulky, black and has a kindly smile. He doesn't mention the fact that we've been waiting an hour for him. To avoid conflict, I tell him straight away why I'm on the bus.

'No worries. You're welcome,' he replies.

I start by interviewing the guy sitting behind me. Gonzales is thirty-two, and was born in one of the city's many suburbs after his family moved there in the mid-1970s. He went through the initiation ceremony all members have to partake in three years ago. He makes a paltry living respraying cars, working on construction sites and odd-jobbing. One of his forearms bears the tattoo 'TEREZA' in large letters. That's his daughter. On the other arm it says 'ANA BEATRIZE'. That's his wife. Gonzalez answers my questions, but all he really wants to talk about is girls and cocaine. Sócrates doesn't appear to interest him in the least, and he barely seems aware that the club's $20 million investment is going to start his first match tonight.

On the other side of the gangway, a guy sits on the roof of the toilet. He has a tattoo across his eyebrow, and a lip piercing. A scar runs along his left cheek from the corner of his mouth to his ear; it looks like a halter. I ask if he knows why the hawk became the supporters' club symbol. He doesn't seem to understand the question.

'I mean, why was the hawk chosen? Why wasn't it some other animal? A tiger, a lion, or something else? Was it because the hawk has a keen eye, dives from high up and catches snakes?'

Instead of answering me, the guy turns to the leader who is sitting at the front with the sixteen-year-old girl.

'Boss, this gringo says we eat snakes.'

The leader turns around and looks at him.

'What did you say?'

'The gringo says we eat snakes.'

The leader catches my eye and takes a toke on the joint. He tries to look angry.

'Sorry, it came out wrong,' I say. 'I was asking why you were called the Hawks, and wondered if it was because you are strong and kill snakes and so on. I didn't say you ate snakes.'

'Are you stupid, or what? Hawks don't eat snakes,' he says, blowing out the smoke.

I put down my notepad and look out of the window. It's started to rain. The bus still hasn't made it out of the megalopolis, and everything looks grey and dreary. On the periphery of São Paulo, there's no samba, sun or sand. This place is dominated by concrete, queues and chaos. I try to catch the leader's eye again to see if he's calmed down. He has.

A while later, he pours himself a vodka Red Bull in a cut-down plastic bottle and asks if I know who 'Nem' in Rio is. I nod and tell him I bumped into his right-hand man – 'Coelho', the Rabbit – in Rocinha, Brazil's biggest favela, a year ago.

The boss seems impressed:

'Nem's my friend. He's invited me to Rio several times.'

Nem is one of Brazil's most infamous drug lords, and leader of the crime syndicate Amigos dos Amigos, Friends of Friends, who control several of Rio's favelas. When I wrote a story about the clean-up of the Rocinha favela a few years ago, I met 'the Rabbit' in one of the alleyways. He was out with his dog, walking completely undisturbed on the streets, not far away from the cafés where the police come for coffee.

The boss asks which other favelas I've been to, and I tell him I've visited a couple of dozen others, including the former Brazil striker Adriano's deadly favela, Vila Cruzeiro, before the marines took it over in 2010. The leader holds out his hand. It feels like I've finally got approval, and can sit back and relax.

I'm awoken an hour later. The gang at the back of the bus are drumming up a samba, and the driver's cab has been turned into a bar. Three Hawks are sitting on the dashboard beside the driver, hotboxing a joint. Two others are refilling the cut-down plastic bottles with vodka and energy drink, and in the gangway a guy is distributing cocaine from a test tube. When he gets to me I decline politely. He takes it as an insult.

'Hey, it's my shout, yeah!'

'I know, but I'm working. Save it for the match.'

The guy racks up a line for himself in the crack between his thumb and index finger and snorts it.

'Go on, give me your hand,' he says.

'I don't want any,' I say.

'Did you hear that? Gringo doesn't want any powder!'

The samba section at the back takes up the phrase and starts up a new samba. 'Gringo doesn't want any powder. Gringo doesn't want any powder. Gringo doesn't want . . .'

I try to smile, but am not really sure how to deal with the situation. The boss rolls a joint, lights it and passes it to me.

'Don't you want a bit of green at least?'

I know that if I decline this as well they'll lampoon me as the most boring reporter they've ever met. I take two deep tokes and pass the joint on. No one wants it. I pass it over to the boss.

'No, no, that's yours,' he says.

I look at the joint. It's ten centimetres long. If I smoke it all I can forget finishing my story.

'Doesn't anyone want any?' I ask, stretching the joint across the gangway.

No one takes it.

I take a third draw and feel the rush spreading through my body. I start to relax and think that I should probably write this chapter some other time. There'll be another match, another day, I can go along to.

The journalist in me is stronger. I pass the joint over to the boss, who smokes the rest himself.

One of the younger guys, who's previously stayed in the background, taps me on the shoulder.

'Gringo, repeat after me: "I am a *boiola*."'

His pupils are enormous.

'Gringo, Gringo, repeat after me: "I am a *boiola*."'

I know very well what '*boiola*' means, and don't intend to answer him. Instead I feel it's time to react, or I'll be the bus's whipping boy again.

'Sorry, but I know very well what *boiola* means. It means gay. In Swedish we say *bög*. Can you say that? *Böööög*!!!'

The wasted guy backs off.

'Oops, Gringo's getting mad,' he says.

'OK, now I've had enough. My name isn't Gringo. I'm called Henrique and I've lived in Rio for ten years. I speak fluent Portuguese, have travelled round Brazil more than most of you and I'm married to a Brazilian. My daughter was born in Rio and now I'm here to write a chapter on Democracia Corinthiana. Could you just RESPECT THAT?'

Silence descends on the bus. No one knows how to react. Should they knock me out or leave me be? Their eyes turn to the boss, who nods curtly and asks the Hawks who've been hanging out in the gangway to go back to their seats. I turn towards the window and am lulled back to sleep by the marijuana smoke.

When I wake, darkness has fallen. Ribeirão Preto, with 620,000 inhabitants, is twinkling in the valley below us. This is the heart of the agricultural industry that has made Brazil one of the world's biggest exporters of produce. Every year, Ribeirão Preto holds the world's second largest agricultural fair, Agrishow, which has helped to give the city the country's eighth highest GDP per capita. Aside from rising prices on the world market, the thing that delights residents most is the fact that it was with their club, Botafogo-SP, that Sócrates started his career.

The Hawks' bus turns into the road that leads to the stadium, and I wonder how the members are going to get in: has the club management put aside tickets to be collected at the gates, or are they going to buy them outside?

Ten years ago, a standing ticket in the stadiums of São Paulo state cost around $3. It wasn't a big deal for guys from the suburbs to take a train into town and go to a match. Now the cheapest ticket in the Campeonato Paulista costs around $30. Admittedly, the minimum wage has more than tripled during that time, but it's still not enough.

A number of the clubs have raised prices out of pure greed, others have been more calculating. They want to limit the number of aggressive supporters at their stadiums in order to do what Europe has done: tempt wealthy families and businessmen to the football. Clubs hand out free tickets to their most established supporters' organisations, so as not to lose that all-important atmosphere, with fans singing, jumping around and waving banners. The problem is that some clubs give only a hundred or so tickets. That doesn't go far. For the Hawks, with 96,000 members, not even a thousand tickets a match would help much. What's more, for this match the hosts have exploited the fact that Brazil's second biggest club are visiting; Sócrates' club has raised the price of a standing ticket to almost $40.

'We'll sort the tickets out when we arrive,' the boss says.

I wonder how they'll go about it – do the Hawks have some kind of fund to buy tickets for their most loyal members?

Suddenly, a few Hawks shout at the driver to slow down and open the central door. I catch sight of a family, all dressed in Botafogo-SP's red, white and black kit, in the middle of unpacking their car, before three Hawks jump out of the moving bus. They punch the dad and the son, and jump back in through the central door. A battle cry fills the bus.

The traffic gets busier, and the sides of the road are lined with *corinthianos* who've left their cars parked down the road. Everyone apart from the Hawks walks the last kilometre to the stadium. It's obvious it's going to feel like an away match for the home team. Two-thirds of the 26,000 fans who got tickets to this match are wearing Corinthians shirts.

In the midst of the flow of people stands a *cambista*, a black-market vendor, in a blue wig and a clown suit. He is trying to earn money from tonight's sold-out match. The bus driver catches sight of him, opens the bus doors and shrieks:

'*Cambista* on my left!'

Three Hawks jump out of the bus, catch up with the old guy and hold him down, while two other Hawks fish for tickets in his pockets. Another battle cry goes up. A little further on there's another man selling tickets. Eight Hawks run out and form a tight ring around the man. The vendor gives up and voluntarily gives his tickets to the Hawks.

'How many've we got now?' asks the boss.

'Twenty to go,' replies the guy with the bashed-in teeth.

The chubby high-school kid with rosy cheeks, who seemed like a prime bullying target when he boarded the bus in São Paulo, volunteers to lead the next raid. He stands on the bottom step of the bus, waiting for the signal. Half a minute later the driver shouts from behind the wheel:

'*Cambista* on my right!'

The high-school kid jumps out, kicks the guy to the floor, steals his tickets and holds a bunch of them up towards the bus's windows. The Hawks cheer. Now they only need ten more tickets to get everyone into the game.

Shocked by the Hawks' raids, I tap eighty-year-old Lourdes on the shoulder.

'Do they always do this?'

She smiles.

'Yes, the tickets have got so expensive. No one feels sorry for those black-market guys anyway.'

Further on, a man is holding tickets in the air, shouting '*Ingressos! Ingressos!*' Tickets! Tickets! What he doesn't know is that his salesman's voice is a siren call for the Hawks, who dive down on him with frightening precision and take the last tickets. In less than a quarter of an hour, the Hawks have got hold of fifty tickets, and, with that, saved themselves over $2,000.

Five hundred metres from the stadium, police have set up a barricade of two jeeps with flashing blue lights. The Hawks' vice-president gets out of the bus and demands permission to drive the last stretch up to the stadium to drop off the biggest of the banners, which is almost forty metres long and is unfurled when Corinthians score a goal. The police officers shake their heads determinedly. The vice-president tries to convince them, but is instead informed that the Hawks are to be searched before they can enter the stadium. The fear the PCC arouse in São Paulo counts for nothing here. The vice-president selects ten Hawks, who form a chain and march the banner up towards the stadium. The rest of us follow behind at a more leisurely pace.

When an old popcorn vendor spots the clump of Hawks approaching, he tries to escape with his stand. He doesn't make it. The Hawk who was offering me cocaine in the bus catches up and stops the stand. Desperately, the man cries that the popcorn costs a dollar a bag, but the Hawk doesn't even look at him as he serves up popcorn for the whole gang. When the vice-president comes up I think: 'Right, you bastards, now he's going to come and ask that guy to give the bags back.' Instead, he goes up to the old man, takes a bag of popcorn and asks for salt. The drugs, the violence, the attitude towards women . . . for some reason this is the moment I decide I've had enough. The people who sell popcorn in Brazil are among the poorest in society. You don't steal from them.

For the last stretch of the slope I walk with Lourdes. Her hips are worn out by physical labour, and she supports herself against me. When we get to the top, I pull her away from the crush and put her behind a tree as protection from the thousands of supporters who are pushing from behind. The Hawk with the scar across his cheek, who couldn't explain why they were called the Hawks, comes over and asks how Tia is.

'I'm fine,' she replies, and takes a ticket from him.

My journey with the Hawks has come to an end; I intend to watch the match from the press box. I give Lourdes a hug.

'Don't be angry with them. They just wanted to test you. They're nice boys really,' she says.

A quarter of an hour later, the rain starts to bucket down. Everyone queuing gets soaked to the skin. I've managed to make it into the stadium, which is in a terrible condition. Rainwater forms puddles on the stairwells. It isn't until I get to the top that I realise there is no press box. The press seats are housed in a concrete booth, where five TV cameras on tripods take up almost all the space. Two of them are going to be following Pato. The other three will be showing the match to several million viewers.

When Pato runs on to the pitch, the Hawks jump around in the packed standing-room only terrace opposite me like a punk gang at a concert, despite the fact that none of them came here to see him. Pato works the pitch and plays really well. Twice in the first half he comes close to scoring. But then nothing much happens. In the second half, the home team's defenders have him in lock-down, and in the seventy-fifth minute he's subbed. Corinthians continue to have possession almost all the time, and yet it's still Botafogo-SP who come closest to taking the lead. With ten minutes remaining, the Hawks can no longer wait for a goal and unfurl their enormous banner over the sea of people. It is shaped like a shirt with an aggressive hawk on the front. Then the Hawks let off the rockets they have smuggled in. But it doesn't help. One of the Campeonato Paulista's smallest clubs has claimed a point from the world champions.

The next day I wake up in central Ribeirão Preto and thank myself for paying for a clean, pleasant hotel instead of travelling back to São Paulo with a gang of hungover, bitter, damp Hawks. I enjoy a long, luxurious breakfast before asking Reception to order me a taxi. The rain has passed and the sun is peeping out. We drive through a middle-class area of detached houses, the walls around which have grown taller as economic prosperity has increased. The taxi driver drops me off at a cemetery on the edge of town. I look for the administration building, and approach the lady at the desk.

'I was thinking of visiting Sócrates. *Doutor* Sócrates. Do you know where he's buried?'

The lady types the Greek philosopher's name into the computer and looks thoughtful. She turns to her boss.

'It says "Dr Sócrates Brasileiro" here. Was that really his name?'

'Yes, Brasileiro was his surname,' her boss replies.

The cemetery is like an enormous park. Several thousand graves are lined up in a considered but complicated geometric system. Sócrates lies buried in block H, row 27, grave 1,126.

In his last interview, with the Englishman David Tryhorn, Sócrates told him how proud he was of his time with Democracia Corinthiana. 'It's the greatest thing I've ever been part of. We set up our own little democracy in the middle of a far-right military dictatorship. There's no doubt that we, as popular role models, in a football club for the people, contributed to the spread of democratic ideas. We were close to the fledgling workers' party, and collected money for Lula's first electoral campaign. And twenty years later, he became president.'

Sócrates thought football was ordinarily reactionary by nature; that now, more than ever, both managers and players ought to engage with social issues. He felt that the recent decline of Brazilian football could be explained by the fact that the middle and upper classes had taken control of the kind of football that clubs were playing, putting a stranglehold on working-class talent. But he still thought there was something fundamentally positive about football: 'When I played in the youth team at Botafogo-SP, I was at the home of a team-mate who couldn't afford to eat, while I was studying to be a doctor. It made me think and I realised that football brings classes and races together. In that way it's a very democratic pastime.'

As I walk towards Sócrates' grave, images from the Hawks' sizzling carnival show combine with those of the people beaten up during the bus journey. I think of the supporters who sold their cars to go to Japan and what their families thought about it. I also think about the video Washington Olivetto showed me before we parted. Sócrates filmed it for the advertising company's

2011 Christmas party; Olivetto wanted him to send a message about creativity to the employees. The video was made just after Sócrates was discharged from hospital, where he was being treated for internal bleeding. His scarred face hung slack, his eyes were bloodshot and his hair greasy. You could see that alcohol abuse had taken its toll on him. Still, his eyes were sharp as he looked into the camera and said: 'Life isn't black and white, winning or losing. Life is like a rainbow. A combination of colours. Creativity is the same. It's about inventing, showing something new that's never been done before.' A month later, Sócrates was in hospital again. He'd had a dodgy beef stroganoff at a restaurant and thrown up. The doctors diagnosed food poisoning and said it would pass in a few days. But Sócrates' health was so poor that his body couldn't handle a simple gastric infection. Despite being moved to one of the world's best hospitals, the Albert Einstein Hospital in São Paulo, he died three days later.

The headstone is no bigger than anyone else's. It measures only forty by fifty centimetres. Sócrates was democratic even in death. I lay my hand on the stone and give thanks for the 1982 and 1986 World Cups, the first two I ever followed. Someone has put a vase of fresh ox-eye daisies on his grave. It's tipped over in the rain. I right it and notice a bird sitting on a branch nearby. I watch it, and have a spontaneous sense that Sócrates was no hawk. He was a strange bird, with skinny legs. His democratic revolution claimed no victims. His only weapons were his bandana, on which he wrote his slogans, and his unusually small feet.

On the way out of the graveyard, I stop to talk to the gardeners. Most of them are *corinthianos*, and tend to argue about whose turn it is to trim the bushes that grow around Sócrates' stone. I ask whether many people come to visit the legendary footballer.

'Someone comes more or less every day. Lots of foreigners, actually. Last week we had two Italians here,' says one of the men.

The other gardener snorts. He can't understand why Italians come. It was they who put paid to the World Cup victory the Magic Square so deserved.

6

'In the end, the whole of Brazil was flashing'
The biggest football commentator in the
world bewitches his country

It's twenty-five minutes until live broadcast and the host still hasn't turned up. The studio manager wanders back and forth, reassuring the guests. It's Monday evening at the TV centre in São Paulo, and time for Galvão Bueno's talk show *Bem, amigos!* – Well, friends!

One of this evening's guests is Alexandre Pato. As is one of Brazil's most popular singers, Zezé di Camargo, who, like Pato, sits, made up and ready for the broadcast, before the host's even shown his face. There's no doubt who the evening's biggest star is.

'It's fine, it's fine, he'll be here soon,' the studio manager Sassa says.

Sassa was a friend of Galvão Bueno's in high school at the end of the 1960s. When they bumped into one another again after the millennium, Galvão Bueno offered him the job of studio manager on the spot.

'I'm the only one who's been here since the programme started. No one else has been able to put up with him,' Sassa says, smiling.

Finally, Galvão Bueno saunters down the corridor with slicked back black hair, his favourite black jacket, a pair of new black jeans, a shiny black polo shirt and a pair of black patent leather shoes with black suede detailing. He is tanned, sixty-three years old, and on a vain hunt for the looks he had when he made his breakthrough thirty years ago. His personal security guard, who is almost two metres tall and comes from the German colony in southern Brazil, marches along behind him. Galvão Bueno chews determinedly on some chewing gum, shakes hands with Pato and exchanges a few words with Zezé di Camargo, who has sold thirty-six million records and will be performing with his band this evening. He checks with Sassa that everything is ready for tonight's broadcast and then comes up to me and adjusts his Italian designer sunglasses.

'So, you're the one who wants to talk to me. We'll do it after my show.'

I breathe out. Admittedly he hasn't promised anything, but he's given me at least a little optimism after a hunt that's lasted several months.

First I spoke to the press office at Rede Globo in Rio, where he's employed. They weren't permitted to book an interview with him, but suggested I speak to the TV man's own company, Grupo Galvão Bueno in São Paulo. They introduced Burger King to Brazil in the 1990s and are now investing in the growing Brazilian wine industry. Not even their press secretary could arrange an interview, and had to check with his daughter, Leticia Galvão Bueno, who runs the marketing company The Aubergine Panda. After jumping through that particular hoop I was back to square one: Rede Globo. I realised it was much harder to get a meeting with Brazil's best-known football commentator than it is to book an interview with the best football players.

The name I was given at Rede Globo gave me a little hope,

at least. Ingo Ostrovsky is a popular journalist and author who was employed as Nike's press chief in Brazil after the American sports company took the blame for the 1998 defeat in the World Cup final in France. The media accused Nike of forcing the manager Zagallo to play their poster boy Ronaldo in the final, despite the fact that the star had collapsed the evening before. The accusations led Congress to announce an inquiry into the relationship between the Brazilian team's biggest sponsor and the Brazilian football association, CBF. After three years, the commission was suspended, and Ostrovsky was hired to improve the company's relationship with the media. At national team gatherings at CBF's training ground in the mountains north of Rio he gave out shirts and shoes to journalists, and before the qualifying rounds for the 2006 World Cup I met him a few times at training sessions in Teresópolis. When I rang him, seven years later, he had returned to journalism and was the producer on Galvão Bueno's talk show. 'I can't promise you an exclusive interview, but next time there's space I'll get you into the studio,' he said.

And now here I am. The third guest on the programme is the former star striker Casagrande, who was Sócrates' right-hand man in Democracia Corinthiana in the 1980s. He is one of Corinthians' greatest idols of all time, was in the Brazilian team in the 1986 World Cup, and lifted the European Cup for Porto in 1987. But now he's just turned fifty, and is marked by his long-term cocaine and heroin addiction, which meant that he sometimes failed to turn up to his job as Galvão Bueno's co-host. This evening, he'll be introducing his autobiography, *Casagrande e seus demônios*, Casagrande and his demons, which includes an account of his time in the rehab clinic to which he was confined for a year.

Galvão Bueno, who has a gently teasing manner with most

of his guests, treats his colleague with the greatest respect. His voice drops, and he tells his viewers how the two of them, during the 2010 World Cup in South Africa, celebrated Casagrande's first drug-free year.

'I remember you ringing up to my room and saying "Come down! We've got something to celebrate." I went down, we opened a bottle of wine, drank a toast, embraced and cried. We celebrated the fact that you'd got your life back,' says Galvão Bueno.

The camera zooms in on Casagrande, who, with tears in his eyes, describes how the drugs filled a void that opened up when his footballing career ended, and how he still has to overcome his addiction every day. Galvão Bueno nods encouragingly. He knows he's got the emotions of Brazil's TV viewers flowing once again.

Carlos Eduardo dos Santos Galvão Bueno grew up in the borough of Tijuca in Rio, near the Maracanã. He was interested in sport from any early age. He swam, raced go-karts and played volleyball, handball, football and tennis, before settling on a career in basketball. He reached the highest level and trained as a gymnastics teacher at the same time.

When Galvão Bueno was twenty-three he gave up basketball and took a job at a factory making plastic tubs for the pharmaceuticals industry while waiting to get a job as a gym teacher. In the afternoons he and his colleagues listened to sport on the radio. One day, Rádio Gazeta were looking for a new sports commentator and invited listeners to audition. Galvão Bueno's colleagues signed him up for the auditions, which attracted almost three thousand hopefuls. When the number of candidates on stage got down to three, the former basketball player was one of them.

The radio director asked which sport he was best at. 'All of them,' he replied, and got the job.

Galvão Bueno's first assignment was a nightmare. He was commentating on the final of the international tennis tournament in São Paulo 1974, in which Arthur Ashe was to face an eighteen-year-old Swede. Galvão Bueno had done his research on Ashe, who he saw as the obvious winner. When the Swede started to dominate the match, Galvão Bueno could give the listeners almost no information about him. His only solace was the fact that the match was over quickly: Björn Borg won easily.

A few months later, Sweden screwed things up for Galvão Bueno again. The Brazilian was about to commentate on his first World Cup match, and drew a match that was insignificant for Brazil, Sweden vs Bulgaria. It was one of the first matches of the 1974 World Cup in West Germany, and Galvão sat in a TV studio in São Paulo, watching a team in white and a team in yellow walking on to the pitch.

'There was no doubt about it. White was Bulgaria and yellow was Sweden. So I started off "Ericsson to Singstrom who passed to Ergsson", "Bulgarov to Romanov", and so on. It wasn't until the end of the second half that the camera showed the match scoreboard in the stadium. It said East Germany – Australia. I'd commentated on the wrong match.'

In spite of the bloomers, his star kept rising. During the 1978 World Cup in Argentina, he was in the studio in Buenos Aires, with the former Brazil manager João Saldanha as guest pundit by his side. The same year, the channel he worked for bought the TV rights to Formula 1, which had become one of Brazil's national sports ever since Emerson Fittipaldi became world champion in 1972 and 1974. When Galvão Bueno started commentating on the races, his compatriot Nelson Piquet had just joined the elite, and viewing figures sky-rocketed. In 1981, the same year Piquet became F1 champion for the first time, Rede Globo signed Galvão Bueno, and he's been loyal to the channel ever since.

The first time he was entrusted with commentating on a World Cup match featuring *A Seleção* was in Mexico in 1986. The Sócrates generation were seeking revenge for the unfair defeat in Spain in 1982, and won their group, but in the quarter-final their run came to an end: France won after extra time and penalties. Brazilian football plunged into its deepest ever crisis. For seven years, not a single Brazilian club reached the final in the Copa Libertadores, which had never happened before. The national team hadn't much to celebrate either. Instead it was their arch-rivals Argentina who won the 1986 World Cup, reaching the final again in 1990, and rejoicing in Diego Maradona, the decade's best footballer by a long way.

The problems on the football pitch coincided with Brazil's worst ever financial crisis. Galloping inflation, which had been an issue since 1980, spiralled out of control. At its worst, Brazil's inflation was over 2,000 per cent a year. If you didn't buy food with your wages the day you were paid, your money bought you a lot less the following day. This hyperinflation meant that the working class became poor and large sections of the middle class disappeared. The only people who could inspire any pride in South America's largest country were the racing drivers. Nelson Piquet took his third F1 title in 1987, and, the year after, he passed the baton to Ayrton Senna, who was champion in 1988. On Sunday mornings, Brazilians woke up to hear Galvão Bueno reporting on Ayrton Senna's duels with the Frenchman Alain Prost.

Senna's bold – sometimes too bold – overtaking manoeuvres and his strong Catholic faith made him Brazil's biggest idol since Pelé. The fact that he was as white as a European and the best in a sport that was synonymous with the industrialised world meant that in certain circles he was even bigger than Pelé. Senna's three F1 titles helped the Brazilian people forget that the country had changed currency five times in ten years. When Senna fatally crashed at the San Marino Grand Prix on 1 May 1994, it was Galvão Bueno who announced the news of his death to the viewers. Many felt the country had sunk as far as it could, and when Senna's body arrived back in Brazil, hundreds of thousands of people lined the funeral route in São Paulo to bid farewell to the cocky racing driver who'd given the country the self-confidence and the victories the football republic hadn't delivered since 1970. On TV, a tearful woman was interviewed along the funeral route: 'Brazil needs healthcare, education and justice – but we need a little fun sometimes too. And now our only fun has gone.'

When the 1994 World Cup started a month and a half later, *A Seleção* had no wish to make fools of themselves. The former fitness coach Carlos Alberto Parreira had been made manager, and presented a team that took no defensive chances. Brazil won their group, losing points only to Sweden. In the last sixteen, they narrowly beat hosts the USA 1-0, and then trampled over Holland in one of the championship's best matches. For the first time in twenty-four years, Brazil were close to a place on the podium.

Ahead of the semi-final against Sweden, seventy-eight-year-old FIFA swapped the appointed referee with the Colombian José Torres Cadena. In the second half, the Swedish captain Jonas Thern was sent off after a stamp on his counterpart, Dunga. 'I'm not denying that he should have got a yellow card after that tackle, but it wasn't worth a red,' said the Swedish UEFA chairman Lennart Johansson. A quarter of an hour later, a header from Romário made it 1-0, and Brazil were in the World Cup final.

In the final Brazil got the chance to settle things with Italy for knocking out Sócrates, Zico and the others in 1982. At full time it was still 0-0, and Galvão Bueno's nerves were in pieces. He remembered the match twelve years previously, and fired up the audience at home in Brazil. Pelé sat beside him as studio guest in a suit and tie, but inside the legend was on the pitch – under the table his legs were shooting and passing along with the players. It didn't help. Brazil had more chances on goal, but the World Cup final went, for the first time, to penalties.

After both teams missed their first penalties the tension became unbearable. Before every Italian penalty, Galvão Bueno cried: '*Sai, que é sua, Taffarel!*', Take it, it's yours, Taffarel!, coining one of his most famous catchphrases. When Massaro took Italy's fourth penalty, Galvão Bueno cried out again, and the viewers thought a miracle had occurred. Taffarel saved the penalty, and Brazil were ahead 3-2. However, Italy had saved their best player until last. As Roberto Baggio ran up, Galvão shouted out once again: 'Take it, it's yours, Taffarel!' Baggio hit the ball into the stands and the longest ever World Cup final was over.

The Brazilian TV booth exploded with joy. 'It's oveeeeeeeeer! It's oveeeeeeeeer!' Galvão roared, and got such a hard hug from Pelé that his glasses fell off. 'Four-time winners! Four-time winners! Four-time winners!' Galvão went on. After twenty-four long years, the football republic were once again the best in the world.

For an outsider, Galvão Bueno might seem like any other sports commentator who has made the leap to entertainment TV when his popularity was great enough. But there are a few specifically Brazilian reasons why Galvão Bueno plays in a different league altogether. Brazil doesn't have as much in common with its South American neighbours as many people think. Brazil is actually closer to the USA in many ways. Both countries are as big as continents – if you take away Alaska, Brazil is actually bigger. The countries' histories are also very similar. America's two biggest nations were conquered by Europeans who killed the indigenous peoples and then made their livings as cowboys. After that the coastal areas were developed agriculturally. In the USA it was cotton plantations, in Brazil, sugar cane fields. In both cases, hoards of workers were needed, and in both cases they were brought from Africa. A million slaves were transported to the USA; three million to Brazil. When slavery was abolished, both countries reacted in the same way: instead of employing their former slaves, workers were encouraged to emigrate from Europe. Poor Italians, Germans, Spaniards and Poles took jobs in America's two biggest economies. Chicago is still the city with more Poles than any other outside Poland. The next biggest Polish city outside Poland is Curitiba in southern Brazil.

Brazil also has the same capitalist drive as the USA. Shopping malls are open around the clock, advertising can be seen everywhere and the parking lots are huge. The country's economy is dependent on car sales, powerful lobbying groups direct Congress, and anything can be bought if you have enough money. On the other hand, Brazil is also one of the world's most complicated countries. Bureaucracy makes company start-up difficult, the tax regulations are the most complex in the western world, the justice system is arbitrary and the laws governing labour rights, which were handed down from the Vargas dictatorship in the 1930s, make employing staff painful. And things can end badly for anyone who protests against the way things are – criticising a state employee is punishable by imprisonment.

I would say that Brazil is a cross between the USA and the USSR. The country has both neoliberal and totalitarian elements.

Anyone who can master both playing fields at once has a good chance of achieving total dominance, putting a stop to the competition.

One of the clearest examples of this is the media group Organizações Globo, Galvão Bueno's employer. Rede Globo, the group's television company, reaches 99.5 per cent of the country's residents, and more or less has the monopoly on information in the world's fifth biggest country. In the US, ABC, CBS, CNN, Fox and NBC compete for viewers. In Brazil there's just one major TV company. The monopoly means that it is impossible to communicate with the country's two hundred million inhabitants without dealing with Globo, a fact which has turned the commercial station into the second most profitable television company in the world.

The media group, which also runs Rio's largest daily newspaper and a host of radio stations, makes its biggest profits through the product placement of cars, clothing and household objects in its soap operas, the so-called *telenovelas*. Revenue from product placement and advertising can be ten times the production cost of these predictable soaps. Not even Mexican drug cartels have those kinds of profit margins.

Telenovelas are normally filmed in 180 episodes, and broadcast every day, Monday to Saturday. The plots can be about anything from early nineteenth-century coffee barons to life in a plastic-surgery clinic, and screenwriters often weave in topical debates and social issues. The day's first *telenovela* starts at 2.40 p.m., and they run, one after another, until 9.50 p.m. The only interruptions are for evening news broadcasts. Globo shows no documentaries or quality films, and the week's only programme focusing on societal issues is on Friday evenings at 10.20, when the country's youth are out having fun. When political scientists discuss why

Brazil has yet to reach the same level as the world's more developed countries, a flawed education system is generally top of the list, followed by corruption, with the Globo media monopoly in third place.

In the 1990s, Channel Four produced a documentary on how the Marinho family, the founders and owners of Organizações Globo, control opinion in Brazil. The documentary compared the head of the family, Roberto Marinho, with the fictional media magnate Charles Foster Kane in the Oscar-winning classic *Citizen Kane*, and purported to show how Marinho manipulated the news in the same way Kane does in the film. The documentary, called *Beyond Citizen Kane*, premiered on British television in 1993 and has never been shown in Brazil. The Marinho family convinced the courts to proscribe the documentary, as it contains images to which Globo own the rights. The media group's power is such that no Brazilian president, minister, business leader, musician, footballer or stand-up comedian can have a career in Brazil without Globo. There's a saying that goes: 'It's not the voters who appoint or remove presidents in Brazil. It's Globo.' When Diretas Já organised their first big demonstration in São Paulo, Rede Globo reported that it was a celebration of the city's 430th anniversary that had caused 300,000 people to take to the streets. In 1989, during the first election after the dictatorship ended, the station invited in a former girlfriend of the worker's leader Lula da Silva, so that she could tell viewers about the time Lula suggested she should have an abortion. That didn't go down well in the world's biggest Catholic country, and the young, sporty entrepreneur Fernando Collor de Mello became Brazil's first democratically elected president in thirty years instead. Globo later withdrew their support of Collor de Mello, reporting on a corruption scandal, which led to the president being deposed.

The other reason behind Galvão Bueno's prominence is the role of football within Globo. The three Marinho sons, who run the company today, know that they can let actors come and go in their *telenovelas*, but they can't take any risks with their football audience. When there are big matches in the World Cup, Libertadores or Champions League, more than a hundred million viewers follow the matches, and, without exception, it's Galvão Bueno who does the talking. No commentator in any other country is followed by as many of their compatriots. That's why Globo tends to call him 'the world's biggest football commentator'. Globo also owns all broadcasting rights in Brazil, and dictates league match timings. Weekday matches can only begin after the evening's last *telenovela* has been screened, and, when Brazilian clubs play in South America, the clubs of the neighbouring countries have to keep to Globo's times. Goals are generally presented by a sponsor, and when the referee signals a throw-in or a free-kick, adverts are shown in the left-hand corner.

The big matches of the Brasileirão, Libertadores and Champions League are shown for free, while most of the matches in the state championships are shown on Globo's subscription-only network, SporTV. The network shows football and other sports twenty-four hours a day on three channels, and also screens Galvão Bueno's *Bem, amigos!* – which got its name from the phrase with which Galvão Bueno always introduces matches: *Bem, amigos de Rede Globo* . . . , Well, friends of Rede Globo . . .

The third reason Brazilians, and not just those who are interested in football, have a relationship with Galvão Bueno, is the special Brazilian commentating technique.

Even during the 1958 World Cup in Sweden, broadcasters from other countries were amazed by how Brazilian commentators could make an ordinary match sound like a total adventure. The style has its roots in the Latin American *radionovelas* that took over the continent in the 1920s. These radio series, ancestors of today's *telenovelas*, were dramatised novels that were read aloud in a live broadcast every day. Football commentators started to imitate the dramatic style, and managed to channel the emotions on the pitch into the listeners' body and soul. A Brazilian football commentator is still known as the *narrador*, narrator, and is tasked with giving an account of the course of events during the match. He – and it is really only men – often has two pundits by his side, and for this reason, a *narrador* isn't judged on his knowledge of football or his analytical skill; the key to success is *emoção*.

The concept of *emoção* is central to Brazilian identity, and centres around showing your feelings, as many and as intensely as possible. A *narrador*'s task is to unleash the feelings of the viewers and listeners. It makes no difference whether it's tears or laughter. The main thing is that the emotions flow. If the referee makes a mistake, the crowd's rage must ignite the rage of the viewers at home. If there's an offside, the player's angst must be injected into the viewers' souls. If there's a great goal, the commentator has to shout '*GOOOOOOOOOOL!!!*' longer than anyone else can manage.

Galvão is the master of *emoção*. He's particularly famous for his machine-gun 'R'. Appropriately enough, to the point where it could almost have been at Globo's behest, the four biggest Brazilian stars of the last decades have started with the right letter.

The man who took Brazil to World Cup victory in 1994: RRRRRRRRRRRRomário!

The player who scored both goals in the 2002 World Cup final: RRRRRRRRRRRRonaldo!

And two guys who've both been named the best player in the world: RRRRRRRRRRRRRivaldo and RRRRRRRRRRRRRonaldinho!

When Galvão Bueno had put on his glasses again after Pelé knocked them off at the end of the 1994 final, and the players had unfurled the banner in honour of Ayrton Senna, the emotional virtuoso Galvão Bueno understood that it was time for a change of tone. His voice trembled as he treated the Brazilians to a personal memorial of Senna. The rest of the world had seen one of the world's most underwhelming finals. The Brazilians had experienced an emotional rollercoaster of breathtaking joy and numbing sorrow. Never has a Brazilian World Cup final had so much *emoção*.

After the 1994 World Cup, Galvão Bueno took his place in Brazil's heart, and Globo gave him sole rights to Libertadores, Champions League, Olympic football and Formula 1. The Marinho family knew the value of having someone who could engender emotions and be a point of reference for all classes and races in multicultural Brazil.

During the live broadcasts, the audience feted him with posters saying: 'Hi, Galvão, say hi to my Mum!', and 'Galvão, I love you!' When his contract was extended in 2005, he had become so important to Globo that the Marinho family guaranteed him $500,000 a month. No other commentator has ever received anything in the region of this sum, not in the USA, not in England, not in Japan. This record amount was conditional on him not endorsing any other products. Globo don't want to share their golden egg with anyone else. In order to avoid losing too many of his millions in tax, Galvão Bueno did what F1 stars do, and moved to Monaco. He rented a large flat with a gigantic balcony, and became neighbours with Felipe Massa, Brazil's best racing driver since Senna. Every time there was a match, Galvão flew home to Brazil.

A few years later, it turned out his move was more practical than many people thought. The global rights to *A Seleção*'s friendlies are now owned by International Sports Events, whose head office is in Saudi Arabia. Because the sponsors decide where they want the matches to be held, Brazil's most recent internationals have been played in London, Geneva, Hamburg, Wroclaw, Malmö and Qatar. Galvão, who has had the monopoly on *A Seleção* games at Globo for over twenty-five years, is now often closer to work than his colleagues.

There's an ad break in *Bem, amigos!* at Globo's TV studio. I go up to Ingo Ostrovsky and thank him for inviting me to the studio. I ask him whether he thinks there'll be time for me to interview Galvão after the show.

'Calm down, I've fixed it so you can come along to dinner after the show. We're going to his favourite Italian restaurant.'

Brazil may be one of the most difficult countries in the world, but it's also an unusually flexible country. There is always room for exceptions and surprises.

After the talk show, Galvão is on a high, receiving gifts from fans who've been waiting outside the studio. He passes the presents to his enormous bodyguard, and then points at me:

'You're coming with us. No problem.'

We go down into the bomb-proof garage, where the driver has opened the doors and started Galvão's black Mercedes. The presenter sits in the back and looks through his missed calls. He gives a curt nod when I ask whether he's happy with tonight's broadcast, but gets nervous when he realises he's forgotten to bring the copy of Casagrande's autobiography the author had signed for his wife. The bodyguard takes the rap:

'I told you to bring the book! I put it on the table. Ring Sassa!'

The two-metre-tall guy rings the studio manager, who runs in to look for the book. It's no longer there.

'Ring Ingo, maybe he took it.'

Ingo's not answering.

'We're not leaving here until the book has been found. Ring Casagrande, maybe it ended up with him.'

Casagrande has turned his phone off.

'What a fucking pain. How can it be so hard to get hold of a book?!'

The bodyguard goes to the boot and looks through the presents Galvão was given after the day's show. A few CDs from Zezé di Camargo, a book by a sports journalist, two signed Corinthians shirts from Pato, and there, among the shirts, Casagrande's book. The bodyguard – who has been following Galvão in Brazil and the rest of Latin America round the clock for fifteen years, but has time off when the TV star is in Monaco – passes the book to his employer.

'Right, let's go,' Galvão says.

The back seat is upholstered in black leather and between us there is a stowable armrest with space for two glasses. It's midnight, and the black car with tinted windows glides silently through the avenues of São Paulo. I perch my A4 pad on my knee and ask how it feels to be one of Brazil's most famous personalities.

'I can tell you that I really hadn't expected this. Could never have imagined it.'

He interrupts himself.

'Do you want me to put the light on so you can see what you're writing?'

'No, that's OK. I'm used to writing in the dark.'

He puts the light on anyway.

'Where were we?' he asks.

'That you could never have imagined this,' I reply.

'Of course. Once, when I was in São Luís during the World

Cup qualifiers in 2002, the last one, the one that qualified us, the whole stadium was calling my name. It was crazy. They made me run a victory lap after we'd won 3-0 over Venezuela. I talked to Pelé about it afterwards. He just said "That's what it's like, being an idol". Another time, in Belém, there was the same atmosphere. The whole stadium wanted to embrace me after we'd won. The organisers had to smuggle me out in the stadium's ambulance.'

Galvão looks contentedly out through the window, and continues his tale about the 2002 World Cup.

'I don't know if you were here then, but during the World Cup in Japan and South Korea, the matches took place in the middle of the night. Before a broadcast, our helicopter flew out over São Paulo to see how many people had got up to watch the match. Everywhere in the tower blocks, lights were on, and I had an idea and said, live on air: "Good morning friends of Globo! Can everyone who's got up in the middle of the night to watch this match turn their light on and off, so we know you're awake." It was magical. The whole city flashed.'

Galvão repeated the challenge ahead of every match.

'It became a mass movement. In the end, the whole of Brazil was flashing,' he says. I ask how he views his role as the country's foremost sports commentator. He takes a while to reply.

'A colleague of mine, who wrote a book on us *narradores*, said that I'm the singer in the band. I like that description. I'm the band's singer. It's me who conveys the emotions.'

'Like a kind of Bono,' I suggest.

'Exactly.'

'But you see,' continues Galvão, 'this country is made of football. It's not just me who's big. It's football, too. And then, of course, Globo are powerful, too. We have almost all the viewers.'

I ask him how he prepares for a match.

'Not everyone thinks so, but I always prepare well for my broadcasts. I do my research and always try to speak to the players when we meet. When the broadcast starts, I think of myself as a salesman, selling emotion. How do I get people at home to really feel what's happening on the pitch? It all comes down to that.'

The driver stops outside Lellis Trattoria in Jardim Paulista, one of São Paulo's most fashionable districts. The restaurant's suit-clad valets rush up and open the car doors. The bodyguard gets out and stands on the pavement, then Galvão gets out. A few diners smoking outside fall silent as the restaurant owner opens the door.

Ingo Ostrovsky and the rest of the team are already seated at the usual table, helping themselves to Parma ham, parmesan and olives. Galvão sits me to his right, leaving the space to his left empty. The waiter shakes his hand, and the TV commentator asks him to fetch a bottle from Galvão's own vineyard.

'Now it's time for you all to taste some real wine,' he says.

Opposite the presenter sits the sixty-year-old channel director for SporTV. He's a regular guest on the programme, and is given the honour of tasting the wine. Beside him sits Cleber Machado, the commentator who's expected to get his break when Galvão retires. Cleber is ten times more knowledgeable about football than Galvão, but he's never even got the chance to commentate on an *A Seleção* friendly. Cleber does the league derbies, Paulista finals, group-round matches in the Libertadores and the World Cup matches Brazil doesn't play in. The waiter pours him a glass.

'Your wine is very good,' fifty-year-old Cleber says, putting down his glass.

The wine is called Bueno Paralelo 31, and comes from Galvão Bueno's vineyard on the border with Uruguay, along latitude 31. Bueno Paralelo 31 is a blend of Cabernet Sauvignon, Merlot and Petit Verdot, and was created by the extremely expensive French oenologist Michel Rolland.

Galvão calls the waiter over to find out what the restaurant charges for his wine. A bottle costs $75.

'That's cheap,' Galvão says.

When Bueno Paralelo 31 was launched a few months after the World Cup fiasco in South Africa in 2010, many of Brazil's biggest star footballers turned up. Ronaldo arrived with his wife, and tasted the wine for the cameras.

'Weren't you there, too?' Galvão says, nodding at Cleber Machado.

'Of course! It was really fun,' he says.

The plates of Parma ham and parmesan are refilled and the TV crew recount old memories.

'Do you remember when Pelé was a studio guest for the first time, during the 1990 World Cup in Italy? We were going to go out and eat together after the final. We chose the fanciest restaurant, ordered the most delicious food and the most expensive wine, and then we let Pelé pick up the whole bill,' says Galvão.

The table dissolves with laughter. Pelé's miserliness is supposedly well known in the business.

'We just pointed. "He's paying,"' the channel director says.

Renewed laughter.

When the waiter saw who was going to pay the bill, he called his boss over.

'The owner came out, stood behind Pelé and laid his hands on his shoulders. I think one of the waiters took the picture. And that paid the bill,' Galvão says.

Two women come over to our table and want to have their photograph taken with Brazil's biggest TV star. Galvão stands up with all the vigour his sixty-three-year-old body can muster and puts his arms around the women. When he has sat down again he turns to me.

'That's what I mean about being the band's singer. I'm not the guy, what was his name again, the guitarist in U2? The guy with the hat.'

'The Edge.'

'Exactly, I'm not The Edge. I'm Bono,' he says, and takes a gulp of wine.

Galvão's ego is larger than most people's. When he makes a joke and no one laughs, he tells the joke again until someone does. Despite the fact that he is already one of Brazil's most famous people, he wants the spotlight to be on him.

The biggest setback to his career came during the opening ceremony of the 2010 World Cup in South Africa. Galvão had visited some South African vineyards and was in a good mood. In the TV studio he chatted away, interrupting the opening concert by Shakira. A Brazilian viewer tweeted '*Cala a boca #Galvao*' – Shut your mouth, Galvão – and unleashed a tidal wave. In a few hours, #Galvao became the hottest hashtag on Twitter in Brazil. Some Brazilian Twitter users, who wanted to spread the meme internationally, pretended that Galvão was the name of an Amazonian bird threatened with extinction, and put together a video with an English voiceover in which they encouraged people to tweet about the campaign. For every tweet containing the words '*Cala a boca #Galvao*', fifteen cents would go to the Save Galvão Birds Campaign. The video went viral and the Brazilian football commentator became one of Twitter's highest trending topics of the 2010 World Cup.

A month later, he gave one of his rare interviews, to Brazil's biggest daily paper: 'For me it was a real knock, of course. Twitter's a crazy thing. When I looked through my email, I saw that you

[*Folha de São Paulo*], *Globo*, *El País* and *New York Times* had been trying to get hold of me. To put it simply, I thought: "I'm through." And then I thought: "What shall I do now? Send out a press release?" But I'm not a politician. I haven't committed a crime. We decided to make a joke about it on the next broadcast. We did, and it turned out fine. That video *Save the Birds* was actually really funny. I became a cult figure.'

It was also during the World Cup in South Africa that Galvão Bueno came close to missing one of *A Seleção*'s World Cup matches for the first time in twenty-four years. Like many other members of the Brazilian press corps, he had underestimated the South African winter and not dressed warmly enough. Before the quarter-final against Holland he had a terrible cold. 'My voice was slipping like a car's clutch. It kept cracking and sticking. Cleber got ready to replace me and I was absolutely terrified. When I got home to Brazil, I rang Zezé di Camargo, who asked his voice doctor to have a look at me. He put a camera down my throat and found a load of white spots. I'd picked up some kind of flu thrush in my vocal cords,' he told *Folha de São Paulo*.

The Twitter campaign, the cold and Globo's row with Brazil manager Dunga, who refused to give interviews, made the 2010 World Cup the first championship Galvão Bueno did not enjoy. After the final he told his viewers live on air that he was thinking of quitting. 'My last World Cup will be on home ground. I won't be there in Russia in 2018. I've had enough,' he said. In broadcasts from the London Olympics in 2012, it was clear he was scarred by the Twitter storm. He wasn't as extravagant as usual, and thought people were out to criticise him. During a live studio programme he lost it when one of the invited studio guests made a joke about how Galvão had once said that the Brazilian volleyball team only won their silver medal at the 1984 Los Angeles Olympics because the Soviet Union were boycotting the Games. 'I think that's an appalling thing for you to say. Because I never said that, and would never think of saying such a thing. Now please say I didn't say that,' snapped Galvão Bueno.

The guest tried to calm him down.

'Hey, it was a joke.'

Galvão Bueno waved his finger in front of his face.

'No, no, no. It was no joke! A joke has to be a joke. We're talking in front of millions of people.'

'Yeah, but for Christ's sake, Galvão! The whole programme has a light-hearted tone. I made a little joke and you went totally crazy. Christ!'

Galvão didn't give up.

'A joke when the cameras are rolling is one thing. A joke when the cameras aren't rolling is another.'

When the programme finished, the studio guest, who was also a regular on Galvão's talk show, left the studio without a word. The papers wrote that Galvão was out of sorts, and the guest demanded an apology before he would return to work. The television management tried to mediate, but Galvão refused to say sorry. The result of his outburst was that the guest's contract wasn't renewed.

Galvão waves for another bottle of his wine and points at his colleagues' empty glasses. Then the guest of honour shows up. Galvão pulls out the chair to his left and Zezé di Camargo takes a seat. The waiter pours a glass of wine.

'No, no! I can't drink any alcohol,' the singer says, and orders a Coca-Cola.

Zezé di Camargo and his brother Luciano sing *sertanejo*, a popular Brazilian music genre that fuses pop and country. The style is most popular in rural areas, but has at least one fan in the urban centres. Neymar loves *sertanejo*. Zezé di Camargo and his brother play concerts almost every night all year round. Sometimes the duo do two concerts in an evening, playing their cheesy ballads to thousands of fans. In order to fit it all in, they have a private jet. Galvão, who, after Neymar, earns more than anyone else in Brazilian football, also has a private jet. He asks the singer how things are with the brothers' plane.

'Great,' says Zezé di Camargo.

Cleber Machado exchanges a weary glance with one of the production team at the table. It's not hard to catch his drift. 'Here we sit, us ordinary mortals, discussing SUVs, while our colleague is talking private jets with Zezé di Camargo.'

Cleber Machado turns to me and asks how the Swedish team are doing in the World Cup qualifying rounds. He talks up Zlatan's bicycle kick against England as a real *golaço*. The waiter fills our glasses, and I feel myself starting to lose control of the interview. While I try to find a way into Galvão's conversation about different models of jet, the team want to know how I find living in Brazil. When the food is cleared away I haven't written anything for some time.

Two new women come over to have a photo taken – this time with Zezé di Camargo. Galvão is a bit offended, and when the women realise this, they ask to have another photo taken with him.

To accompany dessert, Galvão asks the waiter to bring out his latest product – a sparkling wine which was also a collaboration with the Frenchman Michel Rolland. Galvão puts his hand on the bottle to check that it is properly chilled, and asks for eight glasses. I'm given the honour of tasting.

'Really delicious! Dry and crisp. Just as it should be,' I say.

Every time Galvão is in São Paulo for a live broadcast of his show, he invites his guests and colleagues to dinner at Lellis afterwards. The agreement is that the restaurant's owner takes care of the food and Galvão pays for the drinks. Since Lellis doesn't have many customers on a Monday evening, Galvão and his guests tend to have the restaurant to themselves after a while. Closing times are always flexible. When I look at the clock it's past two in the morning, and the staff have changed out of their work clothes. According to the rest of the party at the table, former Brazil manager Vanderlei Luxemburgo holds the record for stamina. He left the restaurant at eight in the morning.

To accompany the coffee, Galvão orders us a bottle of hazelnut liqueur. Then he sees one of Brazil's public prosecutors sitting at another table. The man is well known for managing to get the controversial banker Salvatore Cacciola extradited from Italy in 2008. Galvão raises a toast to the prosecutor and invites him over for some hazelnut liqueur.

The discussion covers everything from the guest pundit whose contract wasn't renewed by Globo, to the Brazil manager Luiz Felipe Scolari, who no one seems to believe in. Soon it is 3.30, and Zezé di Camargo leaves the table and drives home in his red Ferrari. Ingo Ostrovsky takes a taxi to his hotel and Cleber Machado goes home to his wife, who's been ringing, wondering where he's got to. The station director leaves, too, and only Galvão Bueno, the public prosecutor and I remain. We finish up the hazelnut liqueur, and the TV star asks for a new bottle. When I reach over the table to charge my mobile, I knock over a wine glass which smashes on the floor. I sense it's time for me to go home, too.

When we get out on to the pavement, I turn to Galvão and ask him what the greatest moment in his career was. He puts his arm around me.

'As a Swede it might be hard for you to understand, but the 1994 victory has probably been the biggest. We hadn't been in a final in twenty-four years. Can you imagine? Twenty-four years! It's like Sweden not being in an ice hockey final for all that time. Between 1950 and 1970, we'd been in four of six possible finals. We'd grown used to it. Then came over two decades without a single final. Everything was unleashed in 1994. We sat in this cramped, sweaty TV booth, and Pelé kept kicking me in his keenness to correct the players' passes. It was unbelievable. I just screamed: "Four-time winners! Four-time winners!"'

Galvão turns around and puts his arm around the public prosecutor.

'That was another time, wasn't it? You couldn't get anyone into prison. Everyone was acquitted. And then we had inflation at over 1,000 per cent a year. We needed that World Cup victory. Right?'

The public prosecutor nods and I scribble everything down as fast as I can. The hazelnut liqueur makes my letters large and formless. Galvão sees my scribblings and asks the doorman to put the lights back on in the restaurant.

'This Swede needs to sit at a proper table so he can make notes.'

The waiter is somewhat amused when he sees Galvão enter the restaurant again and stick three fingers in the air.

'Three espressos and three liqueurs. For me, the public prosecutor and the Swede.'

The time is 4.25 and I really only have one more question to ask: what's he going to do after the 2014 World Cup?

Galvão squirms in his seat.

'OK, all that was a misunderstanding. What I said in South Africa was that I found it really hard to see myself as a commentator in Russia in 2018. So Cleber or someone else can take over. But that doesn't mean I'm going to stop. I can't. I'm addicted to the adrenaline,' he says, drawing his fingers along his forearm.

'I might lead the studio broadcasts, or have my own programme where I interview the players. Or a new talk show. And I'm not planning to miss the Rio Olympics in 2016. You can put that in! All this stuff about Galvão Bueno retiring is just plain wrong. I'll never retire!'

7

7

'I pity the countries who get drawn to play here'
Lawless football in Amazonas

About fifty young women are wandering back and forth in
the conference hall of the Tropical Hotel in Manaus, in the heart
of Amazonas state. Most have the features of the indigenous
population as well as the white rubber workers who colonised the
world's biggest rainforest. All of them are focused, and dressed
in black high-leg bodies. Tatiane Reis sticks out her behind and
asks her colleague to spray hairspray over her thighs so the fine
hairs will glimmer in the spotlights.

'I have to get to the final so I can help my team,' she says,
waving her hand behind her thighs so the spray will dry – which
it doesn't do easily in humid Amazonas.

When the preparations are over, the girls skip out in a high-
heeled line on to the hotel's football pitch. A fifteen-metre-wide
stage with a spotlight rig has been built in front of the forest,
which is fading into the advancing evening. This year, the *Peladão*,
the world's largest, most colourful city championship, is celebrating its fortieth birthday, and the beauty contest, which is part
of the tournament, will be broadcast live on prime time. Of the
580 participants, the jury have picked out a total of fifty *rainhas*,

8

beauty queens. This evening, twelve of them will go through to the final.

Tatiane Reis waves the insects away from her face as she walks up towards the catwalk. She's representing Manaus Moderna, an amateur team that was formed at the fruit and vegetable market in the harbour. They are the reigning champions, and have won more titles than any other team since the *Peladão* began. They never leave their choice of *rainha* to chance. There's a priceless bonus to be had if the team's beauty queen goes through to the final – she requalifies her football team for the championship if they go out.

Two hours later, I've almost become inured to all the long legs, backsides and plunging necklines. I walk down from the bleachers to the jury, who are sitting in a row in front of the catwalk. There's a band playing on the stage, and when the jury tot up their points it turns out that the twenty-year-old Tatiana Reis is one of the twelve finalists. The first thing she does is ring the chairman of Manaus Moderna.

'Brilliant!' the chairman shouts down the phone line. 'I'll tell the players at once.'

When Brazilians meet to play a spontaneous game of football it's called a *pelada*. For the big European clubs, that word is a real sticking point – almost all Brazilian stars break the terms of their professional contracts and risk injury by playing a few matches with friends when they're on holiday at home in Brazil. For millions of ordinary Brazilians, though, a *pelada* is the most entertaining way to spend their free time.

The term comes from the late nineteenth century, when rubber workers saw how the British sailors who'd chugged up the Amazon in steamers kicked a leather ball around beside the river as the boats were being loaded. The rubber workers became curious and started enlarging the lumps of natural rubber – *pela* – that formed in the tapping bowls on the rubber trees. The lumps became balls, and rubber workers and Indians spread the new game along the river. That's why anthropologists insist that it was in Amazonas that the Brazilian art of dribbling was born – not in Santos, where football came ashore with Charles Miller.

Still, it's no surprise that it was Charles Miller, and not the rubber guys, who went down in footballing history. What goes on in Amazonas tends to stay in Amazonas. The only way to get to Manaus, which is the biggest city in Amazonas, is by air or several days by boat. Manaus is like an isolated island, with over two million residents in the midst of a green, sparsely populated ocean of rainforest. At the end of the nineteenth century, however, this isolation didn't stop Manaus becoming one of the world's richest cities, at a time when Brazil had a monopoly on one of the industrial world's most sought-after resources. The rubber barons competed over who could live in the most opulent European style, sending their dirty laundry to Paris to have it washed and ironed. In 1896, these nouveaux riches opened South America's first opera house, and paid the opera singer Caruso and the actress Sarah Bernhardt to perform. The party continued until the English smuggled out a cargo boat with tens of thousands of rubber-tree seeds stowed in it. The seeds were planted in Malaysia, and, a generation later, Manaus was a poor city. Nowadays, Manaus residents say: 'The English took the rubber, but they gave us football.'

At the end of the 1960s, the jungle metropolis didn't have many jobs to offer its roughly 300,000 residents, and there was a risk that the population would do what people had done in many other parts of the Amazon – start clearing the rainforest.

The military regime was forced to act, and created a free economic zone where foreign companies who wanted to get into the protected Brazilian market could set up factories. Today, Honda, Nokia, Sony, Samsung, Yamaha and Harley-Davidson have caused the population curve to swing in the other direction. Many of Latin America's biggest manufacturing plants are situated here, and Manaus is Brazil's eleventh largest city, with 2.2 million residents.

Among those who benefit most from the economic growth in Amazonas are the Calderaro family. When the free economic zone was introduced, Umberto Calderaro owned the biggest daily paper in Manaus, *A Crítica*. He was also the editor-in-chief, and hailed the initiative, but was worried about the baggage the thousands of young workers brought with them. The nightlife and the brothels flourished, but Calderaro wanted the workers to have better things to do with their free time. Via adverts in the paper, he encouraged the city's workplaces to start up amateur teams for a football championship. He called the championship *Peladão*, the big amateur tournament, and in 1973, the very first year, 188 teams took part. The following year, he had the idea of inviting the women from the textile factory to enter a beauty contest at the end of the championship.

'Grandad was smart. Brazil's greatest passions are football and women. Here you had it all in one,' Umberto Calderaro's Miami-educated grandson Dissica Calderaro says.

Umberto's grandson is head of the TV division of Rede Calderaro de Comunicação, now the largest media company in Amazonas, with three daily papers, three TV channels, two radio stations and a host of websites. And it's the TV channels that are doing best: they make big money broadcasting adverts for the new residential complexes that are being built in the Ponta Negra district along the white sands of the Amazon. This is where the new middle classes, who've made money from the recent growth, are moving to.

The *Peladão* tournament has been part of thirty-five-year-old Dissica Calderaro's life ever since he was born. The combination of football tournament and beauty contest was a hit, and the tournament's name provided an extra enticement. *Pelada* doesn't only mean amateur football. It is also Brazilian slang for 'starkers'. If you add the suffix *-ão*, it becomes 'super-starkers'. After ten years, over a thousand teams were taking part every year, making the *Peladão* the world's biggest city-wide football championship.

There are still just as many teams competing in the six different competition categories. And yet, few Brazilians outside Amazonas have heard of the tournament. Since the Amazonas tourist board invited the British journalist Alex Bellos to write about *Peladão* in his book *Futebol: The Brazilian Way of Life*, there have been French, German and British documentaries made about the championship. But in Brazil, the tournament is almost unknown. The reason for this is that the Calderaros' media network is connected to the national TV company Rede Record, which is owned by the Pentecostal pastor Edir Macedo. Because Macedo threatens Rede Globo's monopoly position, Globo's sports programmes ignore the tournament.

This year, Dissica Calderaro has a plan for making the championship better known. He has created a docusoap in which viewers get to decide which of the finalists will be voted the tournament's beauty queen. The twelve candidates will live for two weeks on a luxury yacht gliding along the Amazon. Every day, the boat will be visited by a make-up artist, a stylist or a model who will teach the girls the best beauty or modelling tricks. *Peladão a bordo*, Super-starkers Afloat, will be screened on prime time every evening, and will be Amazonas's first reality television show.

'Grandad was an innovator, and now it's my turn,' his grandson says. 'We have sixteen cameras on this luxury yacht. You'll be able to see everything.'

Dissica is trying to sell the concept to the Dutch media giant Endemol, who created the formats for many of the world's most popular reality shows.

'I think our formula is more attractive than *Big Brother* or *I'm a Celebrity* . . . Imagine flying in loads of hot girls from all over the world and having them sail up the Amazon. Who wouldn't want to watch a programme like that?'

So that Dissica Calderaro can concentrate fully on the show, the TV company has put responsibility for the football tournament in the hands of the retired sports commentator Arnaldo Santos. Arnaldo reported from the 1982 World Cup in Spain and the 1986 World Cup in Mexico, and was Coca-Cola's director for the Amazonas market. Fifteen years ago he retired, and since then he's been working overtime trying to get a handle on one of the world's craziest championships. But the odds are stacked against the seventy-four-year-old.

Brazil is a country where the law doesn't always apply. Sometimes some laws apply, sometimes others. Justice is hard to predict. The only thing that's certain is that if you're rich and have contacts, you can more or less get away with any crime at all without going to prison. The fact that the Brazilian justice system is as flexible as natural rubber means that Brazilians have more room for manoeuvre than other westerners. Drink driving was generally accepted up until 2008, and, even today, criminals can avoid the country's infamous prisons if they can show they have a university degree – then they can sit out their sentence in a cleaner, more spacious, less dangerous prison.

Respect for the word of the law is at its weakest in Amazonas. The tentacles of the judicial system seldom find their way here, and the residents are used to taking the law into their own hands. An example of this is the politician and TV personality Wallace Souza. For ten years he was a member of Manaus City Council, before being voted into the state parliament. Alongside his political career, he hosted a popular crime-fighting television show that followed manhunts for criminals in Manaus. When it was alleged that Wallace Souza also had a personal death squad that murdered suspected criminals at his behest in order to increase viewing figures, not everyone in Manaus thought it was a scandal. Many felt his presence helped to maintain order in the city. It wasn't until it emerged that Wallace Souza was suspected of being involved in cocaine smuggling along the Amazon that he was arrested by the police. When he died of a heart attack in 2010, thousands of Manaus residents took to the streets to celebrate his life.

Seeing as the sense of justice in Amazonas' capital city is on a par with the Wild West, Arnaldo Santos has a tough job maintaining order in Brazil's biggest football championship. But he has figured out a few countermeasures. For example, to avoid arguments about linesmen's offside decisions, he's simply removed the offside rule: a striker can spend the whole match hanging around in front of the opposition's goal if he wants. The only thing the linesman has to pay attention to is whether the ball crosses the boundaries. However, because most of the gravel pitches aren't chalked, the edges of the pitch are also fluid. The sidelines consist of markers in the form of items of clothing or water bottles, and the referee tends to give half a metre's grace.

To speed up the game, the halves have also been shortened to thirty minutes each.

'People want energy and movement. Things have to happen on the pitch,' Arnaldo asserts.

We meet in his office on the second floor of the building the *Peladão* rents in the centre of town. It is situated only three blocks from the opera house, and is painted pale blue. Arnaldo sits at the office's only desk, in front of the filing cabinets that hold the championship's results and other documentation.

Arnaldo Santos is extremely careful to ensure that everyone follows the rules. When this year's beauty finalists were selected, I saw how he checked that all the models had been present at their team's first match; if not, they were automatically disqualified. And players who get more than two red cards during the tournament are required to buy twenty footballs and distribute them in Manaus's schools. For more serious disciplinary offences, Arnaldo has instituted a court composed of volunteer referees and lawyers, who decide whether a player, a team or a referee should be excluded from the championship. Two common problems are players who play for more than one team, or are signed to one of Manaus's four professional clubs. Both are strictly prohibited.

Arnaldo gets up from his office chair and takes out a black folder.

'This is where I keep the names and ID numbers of every professional who's cheated over the years. No one gets past me!'

The only thing he's dissatisfied with is the lack of national acknowledgement of the championship. A few years ago, the organisers of Copa Kaiser in the state of São Paulo claimed their amateur tournament was Brazil's biggest.

'I was so angry. They said they had the record attendance for an amateur final. Twenty-one thousand spectators. That's what we have for the last sixteen!'

The finals of the *Peladão* have always filled Manaus's biggest stadium, Vivaldão, which accommodates 50,000 spectators. Not even the national team have attracted a bigger crowd the few times they've played in Amazonas. The fact that this amateur championship can draw a large audience is not only a result of the crazy rules. Professional football in Amazonas is of such a low standard that it's rare for one of the city's four clubs to reach the national leagues. The residents of Manaus have grown accustomed to satisfying their passion for football by watching their friends, neighbours and workmates play.

When I leave Arnaldo's office and go down to the ground floor of the *Peladão* offices, one of the championship's celebs is hanging out by the reception. 'Paulinho', little Paul, who is less than 150 centimetres tall, has refereed almost five thousand matches since the tournament started in 1973. There isn't a situation he hasn't found himself in – or a situation he hasn't been able to get out of.

'Once I felt my pockets and realised I didn't have any cards with me. I went over to the fruit and veg stand beside the pitch and picked the reddest tomato. It worked brilliantly,' he says.

It's also well known that Paulinho takes out his red card faster and more often than Lucky Luke draws his pistol.

'No ref in the world has sent off more players than me. Once I had to disappear for a few days because someone wanted me dead. Another time I had a mafia boss after me, he wanted revenge because I'd sent him off. But I talked him out of it. It ended with him taking me to a brothel.'

The team who have put the most into success this year is Obidense FC, which was founded in 1989 by migrant workers from the town of Óbidos in the state of Pará, two days away by boat down the Amazon. Most of the club's members work in the manufacturing industry in Manaus, and they have a unique cohesiveness. Their parties, with local bands and food from Pará, attract up to five thousand guests. Each pays the equivalent of $15 to get in, and buys twice that sum in beer. This means that the club has a budget of over $150,000, which they can spend on signing Manaus's best amateur players, and renting the only artificially lit grass pitch in Manaus. It's situated in an industrial area, and owned by the oil company Petrobras.

Obidense's chairman is the most successful migrant from Óbidos, and shows it by wearing a gold chain, a gold watch and three gold rings. Donis Bentes runs a chain of shoe shops with fourteen stores in Manaus, and is currently testing the oil company's turf with his crocodile-skin winklepickers. Every Wednesday, he pays Petrobras $300 so that the amateur team can have their evening training sessions on a good surface.

'Most of the players work during the day. This is our only chance to train properly.'

This year, Obidense have also done something else that aroused envy in the 580 other teams in the championship's main tournament. The club signed Amazonas's best professional footballer of all time.

'We heard he was back, and that he was free. So I went round to his house one Sunday and negotiated. What a fantastic palace he's built for himself! He's even got his own sandy beach along the river. We agreed that he would take a certain fee per match and a smaller fee for training sessions,' Donis Bentes says.

Francisco Lima has a long professional career in Europe behind him, and is now the highest paid player in the history of the *Peladão*. A host of successful entrepreneurs from the Óbidos colony have invested the money needed, and so the club's strips are crammed with adverts for a convenience store, an abattoir, a beverage distributor and a video shop.

The club chairman, whose shoe shop chain is the main sponsor, has also employed the coaching team with the most *Peladão* titles to its name.

'This year, nothing's going to go wrong,' he assures me.

A minute later, multi-millionaire Lima glides into the car park in his silver SUV, and grabs his Louis Vuitton bag through the passenger door. He says hi to the coach, the assistant coach, the fitness coach, the goalkeeper's coach and the masseur, and gives a nod to Donis Bentes and the kitman. Then he puts a knee to the ground and laces his boots. When Lima is ready he crosses himself and starts a thorough warm-up.

'I've managed to get by with no injuries throughout my career. I intend to keep it that way,' the forty-one-year-old says as he runs out on to the pitch.

Lima made his name at Roma from 2001, together with Emerson and Cafú, but every time Emerson and Cafú flew home to Brazil to take part in the South American World Cup qualifiers, Lima stayed in Italy. On the other hand, he wasn't missing much. The 2002 World Cup qualifiers were worse than the qualifying rounds for the 1994 World Cup. *A Seleção* used four different managers, and lost 3-0 to Chile, 1-0 to Ecuador and 3-1 to Bolivia. The football republic prepared to exit the World Cup without qualifying for the first time ever – they needed to win the last match to guarantee their place. The team did it in the end – but manager Luiz Felipe Scolari was still mocked by experts and fans. The reason was that he had left out Romário, who the rest of the country thought was on top form, and played Ronaldo, who the rest of the country thought was injured. Scolari justified his decision with the argument that Romário was no longer playing at the same high level, and that he thought Ronaldo would get his speed back before the World Cup.

For the first time in several championships, Brazil weren't among the favourites, and the pressure on the players was less than usual. The day before the first group match, Emerson was so relaxed he played in goal during the training. He dislocated his left shoulder, and the team found themselves without a captain and a midfield dynamo. The armband was switched to Cafú, and Scolari took the chance, with twenty-four hours to go to the first match, to call in a replacement. Francisco Lima thought 'now it's time'. But it wasn't. Scolari called in Ricardinho from Corinthians.

'I thought it was strange. Sometimes Emerson was my back-up at Roma. Why couldn't I be his? I was on top form in 2002. I could have replaced him,' Francisco Lima says at the Petrobras training ground.

Brazil won the first match in the 2002 World Cup 2-1 against Turkey, and Ronaldo proved to be in much better shape than the fans at home in Brazil expected. Up to the quarter-final against England, 'O Fenomeno' scored at least one goal per match. The second time Brazil met Turkey, he scored the only goal in the semi-final, and in the final against Germany he first took advantage of a mishandle by Oliver Kahn to follow up and tuck the ball home, and then slid a cool side-foot in past the post for his second. Ronaldo won the Golden Boot with eight goals, Scolari was vindicated (six of his players were in FIFA's 2002 All-Star team) and Brazil became five-time World Cup champions.

'Of course it would have been awesome to have been part of that gang,' Francisco Lima says. 'But I don't let it get me down. I've had a wonderful career.'

Two years after the 2002 World Cup, Lima went to Lokomotiv Moscow and won the Russian league, paving the way for Brazilian professionals to play in Russia. After two seasons, he was sold to Dynamo Moscow, who later loaned him to Qatar. His career was coming to an end, and Manaus's most successful player rounded off his time in Europe by playing fifty-eight matches with Brescia in Italy's Serie B.

Still, after a few months at home in the rainforest, Lima started to get itchy feet, and he decided to squeeze the last few drops out of his career. He had a season with the San Jose Earthquakes in California, and a year with the Serie D club Taranto in southern Italy. During that time, his family was busy building the palace by the white sands of the Amazon. When Lima finally landed in Amazonas for good, three of Manaus's professional football clubs came queuing up to sign him. The first year, he represented Nacional in the state championship, and the second year he went to Rio Negro. His last club was São Raimundo, the best-known club in Amazonas, who played in the Brazilian Série B up to 2006. São Raimundo's time in the limelight was over, however, and there wasn't enough money to keep Lima. He left after a few months. After that, he had no plans ever to touch a ball again, but then the rumour spread that no professional club had signed him. That meant the green light for the *Peladão*, and the biggest amateur clubs got in touch. The only ones who could cough up the dough Lima demanded were Obidense.

'They want the title this year. It's perfect for me. I get to stay in shape and earn a bit at the same time.'

Before the players part after the training session, the team come together in a circle and put their arms around each other's shoulders. Most close their eyes and speak in tongues, some shriek. Lima waves his hands about like an evangelical preacher, firing up his fellow players. This is a new ritual that's taken hold in Brazilian football over the last ten years. It's come from the wave of Pentecostal churches that has flooded the country: almost a quarter of Brazil's two hundred million inhabitants belong to some form of Protestant congregation. The proportion is even higher among footballers.

When Dunga was managing Brazil, former right-back Jorginho was his assistant coach. Apart from giving the perfect pass to Romário in the semi-final against Sweden in 1994, Jorginho is also famous for being the chairman of the fundamentalist revivalist movement *Atletas de Cristo*, Christ's athletes. The organisation encourages its members to 'spread the Gospel through sport in every conceivable way', and belongs to the Pentecostal Church movement which has come to have so much power in Brazilian society. The Pentecostal church congregations see samba as the music of Satan and carnival as sinful, and think that the Afro-Brazilian religions are the work of the Devil. The congregations vandalise Afro-Brazilian temples, mock homosexuals and fight for tougher abortion laws. One of the most prominent fundamentalists in Brazil is Kaká, who has been involved with the Renascer Church, whose owner has been accused by the Brazilian courts of heading a family-run crime syndicate founded on the exploitation of people's faith. Kaká left the Church in 2010 after their mishandling of money became known.

Lúcio, the former Bayern Munich centre-back, is another of Brazil's most religious players. When Dunga made him captain, almost the whole first eleven was made up of Pentecostalists. After Lúcio headed the winning goal in the final minutes of the Confederations Cup in South Africa, the captain gathered the entire squad in a circle on the pitch. The players took off their team shirts to reveal Jesus t-shirts, then joined hands. Together with their team leaders, masseurs and doctors, the team fell to their knees and thanked God for their victory. Not since the military regime in the 1970s had an organisation so effectively hijacked Brazil's best-known trademark and used it for its own purposes.

The fact that even poor Pentecostalists donate a tenth of their household income to their congregation has meant that becoming a Pentecostal minister is now a desirable career choice in Brazil. In São Paulo, Igreja Universal, one of the world's biggest Pentecostal churches, runs expensive courses where the church hands out tips on becoming a successful Pentecostal minister. The church's founder, Edir Macedo, who bought up Rede Record, tempts people in with a salary of around $10,000 a month. If the new Pentecostal minister reaches the congregation's profit target, they also get a bonus. The billion-dollar industry of the Pentecostal church has also meant that becoming a Pentecostal minister is a possible career choice for former professional footballers. One of them is Francisco Lima. Since the end of his professional career, he has founded his own Pentecostal church in Manaus. Lima is clear as to his motivation.

'It's my turn to give something back. There are many poor people to help on the outskirts of Manaus,' he says.

For six months of the year you can follow the *Peladão* in every possible area of Manaus. The championship starts in August, and goes on until carnival in February. The group stage features over a hundred groups, the winners of which go through to the knockout rounds. The beauty contests are held concurrently, with the jury gradually settling on a winner.

I travel out to Betânia, one of the oldest parts of Manaus, which lies near one of the watercourses which burst their banks and flood nearby houses every year in December. Many of the houses are built on stilts, and the residents walk from house to house on planks. Betânia's gravel pitch occupies the best patch of land in the area, and is surrounded by a concrete wall overlooking a stinking stream that's used as a rubbish dump in the dry season. It's a Saturday, at ten o' clock in the morning, and it's time for round sixty-eight in the final stage.

The home team, a bunch of guys in their twenties who call themselves Furia FC, are warming up on the pitch. They're irritated. The referee hasn't shown up.

'He's stuck in traffic,' says the ref's friend.

Furia's captain looks at the clock. If they don't start playing soon, all the day's matches will be delayed. He looks at the ref's friend.

'Have you ever refereed a match?'

The friend shakes his head.

Furia's captain goes over to the opposing team and asks whether they're happy for the referee's friend to step in. They shake hands and point at the friend.

'You referee.'

A dozen or so supporters try to convince the first-time referee to give the home team the advantage. Even the neighbours closest to the pitch want the ref on Furia's side. The game is tough and you can tell the *Peladão* has entered the knockout phase of the tournament. One of Furia's strikers spends the whole time hanging around the opposition's keeper. He puts his first chance against the post. The second hits the crossbar, and the third goes wide.

'Fucking amateur!' screams Furia's coach, who is just as young as the players.

In the second half, the first-time referee caves in to pressure from the neighbours and gives a cheap penalty to Furia. Even that's botched by the team's forward. Their friends standing by the fence don't know what to do with themselves – if Furia don't win this match, they'll be out of the *Peladão*. When the opposing team, from neighbouring borough Colônia Oliveira Machado, score a goal instead, and eventually win 2-0, it's too much. Furia's captain has a go at the referee for not sending off a player on the opposing team who came on to the pitch wearing cleats. That's forbidden by *Peladão* rules.

'The match has to be replayed,' demands Furia's captain.

'Fat chance,' the winning team's captain replies. 'As soon as the ref told him to take the boots off, he did. He played the whole match barefoot.'

'That makes no difference,' came the Furia reply, 'he went on to the pitch with football boots on and that's forbidden.'

The players gather round the novice referee, who backs towards the exit. The atmosphere has turned sour, and when the winning team start pushing Furia's captain the referee sees his chance to leave the pitch. He waves over a motorbike taxi and flees. The argument on the pitch continues until two jeeps full of policemen turn up with automatic rifles at the ready.

In the afternoon it's time for the pride of the district, BEC, Betânia Esporte Clube, to play their match. They've won the senior championship a few times, and always draw a good crowd. Today, a few hundred friends have spread out their cool bags, full of cans of beer, along the concrete wall that surrounds the pitch. It's 30°C, and the old guys' jerseys, sponsored by one of Betânia's bars, are already soaked through with sweat. BEC will face a team made up of officers from one of Manaus's regiments. These players are also in their fifties, but none of them have beer bellies.

'It's so typical that we'd be up against a gang of muscle-bound officers,' says Maria Machado.

Her husband is BEC's captain, and neither he nor his teammates can stand up to the military's attack. BEC lose 5-1, and the officers gather in a circle on the pitch and let out a confrontational war cry that echoes around the stilt houses of Betânia.

A few hours later, the beer bellies are gathered round a long table outside their clubhouse. It's the first time the club have gone out so early in the tournament, and the only thing that can numb the pain is the heavenly scented fish stew their wives have made.

'We had bad luck this year,' the right-back says, downing a glass of cachaça.

The intention of the *Peladão*'s founder, back in 1973, was that football would put a stop to the drunkenness on the streets. It hasn't worked. On the same day, two of Betânia's best-loved teams have been knocked out of the tournament, and it's hard to find anyone who's sober in the surrounding alleys.

Over the last few years, Arnaldo Santos has also held an Indian championship as part of the *Peladão*. The different tribes that live in and around Manaus play each other in a separate league, their matches take place in a glade in the rainforest that belongs to the university. I follow the rough track and keep my eyes peeled for snakes. The final is being held today.

One of the teams belongs to the Munduruku tribe, who are known for their test of manhood in which a large glove is smeared with a sweet paste favoured by the poisonous giant ant *tocandira*. When enough giant ants have climbed into the glove, the teenager slips it on. Each bite hurts twice as much as a wasp sting. In order to call himself a man, the boy has to wear the glove for twenty-four hours. Anyone who doesn't pass this test has to repeat the procedure until he has learned to handle the pain. This year, Munduruku FC have won all their matches, and they have the best goalkeeper in the championship. They won the semi-final 11-2.

Their opponents are Gaviões FC, the Hawks, made up of players from Sateré-Mawé. This tribe is famous for being the first to us guaraná, an energising berry that's in Brazil's bestselling soft drink. An anthropologist from the elite university USP in São Paulo, who is writing a master's thesis on the Indian tournament, is standing in the shade of the trees, looking worried. Of the championship's twelve teams, the two who really can't stand each other have reached the final. Several generations ago, Munduruku broke with the main tribe Sateré-Mawé. They've been in conflict with one another ever since.

'Fate must have brought them together again,' the anthropologist says.

After a steady first half, the favourites Munduruku are leading 2-0. Sateré-Mawé's manager is goading his players, just as Zagallo did during the semi-final against Uruguay in Mexico in 1970.

'How the hell can you be losing to these idiots? Now you go out there and win this match!'

Five minutes into the second half, the Hawks bring the score to 1-2. Ten minutes later it's 2-2. The last fifteen minutes are a battle that offers up the best football I've seen during my ten days in Manaus. Despite the fact that the pitch is muddy and uneven, they counter quickly, pass professionally and their keeper makes some spectacular saves. Munduruku are the better team, but the Hawks' keeper stops everything. In a last attack, when most people have resigned themselves to penalties, the Hawks make it 3-2. The final whistle is drowned out by the celebrations, as the referee is surrounded by angry Munduruku players. They accuse the Hawks of having signed a professional goalkeeper for the final.

One of the wives of the Hawks' manager breaks through the circle and walks up to the referee.

'Don't listen to them,' she snarls.

'Aha?' replies Munduruku's team captain. 'Then show us your goalkeeper's ID card. Because he's no Sateré-Mawé. He's white!'

'No, no. He's an Indian,' she reassures him.

To play in the Indian championships, players have to be registered with the Indian authorities in Fundai, and carry the ID cards the indigenous peoples have in Brazil. If the goalkeeper can't show his, the whole team should be disqualified, and Munduruku FC be declared this year's champions.

The anthropologist rushes up to stop a full-scale fight breaking out between the tribes. Arnaldo Santos comes running after him.

'Let the courts handle this. We shouldn't spoil the football by fighting!'

He compensates Munduruku by giving them the prize for best player, goal and goalkeeper. To distract the players further, he asks me to administer the prize-giving. I feel like some colonial lord as I place the medals over the Indians' heads. Then Arnaldo passes the winners' cup over to the Hawks. I go up to the goalkeeper who stands accused of not being an Indian, and ask him where his village is.

'It's in the jungle, of course!' he says.

It's obvious that he doesn't belong to the indigenous tribes. Therefore, Sateré-Mawé ought to hand back the cup – as I point out.

'To Munduruku?! Never,' says the manager. 'We won.'

On the way back to town I am once again struck by how bizarre it is to nominate Manaus as one of the host cities for the 2014 World Cup. The city is more or less lawless, there's no professional football to speak of, it has appalling infrastructure and a climate that will make the Dallas matches of the 1994 World Cup seem like a picnic. When you step out through the doors of the plane, if feels as if someone's thrown a soaking wet woollen blanket over you. At the same time, your hair frizzes up and it feels like you're wading through sand.

Another problem for the teams who will be playing there is the lack of training options. The stadium offered by the Brazilian football association to FIFA as a training ground is falling to bits. The only grass pitch that's good enough is the Petrobras pitch, but that won't do as a training ground because it is in the middle of an industrial area which tens of thousands of workers pass through every day. The only possible training ground will be the new World Cup stadium, which was built on the ground that the Vivaldão once stood on. None of the other professional clubs' stadiums have any floodlights.

From a distance, the Arena Amazônia looks like a spaceship that's landed in the rainforest. It was designed by the German architects GMP, who built three of South Africa's stadiums for the 2010 World Cup, including Cape Town's Green Point stadium. In order to avoid the grass pitch turning into a lake during the rainy season, the architects came up with a way of pumping the rainwater out into gigantic underground tanks. During dry periods the stored water will be used to irrigate the pitch. The Germans have dubbed the stadium ecologically sustainable as a result. Alongside the precipitation, lightning is a problem. Germany suffers two or three major thunderstorms a year – in Amazonas, two thunderstorms roll in every week. The architects have equipped the stadium with a roof to which they can attach lightning rods. The problem is that the roof, which is built of thick plastic netting, stops air escaping. When Arena Amazônia is at full capacity, it will turn into a steaming 50°C cauldron.

'I pity the countries who get drawn to play here,' says Orleans Mesquita da Silva, one of the 1,500 construction workers who have erected the stadium.

Ten years ago, he played in the final of the *Peladão* with Manaus Moderna, the fruit and vegetable market's team. The match was played late in the evening at the Vivaldão, so that none of the players or the spectators would collapse in the heat. During the 2014 World Cup, the group-stage matches – including England vs. Italy – will be played in the late afternoon, so European TV viewers can watch the games.

'These will be the worst matches of the World Cup,' he sighs.

They're also concerned about Arena Amazônia at the Brazilian federal accountability office in Brasília. As a result of suspected corruption, the office mothballed a $200 million loan from the Brazilian development bank. The state government had to finance the construction themselves until they could show that the money wasn't finding its way into the politicians' own pockets. Another thing that worries the accountability office is that the stadium, built with taxpayers' money, may turn out to be a white elephant.

They fear that no one will have any use for Arena Amazônia after the 2014 World Cup. None of the professional clubs in Manaus attracts more than a few hundred supporters, and the national team avoid Manaus because of the climate and the distance – the flight between Rio and Manaus takes four hours.

The state government have appointed a former politician to tackle the problem. Miguel Capobiango has government funding to build a conference centre adjacent to the arena.

'This is how I see it: you have a product you want to launch, maybe it's something produced by a company from the industrial areas around here – you can have the whole pitch at your disposal. We can also arrange concerts here. Both Iron Maiden and Megadeth have played in Manaus. We could have a heavy metal festival here. You have to think creatively,' he explains to me, and continues:

'Manaus could become a tourist metropolis.'

I remind him of the statistic that only 4 per cent of domestic tourism reaches Amazonas. Most Brazilians think they'll get yellow fever or malaria as soon as they land in Manaus.

'There are many prejudices. What people don't get is that Manaus is just like any other big city. We have fancy malls and good restaurants. We don't have any wild Indians on the streets.'

The price tag for Arena Amazônia, with room for 42,377 spectators, has amounted to over $250 million, making it the most expensive World Cup stadium per seat. One of the reasons is the cost of transporting building materials here. The concrete, specially manufactured to tolerate the rainforest's humidity, arrived by cargo ship up the Amazon. The steel construction for the stands was sent by boat from Portugal, and the plastic seats were flown in from Germany.

'We tend to joke that this was how things were during the rubber boom, when everything was shipped here from Europe to build the opera house,' Miguel Capobiango says.

The difference is that, then, the bill was footed by a few extremely rich rubber barons. Now the population are having to cough up for a stadium that will only be used for four group-stage matches during the World Cup. Critics point out that the money could have gone into much-needed infrastructure instead. Seventy-eight per cent of the population of Manaus have no access to running water or sewage disposal in their homes.

Capobiango says 'you can't do everything at once', and points out that there is a future for football in the stadium.

'We'll hold the final of the *Peladão* here every year.'

At the popular Italian restaurant Fiorentina, which is by one of the old squares in central Manaus, the guests are waiting to see the first episode of *Super-starkers Afloat*. The programme is scheduled for 7.20 p.m., but when the evening news has finished an animation about Moses in the desert starts instead. The production server has crashed, and the producers have hastily thrown in a replacement programme from the Pentecostal minister's channel Rede Record. The opening credits don't roll until 8.30: twelve half-naked girls wave from a luxury white yacht that glides along the Amazon at dawn. The men in the restaurant whistle and reminisce about the *Peladão* of former years, when the city's prostitutes used to take part in the beauty contest.

'They used to get their tits out back then. Now the *rainhas* don't even have string bikinis – they have to wear those bodies that look like fucking swimming costumes,' one of the men complains.

The cameras that have been set up on the yacht show the participants having breakfast, sunning themselves on the deck and drinking cocktails in the bar. The task for today has been to listen to a former Miss Amazonas explaining the mindset required to win a beauty contest. The mood among the candidates is tense. When two of the girls on the boat became friends on Facebook they realised they had the same boyfriend. The newspaper *A Crítica* exploited the rift to the max and has been baiting the participants.

'I can't understand why they're arguing about dating the same guy. They should both just tell him to go to hell,' one of the girls in the restaurant says.

Her name is Paulina and she texts into the channel to vote off the girl with the dyed blonde hair.

'She looks like she's just stuck her head in a bucket of bleach.'

The ones who do best on the programme are the girls with long, dark, curly hair.

'They should look like they're from Amazonas, you know,' Paulina says.

The programme finishes with the luxury yacht gliding down the Amazon into the sunset, while the participants once again wave from the sun deck.

The following Sunday, more than five hundred Obidense supporters turn up to São Raimundo's home stadium, Colina. Beer is sold from enormous polystyrene boxes for $1.50 a can, and the private security guards who've been hired by the team ensure that no one gets too drunk. No one's allowed into the concrete stands behind the goals and along the far touchline because of the risk of them collapsing – this was the stadium CBF presented as a training ground for FIFA.

Around the pitch, Obidense's shoe king adjusts the advertising banners from the abattoir, the video shop, the convenience store and his chain of shoe shops.

'This is how we want it to be. A family treat for everyone,' he says, looking up at the stands.

The supporters set off fireworks and start chanting. Lima signs autographs for the fans and thirty or so children run on to the pitch with the team. The team they're about to face look on enviously while the well-paid coaching staff put out water bottles along the touchline. When Obidense make it 1-0 in the first half, the fans climb up on the fence to touch the players. In the second half things pick up speed and the final score is chalked up at 8-0. The only one who isn't euphoric afterwards is the coach. There's something about Lima he's worried about.

'I've told him so many times. He doesn't need to set any offside traps any more. It just leads to unnecessary risks.'

Four weeks later, Obidense have made their way into the last sixteen, and I follow the match in Rio via internet radio. The opponents are a simple team founded by a construction firm that made money during the property boom in Manaus. The owner put some of the money into signing former professionals to key positions in the team. The match is being played at Colina, and a family atmosphere has once again taken hold. In the first half, Obidense lead 1-0, and the commentator suggests that they're within reach of the final. During half-time the heavens open. Within a quarter of an hour, the already poor surface is transformed into a muddy puddle. The shoe king tries unsuccessfully to convince the referee to stop the match. Five minutes into the second half, one of Obidense's defenders slips as he's kicking the ball out, and one of the construction firm's players equalises. Ten minutes later, the keeper slips and lets in a goal, making it 2-1.

'We fought like animals in the last fifteen minutes, but it didn't matter what we did. The ball wouldn't go in. It was awful. Children were crying in the stands,' the shoe king tells me on the phone.

The worst thing was the mood in their home town Óbidos, with its 50,000 residents. A celebratory dinner was laid out on the table in the main square, and the whole town listened to the internet radio broadcast. Not even in their wildest dreams had anyone believed the team would be knocked out by a bunch of construction workers.

'They were really, really disappointed,' the shoe king says.

After the championship, the Calderaro family handed out prizes to those who'd stood out during the year's competition. The shoe king won the prize for best club chairman, Obidense's supporters' club won the prize for best fans and their forward was declared top scorer with fourteen goals.

'We have to be content with that, but next year will be better. Lima has already said he's happy to join us again.'

Next year, the shoe king will also put more energy into finding the right beauty queen.

'This year we had the girlfriend of one of the board members. She wasn't ugly or anything, but she was shy. At the first presentation, she didn't even look the jury in the eye. You know? She went out in the very first round.

'Next year we'll pay for a proper professional model. It's worth it. If our beauty queen had got through to the final, we would have been able to erase that match with the rain.'

8

'There's not that much competition'
How Brazilian football's number one rebel
Romário became a respected politician

The caretaker opens the door in the high wall topped with elec-
trified fencing. I go in through the garage entrance where a red
Ferrari is parked. The owner of the car is hanging out by the
pool in shorts, flip-flops and a vest, chatting to a friend. To avoid
disturbing them, I walk to the other end of the terrace and look
out over the artificial lake that was created at the end of the fifties
to provide humidity in the newly built capital Brasília. His motor-
boat lies anchored by the jetty and planted palms rise up along
the shoreline. The pale green villa with white corners is big enough
to house half a dozen families, but here one man rules the roost.
His name is Romário de Souza Faria, and he's a member of the
National Congress of Brazil.

When '*O Baixinho*', Shorty, has finished talking to his friend,
he comes up to me and holds out his hand.

'Welcome,' says Romário and asks if it will be OK to do the
interview in the garden. We go through the kitchen where his
eight-year-old daughter Ivy is having lunch with her nanny and
two of the villa's caretakers. A large volleyball court with imported,

fine white sand opens out at my feet – Romário uses it when he misses life on the beach in Rio too much. Behind the sandy court looms a four-metre-high fence enclosing his private football pitch. The grass is freshly cut and the lines freshly painted.

'I've just sorted it out. This evening we'll be playing a *pelada* here', Romário says, sitting down in the shade of two trees.

I tell him that when I moved to Brazil he was in the papers every week. His former wife had sued him for missing maintenance payments for their son, the tax authorities were demanding retrospective taxes for his time at Flamengo, the co-op association in his apartment block were asking for a six-figure fee for water damage and Fluminense fans were attacking him for not turning up for training – to which he had answered: 'I'm not a sportsman. I'm a striker.'

Romário was known as 'the bad boy of Brazil'.

Now, ten years on, he's the country's golden boy. Romário is one of the best liked people in Congress, and has been awarded top marks by the independent political journal *Congresso em Foco*.

'What happened?' I ask.

Romário guffaws and answers in his lisping favela Portuguese:

'What kind of talk is that? I'm still the bad boy. I always will be. What happened was that I was given this fantastic little girl, a special little girl, who has helped me realise how dumb, crazy and arrogant I've been. A real egotist. It's always been just me, me, me. When Ivy was born, everything changed. She opened my eyes,' he says, leaning back in the garden chair.

Romário de Souza Faria was born in 1966 in Jacarézinho, one of Rio's most densely populated favelas, with 60,000 inhabitants packed into less than half a square kilometre. When he was four years old, his dad managed to find a better home in Vila da Penha, one of the shabby suburbs in Zona Norte. His dad loved playing ball and formed a neighbourhood club where he made sure his son got a chance to play with the older boys. When Romário was a teenager, his father realised his son had talent and took him along to Olaria, a feeder club for Vasco da Gama, which immediately sent Romário over to Vasco for a trial. The old working-class club signed him and the nineteen-year-old joined the A team, together with Roberto Dinamite, Vasco's best striker of all time.

Romário was top scorer in the Campeonato Carioca, with one goal more than Dinamite, and the residents of Rio demanded that Telê Santana take him along as a wild card in the squad for the World Cup in Mexico in 1986. But Santana didn't want to break up his '*Quadrado Mágico*'. His big breakthrough into the national team came instead with the Olympics in Seoul in 1988. Romário took *A Seleção* into the final against the Soviet Union, where he put his team ahead after half an hour. Brazilians watching at home were convinced he was going to give Brazil one of the few medals they've yet to win in the football world – an Olympic gold. But in the second half, the Soviet Union drew level with a penalty and then won in extra time. Romário had to be content with the Golden Boot, and the news that he had caught the attention of PSV Eindhoven, who'd won the European Cup a few months before.

At that time it was still unusual for Brazilian professionals to play in Europe, but the coach Guus Hiddink flew over to Rio to sign Romário. Vasco received the equivalent of $5 million, at that time the highest transfer fee a European club had paid for a Brazilian. Romário thanked them for their confidence in him by scoring 165 goals in the 163 matches he played during his five years in Holland. The success led him to take extraordinary liberties. When he injured his wrist in 1990 and couldn't help his team stay top of the league in the final games of the season, he ran off to Rio, where his injury did not stop him playing sweaty *peladas* on the beach. Ajax overtook PSV and won the Dutch league. Romário shrugged: 'Everyone knows PSV aren't capable of playing without Romário.'

Even though Romário was difficult and referred to himself in the third person like Pelé, Guus Hiddink still thinks Romário is the best player he's ever worked with. 'Before an important match, when everyone was a bit nervous, he would come over to me and say, "Relax, coach, Romário will make sure we win the match", and he did! Of course, it wasn't always like that, but in eight out of ten key matches he scored the winning goal!'

Success at PSV led Barcelona's Dutch coach Johan Cruyff to convince his club that bringing Romário to the club would be a great investment. In his very first season, Romário was top scorer and Barcelona won the league.

Things went a bit more slowly with the national side. His tricky wrist stopped Romário taking part in the 1990 World Cup, and, ahead of the 1994 World Cup, the manager Carlos Alberto Parreira was unconvinced. The two had clashed ever since Parreira benched Romário for a friendly in Brazil. 'I don't fly all this way just to sit on the bench,' Romário had said, and left the ground. Parreira's problem was that his team couldn't manage without their temperamental forward. During the 1994 World Cup qualifying rounds, Brazil drew 0-0 with Ecuador and lost 2-0 to Bolivia, the first defeat *A Seleção* had ever suffered in a World Cup qualifier. With one match remaining, Brazil had to win – or miss a World Cup for the very first time. To make things even more painful, they were to face Uruguay, at the Maracanã, and veteran journalists who remembered *Maracanazo* were doing their best to make the players nervous. Parreira knew only one striker who liked situations like that. Romário was flown in from Barcelona and scored both goals in the match, ensuring Brazil's qualification for the 1994 World Cup.

In the plane on the way to the US, Bebeto boarded first and took the window seat. When Romário came aboard he walked up to his fellow forward and said, 'Hey, that's my seat'. Bebeto didn't know what to do; there were plenty of other empty seats. To avoid an argument he got up and gave the window seat to Romário.

The tension between the pair didn't ease off until the second-round match against the USA on 4 July. Although Romário had had masses of chances, it was still 0-0 a good way into the second half. With little more than a quarter of an hour of the match left he saw yet another chance open up, but he couldn't close it himself. Instead he passed to Bebeto who made it 1-0. Bebeto cried 'I love you, Romário!' and the turbulent duo became Brazil's sharpest pair of strikers since the days of Pelé and Tostão.

After the country's fourth World Cup victory, praise for Romário in Brazil became so universal that it made his playing in Europe seem ridiculous. 'His body was in Barcelona, but his thoughts were in Rio,' said his team-mate Stoichkov. At the start of 1995, Romário couldn't stand it any more: he signed for Flamengo. Brazil's biggest club was celebrating its one hundredth anniversary and convinced the Brazilian brewery giant Ambev, which now owns Budweiser, to sponsor part of the transfer fee demanded by Barcelona. A million *flamenguistas* lined the streets to welcome Romário when he was paraded through his home town.

After this point, Romário became known for his disputes with coaches, players, fans and girlfriends. When he was kept out of the World Cup squad in 1998, the manager said he was injured but everyone knew Zagallo wanted to prevent Romário's undisciplined style rubbing off on the other players.

Despite all the trouble, Romário continued to score goals. As a thirty-five-year-old, he was top scorer in the Brasileirão 2001. When I attended the Rio carnival in February the following year, tens of thousands of people roared 'ROMÁRIO, ROMÁRIO, ROMÁRIO!' from the stands. Not until I looked up at the big screens did I realise what had kicked off the perfectly timed chorus at the Sambódromo da Marquês de Sapucaí. The Brazil manager, Luiz Felipe Scolari had arrived in one of the boxes and the residents of Rio were trying to convince him to take Romário to the 2002 World Cup. But it wasn't to be this time either.

Two years later, when I was writing a story for the Swedish football magazine *Offside* on the tenth anniversary of the 1994 World Cup, I followed Romário around for a few weeks. I wanted to get an interview or at least a comment on the header that sent Sweden out of the semis, taking the shine off one of Sweden's most beautiful summers. At this point, Romário was into his third Rio club, Fluminense, and had just been arrested for punching a supporter who'd been throwing chickens on to the pitch. The chicken attack was the supporters' way of heckling him for caring more about chasing women on the beach than chasing balls on the pitch (the Portuguese word for 'hen' is *galinha*, also Brazilian slang for 'ladies' man'). I went to Fluminense's ground every day, but the few times Romário actually showed up for training he just passed the reporters by, refusing to answer questions. Instead I was invited to the opening night of his new nightclub in Barra da Tijuca, but even there he avoided the media. With my seventh free whisky to buttress my courage I finally got the guts to sneak through the bar into the roped-off VIP area, where Romário was sitting with his friends. I'd barely managed to introduce myself before the bouncers came.

'He came in via the bar,' one of them said.

'Via the bar?' asked Romário.

'Yeah! He climbed over the rail,' replied the bouncer.

'Did you come via the bar?' Romário asked me.

'Does it make any difference how I . . .'

'If you came via the bar I can't talk to you.'

'But . . .'

'No.'

The bouncer dragged me over the dancefloor and threw me out onto the street.

A year later Ivy was born. Romário has said: 'The first hours after the birth I was in shock, thinking: "Why is this happening to me? What have I done wrong?" Then I went in to my wife and told her. "Our little girl's a bit different."'

To stop the rumours spreading, the king of strikers called a press conference the following week. He explained that his daughter had been born with Down's syndrome, and that he was a very happy father. A month later, on 25 April 2005, he said farewell to the national team. After scoring the second goal against Guatemala in a 3-0 win at the Maracanã, he pulled up his shirt to reveal a white vest on which was written: 'I have a little girl who has Down's. She's a little princess'. When he was substituted in the second half, he cried at the standing ovation and blew kisses to the fans. Brazil's biggest football rebel had found his sensitive side.

Romário was thirty-nine years old, had scored 944 goals during his professional career and became ambitious for the first time. Just like Pelé, he wanted to score his thousandth goal. Romário signed once again for the team that had nurtured him, Vasco, and scored eighteen goals during his first season. Becoming uneasy, Pelé urged Romário to hang up his boots 'considering his advanced age' – Pelé himself was twenty-nine when he scored his thousandth goal. Romário replied that he thought someone should stuff a sock in Pelé's mouth, concluding: 'A quiet Pelé is a poet.'

The following year, Romário moved to the US, just as Pelé had done, to wrap up his career. He signed for Miami FC and scored twenty-two goals in twenty-nine matches. One of the reasons for the move was that his daughter would get access to expert advice on Down's syndrome, but when it emerged that Miami had no more, and no better, experts than Rio, the family decided to move home again. Romário signed for Vasco for the fourth time in his career and the club started the campaign Projeto Romário 1000 Gols. There were only sixteen goals to go, and the management of the club encouraged his team-mates to try to let Romário have the final shot. I was at one of these hilarious matches at São Januário and saw how much effort the whole team put in. Many of my neighbours in the stands remembered how a young, energetic Romário had been the Campeonato Carioca's top scorer more than twenty years previously. Now, the forty-one-year-old striker didn't set foot in his own half during the entire match. He stayed with the opposition defenders and waited for the ball.

When Vasco were up against their rivals Flamengo at the Maracanã, Romário scored his 999th goal. There were ten minutes left of the match, and the reporters rushed down from the press box to gather along the pitch in order to be able to run over to Romário when he scored his historic goal. The setting was perfect – a classic derby at the Maracanã, where Pelé had also scored his thousandth goal. Three minutes before full time, Romário freed himself and lured Flamengo's goalkeeper over to the wrong side.

O Baixinho shot, but Bruno stuck out his leg as he hung in the air and saved the ball miraculously with one foot.

The next chance came against Botafogo, but Romário was unsuccessful that time, too. When Vasco were scheduled to play a match in the Brazilian Cup, the conditions were perfect – they would meet second-division Gama. Romário asked for the match to be moved to the Maracanã and his family baked a giant cake bearing the words '*1000 gol*'. His team-mates were so focused on helping him score that Gama knocked Vasco out 2-0. 'It's not worth it. The thousandth goal will come along when God wills it,' Romário said to his wife.

Two weeks later, on 20 May 2007, Vasco faced Sport from Recife in the Brazilian league. Vasco were leading 2-0 in the first half, but neither of the goals had been scored by the team's number eleven. In the second half, one of Sport's defenders brought down a Vasco player and the referee pointed to the penalty spot. The Vasco fans, who'd been following the fraught struggle patiently, screamed 'ROMÁRIO, ROMÁRIO, ROMÁRIO!' as he walked up to the penalty spot at São Januário.

'*GOOOOOOOOOOOOOOOOOL!!!*'

Just like Pelé, he scored his thousandth goal from a penalty, and hundreds of reporters and photographers stormed the pitch. Romário picked up the ball, kissed it and wept. 'I never expected that He up there would give me a chance like this at the age of forty-one,' he said, crouching before the cameras. Then he tore off his shirt and gave it to his mother, who had run down on to the pitch. He gave the ball to his son, Romarinho, Little Romário.

Two matches and two goals after his thousandth goal, he wrapped up his record-breaking career. The occasion coincided with FIFA's decision that Brazil was to host the 2014 World Cup.

To show that the football republic were planning to arrange something out of the ordinary, President Lula da Silva took Romário with him to Zurich, where the former rebel of football held aloft a replica of the World Cup. It was time for the 2014 World Cup preparations to begin.

Then something happened.

The step from football legend to politician is not as big in Brazil as in other countries. It's actually a relatively conventional career path. Football heroes already have their supporters and can easily transform them into voters in the elections. When Roberto Dinamite, Romário's fellow Vasco striker, left the club in 1992 after 702 goals in 1,100 matches, he was voted into Rio's local government. Since then he has been re-elected five terms in a row to the state's legislative assembly, as well as becoming Vasco's club president. Romário's fellow Brazil striker Bebeto has also become a politician. In 2010, he was voted into the state of Rio de Janeiro's legislative assembly, and has since become a member of the organising committee for the 2014 World Cup.

As always, though, Romário had to outdo his fellow strikers. He has gone all the way to the National Congress of Brazil.

When a politician reaches Congress, in the modernist capital Brasília, he or she has no grand expectations. A third of the 594 Congress members stand accused of anything from vote buying and money laundering to kidnapping, cocaine smuggling and murder.

One of the most high-profile cases is that of chief of police Hildebrando Pascoal. In the 1990s, he was linked with an un-official death squad in the state of Acre in the Amazon, which took the lives of more than thirty people. The death squad gouged out their victims' eyes, and dismembered their bodies with a chain saw. Despite the fact that the chief of police was under investigation, he was voted into Congress for the right-wing party Democratas.

Another member of Congress with a heavy weight on his conscience is São Paulo's former governor Paulo Maluf. He has been convicted of stealing $11 million from a road-building project and is facing potential charges of embezzling a further $400 million from the treasury. Although he is wanted, and will be arrested by Interpol if he leaves Brazil, he's secure in his seat in Congress. A third example is the Chair of the Senate, the first house of Congress. In 2007, he was caught up in a corruption scandal and forced to leave his post, but has since returned as Chair, still denying allegations of taking bribes from a construction company to pay the maintenance for children born during his extra-marital affair with a TV reporter who later posed for *Playboy*.

The fact that congressmen and women can seemingly behave however they like with impunity has left citizens feeling unable to take Congress seriously. The same year Romário was elected, the country's most famous clown, Tiririca, also put himself up for a seat in Congress, with the slogan: 'It can't get worse than this – vote for Tiririca!' In spite of the fact that his reading and writing skills are extremely limited, the clown got the highest number of votes in the whole of Brazil.

Brazilians' tendency to elect clowns, footballers and suspected murderers has nothing to do with voters being crazier than in other countries. The fundamental reason is the same as in Italy: the political culture has led to there being exceptionally few honourable politicians to elect. As many of the Brazilian electorate are illiterate or 'functionally illiterate' – they can write their names and read a shopping list, but can't write a letter or read a book – it's easy to buy votes. A large proportion of voters don't believe that politicians can change their lives, and prefer to sell their votes for $20, because at least then they're getting something from the country's political class. And even though it might cost a politician a few million dollars to gather together enough votes to get into Congress, it pays off. The bribes from the construction industry alone, disguised as lobbying, exceed the sums politicians spend on their election campaigns. The media can be manipulated through the placement of state advertising campaigns, and the judicial system is attentive to the needs of those in power. Despite all the evidence, politicians can therefore embezzle tax funds without any real risk of imprisonment. According to FIESP, Brazil's biggest industrial association, up to $30 billion are swallowed up by corruption every year. That money could be used to create 327,000 new hospital beds, provide water and sewage disposal to twenty-three million households, or build 227 new airports.

In light of this, the fact that Congress celebrated FIFA's choosing Brazil as World Cup host is nothing strange. Politicians knew that they would get the chance of the decade to rake in the cash. The decision to grant Rio de Janeiro the 2016 Olympic Games can hardly have made things worse.

At the end of January 2012, I met FIFA's general secretary Jérôme Valcke at a cocktail party at one of the luxury hotels along the beachfront in Ipanema. There was exactly one year to go until the date on which Brazil had promised that all their stadiums would be ready – and the general secretary had just realised this wouldn't be the case. The renovation of the Maracanã was more than six months behind and had become twice as expensive as planned. The construction of the new stadium in São Paulo, where the opening match will be played, was almost two years behind schedule and the work to renovate Beira-Rio in Porto Alegre had been put on hold six months previously.

Brazilians weren't surprised. That's because the most important thing for Brazilian politicians and construction firms when they're dividing up public funds between them is to ensure that the decision-making process and the start of construction are delayed as long as possible. This piles on the pressure, meaning that in the end construction is unable to go through the correct procurement procedures. Planning permission and environmental licences have to be obtained in a hurry and the national auditing body is not allowed the time it needs to check whether the invoices really match up. The politicians and construction companies are then free to share out the spoils in peace.

Jérôme Valcke, in contrast to the Brazilians, was surprised and frustrated. He complained that not even the contract drawn up in 2007 by FIFA and Brazil's former president, Lula, had been ratified by Congress.

'Five years ago, we agreed everything, and now Congress wants to negotiate. It's insane,' Valcke said, as he sipped his caipirinha.

'Lula was different. If we encountered problems, he found a solution. Now Dilma's in charge. I have a lot of respect for her, but she's a very unusual Brazilian. She's not the slightest bit interested in football. Imagine!! The biggest footballing nation in the world is hosting the World Cup and the president's not interested.'

It had also occurred to FIFA's general secretary that 2014 is election year in Brazil. The presidential election campaign begins in July, in the middle of the World Cup, meaning that the current government are planning to use the 2014 World Cup as election propaganda. President Dilma Rousseff's government want to subsidise tickets for those on low incomes, pensioners, students and Indians, and ban the sale of beer in the stadiums to show they care about public health. I wondered what Valcke thought about that.

'Sorry, but beer is not something we can negotiate on. Beer is part of the World Cup.'

A month later, the general secretary could no longer put on a brave face. At a press conference in London, he said that Brazil needed 'a kick in the ass' to get its preparations for the 2014 World Cup underway. His choice of words led the Foreign Policy Adviser to the President of Brazil to call Jérôme Valcke 'a damn fool' and Brazil's sports minister to send FIFA a letter stating that Brazil no longer wished to work with their general secretary. A scheduled inspection of the stadium construction sites was cancelled, and the government's group leader in the Senate stated that the general secretary was no longer welcome to visit Congress. In order to cool things down, FIFA president Sepp Blatter had to cut short a visit to Asia and fly to Brazil to apologise to Dilma Rousseff.

The person who was most angry with FIFA's general secretary was sports minister Aldo Rebelo. He is a member of Partido Comunista do Brasil, which has its roots in Maoism, and led the commission responsible for investigating Nike's actions following Brazil's loss to France in the 1998 final. Nationalist Aldo Rebelo has led a campaign against American words entering into Brazilian Portuguese. He has also tried to ban the celebration of Halloween in Brazil, and supported a bill calling for an amnesty and free land to be granted to illegal loggers in the Amazon rainforest. When the controversial communist was made sports minister, after his predecessor resigned while fighting corruption allegations, he immediately formed a relationship with the Brazilian football association and assumed political responsibility for the 2014 World Cup. Two weeks after Rebelo had said he refused to work with Jérôme Valcke, the International Press Club in Rio managed to get him in for a press conference. I took the chance to ask the minister if there wasn't at least a grain of truth in FIFA's criticism of Brazil.

'Well, we are the only country that has qualified in every World Cup that's been played. We've won five of them. You don't think we'd be capable of organising a World Cup? That's pretty impudent of you. We've organised things much bigger than the World Cup.'

'Like what?' I asked.

'Well, we built Brazil. One of the world's biggest and most beautiful countries.'

No argument can counter nationalism, so I asked instead why the government, who are normally oblivious to the indigenous peoples and build hydroelectric dams over their land in the Amazon, wanted FIFA to provide subsidised tickets for Brazilian Indians.

'Where did you say you came from? Sweden?! Yeah, it's probably not that easy for you to understand, you don't have any Indians, but here in Brazil we were the first to do ethnographic studies of their lives. We care about the Indians. We're going to bus them into the cities so they can watch the matches,' replied the sports minister.

Shortly after the fight between FIFA and the government, the Chair of the Brazilian football association resigned. After twenty-three years in power, Ricardo Teixeira could no longer withstand the corruption accusations, which also implicated his ex-father-in-law, former FIFA chair João Havelange. They both maintained their innocence – and were never convicted of an offence – but forced court action in Switzerland over claims they accepted bribes of around $40 million in connection with the sale of advertising rights. Teixeira was also accused of pocketing $4 million in connection with a friendly against Portugal. In his resignation letter, which Teixeira sent from his luxury villa in Miami, he wrote, 'Our football has always been associated with two things: talent and chaos. When we've won it's been because of talent. When we've lost it's been because of chaos. I've done what I could over the years to bridge that.' On Twitter, Romário celebrated his departure with the words: 'A cancer has been driven out of Brazilian football', but choked on his celebration when he saw who was going to replace Teixeira.

José Maria Marin was born in 1932 and was a state congressman during the dictatorship. In the mid-1970s, Marin gave a speech in which he criticised the editors of TV Cultura in São Paulo, who were politically left-leaning. Within two weeks the editor-in-chief, Vladimir Herzog, was arrested and tortured to death. The case attracted a lot of international attention: Herzog had formerly been the BBC's man in Brazil. José Maria Marin – who denies that his words carried sufficient weight to influence the incarceration of Horzag – went on to become governor of São Paulo in 1982.

When Brazil became a democracy in 1990, José Maria Marin moved to forge a career in São Paulo's football association. He soon rose up through the hierarchy, finally becoming one of the five vice-presidents of the Brazilian football association. In that capacity, he awarded medals to winners of the junior cup in São Paulo in 2012 – and became infamous across the nation for allowing a gold medal to slip into his own pocket. The goalkeeper of Corinthians' junior team went without a medal and José Maria Marin was mocked as a 'medal thief' in the media.

The person who has perhaps suffered most from the selection of José Maria Marin is Brazil's president Dilma Rousseff. She was involved in the armed resistance against the dictatorship and was arrested, tortured and imprisoned. Today she's so scarred by the torture that she's reluctant to talk about it. Instead, it was her cellmate who told of how the military called Dilma Rousseff a 'communist bitch' and tortured her with electric shocks to the breasts and genitals. Dilma's husband was also arrested and tortured in front of an audience consisting of businessmen who had donated money to the military so they could watch the 'communists' suffering.

José Maria Marin continues to deny any wrongdoing and his supporters have cast aspersions in the direction of Romário, but his conflicting position with Rousseff during the dictatorship means that the two people in Brazil most crucial to the World Cup – the country's president and the head of the football association – don't speak to each other.

As if there wasn't enough *emoção* ahead of the championships, manager Mano Menezes was fired a few days before the draw for what was the major dress rehearsal for the World Cup: the 2013 Confederations Cup. FIFA's general secretary was pulling out his hair once again, wondering which manager would represent Brazil at the draw, which was to be aired on TV. The Brazilian football association hadn't thought of that; having promised Luiz Felipe Scolari that they wouldn't be introducing him for a month or so, they were now forced to make the news public immediately. The draw was one of the most chaotic in the history of the Confederation Cup. Brazil's Michelin-starred celebrity chef Alex Atala, who the government had chosen to represent the host country, got so nervous that he confused bowl A with bowl B. If FIFA's general secretary hadn't caught the mix-up at the last minute, Uruguay would have been drawn in the wrong group.

FIFA's newly coined slogan for the 2014 World Cup, 'All In One Rhythm', was turning into a joke.

The thing that has annoyed most Brazilians in the lead-up to the 2014 World Cup is that the government promised that no tax funds would be used to build the new stadiums – the business world were to put up the investment. Today it is obvious that they are all being built and renovated with tax funds. Up to this point, public funds equivalent to around $10 billion have been used to build nine and renovate three stadiums, as well as building roads and infrastructure around them. This is more money than has been spent on the last three World Cups put together.

The Congress member who has most consistently protested against this drain on funds is not a well-read left-wing politician or a hot-tempered environmentalist, or one of the more conservative forces in Congress, or one of its few women. The man who has stood up to the corruption around the 2014 World Cup is the country's number one football rebel.

When Romário was elected to Congress in 2010, Brazilians thought he would do the same as the other members: show up at Congress once a week, take home his salary of $15,000 a month and devote the rest of his time to milking the state of its taxes. But Romário shocked the nation. He became one of the country's most exemplary congressmen.

Politicians who are voted into Congress are granted public funds to run a staff of up to twenty-five people. It is a right that makes Brazil's parliament the world's second most expensive; only the US Congress spends more money on its members. When Romário got the opportunity, he employed the hottest staff in Congress. Wherever he walked through the corridors, *O Baixinho* was followed around by a gang of tall, blonde, competent women, who carried his briefcase and papers. One of those employed was twenty-eight-year-old Janaína. She is my wife's niece, and boasts, as well as her beauty, a law degree. When I found out that she'd got the position, I cheered: 'Yippee! Now I can finally get my Romário interview.' When Janaína put something up on Facebook, I'd 'like' it, and when she visited us I was extra friendly.

When Romário took Janaína to the Olympics in London, where

he was a studio guest on ESPN, I thought: 'Here's my chance to make the most of my family ties.' For over six months I nagged her to get me an interview. A month before the Confederations Cup it paid off. That's why I'm sitting here now, in a garden outside one of Brasília's most luxurious houses, in front of Romário who is sitting in a white vest having just kicked of his flip-flops to scratch his right ankle with his left big toe.

I ask once again how he would explain the way in which he was transformed from football rebel to one of the country's most serious congressmen.

Romário guffaws again.

'There's not much competition.'

Then he becomes serious and looks at his daughter, who's finished her lunch and is now playing ten metres away in the garden.

'It all comes down to her,' he says. 'Ivy made me see that I was needed in another way. When she was born I was in contact with many other parents who had children with Down's syndrome. Everyone kept saying: "You have a voice in society. Can't you help us make this issue more prominent? Society is so full of prejudices, but they listen to you." I thought about it a while and said to myself: "Why not? I used to think about becoming a politician. Why not try it now? I actually have the chance to do something good."'

Romário spoke to a few different parties and decided to stand for Partido Socialista Brasileiro. I ask whether he sees himself as a socialist.

'Depends what you mean by socialist. I'm dark-skinned, come from a poor family and grew up in a favela. I'm no rich, white middle-class guy. I know what it's like to be poor. What I fight for is equality. In that way I'm a socialist.'

A hundred and forty-six thousand residents of Rio voted

Romário into Congress, as many people as the Maracanã held before it was rebuilt. For the last three years he has occupied one of the state of Rio de Janeiro's forty-six seats in Congress. Apart from his attendance statistics being among the highest, he is one of the few congressmen who has achieved something that has improved the lives of the country's population. After just six months, he got a law passed guaranteeing paid parental leave for those who have children with Down's syndrome. When the new law was introduced in the presidential palace, Dilma Rousseff, the world's most powerful woman according to Forbes, chose to attend. Romário brought Ivy along to the ceremony and, when the law was ratified, he lifted his daughter into his arms and kissed her on the cheek. His eyes filled with tears and the images on TV touched people around the country. The egotistical football hero had turned into a politician who fought on the side of the powerless members of society.

'This law is one of my biggest ever victories,' he says.

I ask whether Romário the football player and Romário the politician have anything in common. He thinks for a while.

'Neither of us can keep our mouths shut. If I see something I don't like I say so. I have no problem at all calling congressmen who steal tax funds thieves. That's what they are! Just look at the stadiums built for the World Cup. Take the new national stadium here in Brasília. That's the most expensive one of all. And it's in a city where the best team plays in the third division.

'If we had put a tenth of that money into healthcare, there would have been space to take in all the patients in Brasília. Or imagine if the money had gone into education. Then schools could have offered free school lunches, have air conditioning and pay their teachers properly. I'm just saying what I've said before: the 2014 World Cup is the biggest robbery in Brazil's history.'

'But when Brazil was awarded the World Cup,' I say, 'you, the government and the football association were on the same side. Now you're the competition's biggest critic. Why?'

'I saw what they were up to. It's all about stealing as much money as you can. Several times my colleagues in Congress have tried to rope me into their system of corruption, but I don't want to be involved in it. I want Brazil to host the most beautiful competition ever. That's why I refused to sign the law FIFA wanted to bring in during the World Cup. What FIFA wants is to create a state within a state for the World Cup. I don't want that.

'There are many people who don't always want the best for our football,' Romário continues. 'Just look at the new president of the football association. He's a real thief,' he says referring to the Corinthians medal incident; an act that Marin says has been misinterpreted, whatever the video footage on YouTube shows. Romário goes on to talk about Marin's alleged links to the dictatorship: 'He supported the dictatorship that tortured Dilma's husband. Is she supposed to hand out medals alongside him? Never!'

'But why is it so hard to find a president for the football association who isn't surrounded by allegations?' I wonder.

Romário smiles, leans back in the woven chair and says that it seems that being honourable isn't at the top of the list of criteria for the job.

'Ricardo Teixeira was a real rat who stole money, but at least he made sure Brazil won. But this José Maria Marin – I don't think he gives a shit about the national team. Where are we in the rankings now? Eighteenth! Eighteenth!! It's crazy. Brazil should always be in the top four.'

The conversation drifts on to football, and I take the opportunity to ask the question I didn't manage to ask nine years earlier when I was writing a story about Sweden's woes in the 1994 World Cup.

'Hahaha. Sorry about that header that put us through to the final. But it wasn't what many people think: that I managed to jump higher than your tall defenders. I was just in exactly the right place when the pass came from Jorginho. The ball came down just where I was. If your defenders had got to the ball there, it would have hit them in the chest. For me it was at exactly the right height,' laughs the striker who's no taller than five foot six.

'Alongside the goals against Uruguay, which qualified us for the 1994 World Cup, and the penalty against Italy in the World Cup final, that went in off the post, it was the most important goal of my life.'

Ivy comes running across the lawn and sits on her dad's lap. She gets a kiss on the cheek and he gets one in return. It's clear that Romário has finally found his way home after all these years. He has even been on better terms with his other five children. The nineteen-year-old Romarinho, for whom he failed to pay maintenance for many years, has moved with him to Brasília, and plays for Brasiliense FC, the biggest club in the capital. During the final of the state championship Candangão 2013, he set up one and scored another of the goals that gave Brasiliense the title.

'It was as though my whole life passed before my eyes,' Romário says. 'For the first time I understood how it must have felt for my parents when I scored a goal. It was a fantastic feeling. I picked up Ivy and smashed my champagne glass on the floor. That's more or less how my mum used to celebrate my goals. She always threw a beer bottle at the TV,' he says and grins.

'When Romário went down on to the pitch he couldn't say a word. 'He just cried and cried,' Romarinho said afterwards.

My forty minutes with Romário are over, and my German colleague from the newspaper *Die Zeit*, who has shared my interview time, asks if we can stay and watch the afternoon's amateur match on Romário's football pitch.

'Of course, no problem!'

My colleague looks at him again beseechingly and asks if the team has enough players, or if there's space for another. Romário doesn't hesitate.

'Of course, no problem! You're welcome to play. Ask the caretaker for a pair of shorts!'

Romário has just given Marian Blasberg his happiest day on the job. My colleague springs across the grass in search of the caretaker and comes back with a pair of white shorts and a red shirt.

'You have to film me. You have to film,' he says, and looks nervously at the smooth-worn soles of his tennis shoes.

One after another, the players in Romário's amateur team roll in and sit on the terrace. One of them has played professionally. The others are in their forties and play for fun. The opposition arrive at four on the dot and are just as excited as the German. It's the first time they'll be playing Amigos do Romário, Romário's Friends. When Romário goes down to the pitch he shakes hands with all the members of the opposing team and agrees to be in a team photo. Then he goes over to his team and gives every player a manly box on the arm. He introduces *Die Zeit*'s correspondent as back-up for the day and warms up.

I can see that my colleague, who lives on the same street as me in Rio, is nervous. When he receives his first pass I worry he'll make a fool of himself, but he turns it past his opponent and passes confidently to a team-mate. The next time he gets the ball he pushes up the left wing and does exactly what the Vasco players did – the last pass to number eleven, who scores. In the second half, Romário's Friends have a comfortable lead of 7-4 as dusk approaches. The mosquitos sweep in from the lake, the grass gets damp and Marian Blasberg's tennis shoes get worse and worse. Ivy comes to hang out with me by the fence. I show her a picture of my daughter, who's the same age as her, and Ivy runs off to get a ball.

'Do you want to play with me?' she asks.

It almost feels too perfect. Ever since I moved to Brazil more than a decade ago I've been chasing an interview with Brazil's bad boy of football. Now I'm standing in the garden of his villa, kicking a ball with his daughter.

Three days later, Romário is adjusting his tie as he walks up to the rostrum in Congress. He looks at the speaker for a moment before turning to the Congress members scattered around the benches.

'Honourable colleagues, just a short time ago, selling players and TV rights were the best ways to make money in our football world. That has changed. Now, the businessmen are after the supporters' wallets. There are no terraces any more. They've been stripped out. Our most dedicated fans, who live to see the week-end's match, can't afford to go to the football. I want to bring to your attention a phenomenon that makes me sad: the elite are taking over our game.'

Romário takes the first big match of the year – Santos vs Flamengo – as an example. The businessman Wagner Abrahão bought the rights to the game and moved it 1,100 kilometres from Santos's home ground to the new World Cup stadium, Mané Garrincha in Brasília. The businessman knew that the capital is overflowing with money, but that its residents rarely have the chance to see major matches. Although the cheapest ticket cost $70 and the most expensive $160, the 77,400 tickets were sold in no time at all. After paying the football association around $400,000 for the match rights, Wagner Abrahão made a profit of two million.

'And these stadiums are built with public funds. With our money,' Romário rages.

Most of those in Congress belong to families who have controlled Brazilian politics for generations, and call one another 'Your Highness'. They dress in conservative suits and only vote for the government's suggestions when they see some personal advantage in them. Romário, who's never been accused of bribe taking, is the sharpest dressed man in Congress, and debates in his lisping favela Portuguese. It's like Wayne Rooney walking up to the rostrum in the House of Commons and telling the government what's what in a Scouse accent.

Romário flicks through his papers and takes aim at the Brazilian football association. He demands that CBF should start revealing their income and expenses publicly. He also criticises CBF's president and vice-president; the latter was called in for questioning by police, though released, during a national raid against organised financial crime at the end of 2012.

'CBF have control over our main sporting heritage and choose the players who represent our country beneath our flag. They sing the national anthem and dress in our country's most prominent colours, green and yellow. But are we sure that the football association are really doing their job? No, no! We are not. The

Brazilian football association should be renamed the Brazilian Fake Invoice Association,' Romário says, producing a laugh from the congressmen.

'Mr Speaker, can you picture our president, Dilma Rousseff, being seen with these individuals when she welcomes the world's national teams during the World Cup? You don't think that would be embarrassing for her, and damaging to Brazil's image?'

9

'The giant has awoken'
How football gave people their faith back

Expectations for *A Seleção* weren't high ahead of the 2013 Confederations Cup, the major dress rehearsal before the World Cup. Brazil hadn't beaten any of the other top nations – Italy, Germany, Argentina, France and England – in several years, and self-confidence was at rock bottom.

The last time the Brazilian team had shone was during the Confederations Cup in Germany in 2005, when Carlos Alberto Parreira served up his own variation of Telê Santana's Magic Square from the 1982 World Cup. Ronaldinho, Kaká, Robinho and Adriano made up '*O Quarteto Mágico*', the Magic Quartet, as they were referred to by the media, and *A Seleção* walked all over their arch-rivals Argentina in a 4-1 dream final. The Brazilians thought they would defend their World Cup title from 2002, and so the disappointment was all the greater when *A Seleção* went out in the quarter-final against France in the 2006 World Cup in Germany.

Carlos Alberto Parreira got the sack, and the football association went on the hunt for a replacement. A columnist for the Brazilian current affairs magazine *Veja* listed a few rules that Parreira's successor should follow:

1. No players from Real Madrid. That's a losers' club. [Both Kaká and Robinho played with Real Madrid.]
2. No sleeping on the bench. The manager has to be awake the whole match. [Parreira took his time with substitutions.]
3. Players should be chosen from those who play in Brazil. Only they know the wrongs their football can right. [From the World Cup squad's twenty-three players, only three played in Brazil. In the 2002 World Cup, half the squad were from Brazilian clubs.]
4. No players can be in advertising campaigns before they've won the World Cup. [The Magic Quartet spent more time selling toothpaste and cars than performing on the pitch.]
5. The players selected should be poorer than those in the 2006 crop. [Much of the blame for the World Cup fiasco was laid on spoilt players who partied their way round Zurich's nightclubs during the preparatory training camp.]

From the hundreds of experienced candidates, the football association chose one who'd never been a coach: Carlos Caetano Bledorn Verri, or Dunga (the Portuguese name for Dopey in *Snow White and the Seven Dwarfs*). Brazilians know him as the man who put the nail in the coffin of samba football. When Telê Santana failed to win the World Cup with his Magic Square, it was Dunga who personified the concession that was made: the introduction of European results-based football into *A Seleção*. The stiff-necked, crop-haired midfielder slaughtered his opponents on the pitch, and became captain of the team who gave Brazil their most longed-for World Cup title, in 1994. Just over ten years later, the football association wanted Dunga to inject a bit of pizzazz into the team, phase out the old stars and prioritise young players from Brazilian clubs.

Dunga's team won the South American championship, the Copa América, in 2007, and the Confederations Cup in 2009, but Dunga didn't follow the football association's instructions. The 2010 World Cup squad was just as European as Parreira's had been four years earlier. Nor had Dunga made the team younger, instead raising the average age to twenty-nine. The fact that he didn't select Neymar, who was a shining star for Santos, provoked rage in Brazil. An ad agency in Campo Grande took five of the town's advertising hoardings and created a play on the words of the health ministry's anti-drugs campaign '*Não use craque*', Don't use crack. In Portuguese, *craque* also means football star, and the ad agency's campaign went: '*Faça como o dunga. Não use craque*', Be like Dunga. Don't use stars.

After the 2-1 win against North Korea in the first group-stage matches, Dunga was a much-doubted man in Brazil. He still managed to top the group after winning 3-1 against Sven-Göran Eriksson's Ivory Coast and drawing 0-0 against Portugal. In the last sixteen, *A Seleção* secured an easy victory over Chile and, just as in 1994, Holland awaited them in the quarter-final. Ten minutes into the match at Nelson Mandela Bay stadium in Port Elizabeth, Dunga's favourite player Felipe 'Pitbull' Melo crossed perfectly to Robinho, who shot through the goalkeeper's legs to make it 1-0. Shortly afterwards, Juan put a header over the bar, and, just before half-time, Kaká come close to netting. Brazil had one foot in the semi-final, and Holland had only managed one respectable attack.

Eight minutes into the second half, Sneijder lobbed a ball towards the goal and Brazil's keeper came to punch the ball out. A moment before the ball reached him, however, Felipe Melo jumped up and headed the ball into his own goal. It was Brazil's first own goal in a World Cup and it gave Holland new-found energy. Fifteen minutes later, Robben took a corner which the diminutive Sneijder headed in unmarked. Behind him stood Felipe Melo. The Juventus midfielder realised he was responsible for both goals, lost his temper and began to live up to his nickname. After Melo knocked Robben over in the seventy-third minute, he stood on the Dutchman's thigh as he lay on the ground. The Brazilian was sent off.

'If there'd been any men in the team, they would have ripped him apart in the dressing room,' Vampeta, one of the 2002 World Cup-winning team, said after the match.

The Brazilian media took their frustration out on Dunga, and suggested that the only reason the manager had decided to have Felipe Melo in the first eleven, despite a bad season for Juventus, was that the player reminded Dunga of himself: tough, defensive and leaden. Another person who got the blame for Brazil's exit was Mick Jagger, who has a son with Brazilian TV star Luciana Gimenez. 'He sat in the stands and cheered for the USA when they lost against Ghana. He sat in the stands and cheered for England when they went out against Germany. Our problem is that now he's sitting in the stands cheering for us,' *O Globo* wrote ahead of the quarter-final. Superstitious Brazilian supporters still call the Rolling Stones frontman a '*pé-frio*', someone who brings bad luck.

Dunga got the sack, and the football association rang the golden boy of the 2002 World Cup, Luiz Felipe Scolari, to ask if he felt like taking over the team again. Scolari informed them that he was perfectly happy coaching Palmeiras, and declined. The second choice, Muricy Ramalho, who had a gold-plated contract with Fluminense, gave the same answer. Third in line was Corinthians coach Mano Menezes, who accepted. For his first international match, just a month after the 2010 World Cup, he had already put together an entirely new team, which included seventeen-year-old

Lucas, eighteen-year-old Neymar and twenty-three-year-old David Luiz. The young first eleven beat the USA 2-0, and *Marca*, the biggest sports paper in Spain, ran the headline '*Con Menezes vuelve el "jogo bonito"*', With Menezes, the beautiful game is back.

Because Brazil automatically qualified for the 2014 World Cup as host nation, and therefore did not take part in the match-intensive South American qualifying rounds, the manager didn't have many chances to test his new team under tough conditions. The 2011 Copa América was a fiasco, just one win in three matches and then a defeat on penalties in the quarter-final against Paraguay. Neither did a number of peculiar friendlies in Qatar, Gabon, Sweden and Switzerland provide any positive results, and so the 2012 London Olympics, an under-23s tournament with allowance for three overage players, became an incredibly important tournament for the Brazilian team. Menezes selected centre-back Thiago Silva as captain, and created a team of sharp, young forwards, with Neymar, Oscar, Hulk and Leandro Damião. In order to ensure stability, Menezes wanted to have two additional stars, Marcelo and Dani Alves, in key positions as *laterais* – the typical Brazilian offensive wing-back role. But Barcelona's Dani Alves injured himself and pulled out at the last minute. Instead, Menezes chose the right-back Rafael from Manchester United, who was totally unknown in Brazil.

The new team won all their matches on the way to Brazil's first Olympic final in twenty-four years. The Brazilian media remembered the defeats of 1984 against France and 1988 against the Soviet Union, and declared that this time Brazil would finally win one of the few titles the football republic hadn't already taken home. The new forwards had scored fifteen goals in five matches, and awaiting them in the final were Mexico, who'd never won an international championship.

Twenty-eight seconds into the final at Wembley, Rafael received a pass and didn't know what to do with the ball. He passed backwards without checking. Peralta stole the ball, and scored, making it 1–0. In the second half, Peralta increased the lead to 2-0, and Hulk's goal didn't come until injury time. Once again, Brazil had missed out on Olympic gold, and CBF's official website bore the header: 'Rafael, a mistake to learn from.' No one seemed to notice the fact that the team had had over ninety minutes to correct the mistake – the scapegoat had been chosen. Just like Felipe Melo, Rafael was no longer welcome in *A Seleção*.

Mano Menezes survived for a few more months, but after a 1–1 draw against Colombia and a defeat against Argentina he got the boot. Despite the fact that Scolari had just dragged Palmeiras down to the second division, he was offered the job of manager once again. This time he said yes. In order to improve their chances, Carlos Alberta Parreira was appointed as his right-hand man. With the managers who'd won Brazil's last two World Cup titles on the same bench, the association believed they had double the chance of taking the country's first World Cup title on home turf. Tough Scolari, who was known as 'Big Phil' when he coached Chelsea, confirmed this goal at his very first press conference:

'We have a responsibility to win the 2014 World Cup.'

But he realised that it wasn't going to be easy. Before the Confederations Cup, Brazil were in twenty-second place in FIFA's team rankings, the country's worst ever placing.

Even the supporters were losing faith, and they weren't reassured when rumours that Neymar had signed a preliminary contract with Barcelona were confirmed. In the middle of Brazil's training camp ahead of the Confederations Cup, Neymar flew to Barcelona in a private jet and was presented as the club's new acquisition in front of 56,500 Barça supporters at Camp Nou. At home in Santos, the club president Luis Álvaro de Oliveira Ribeiro was off sick after yet another heart attack. He had promised that the country's most sought-after player would be staying at home until after the 2014 World Cup. He'd now broken that promise, and his illness forced him to send Santos's vice-president to sign the contracts in Barcelona.

At the same time, Neymar was facing criticism from both the media and supporters for his lacklustre contributions to the national side. Brazil's most expensive player ever hadn't scored a goal in over ten matches, but found the dissatisfaction exaggerated and counter-productive: 'You can't expect me to be the same player in the national team as I am at Santos. To be honest, sometimes I don't understand what it is you're after! I benefit from a little love and consideration just like everyone else.'

If success on the pitch has often saved the people in power in Brazil, the situation has been reversed over the last decade. The population has been indulgent with regard to the team's fiascos because millions of people have been lifted out of poverty to the lower middle class. While the economies of Europe and the USA have ground to a halt, Brazil has grown to become the world's sixth largest economy. In 2010, growth stood at almost 8 per cent, and, when the world's third largest oil field was discovered off the coast of Rio, the then president Lula da Silva announced: 'We're living in a golden age.'

So when thousands of students in São Paulo take to the streets in protest two days before the Confederations Cup, the police and the government are taken unawares. The police attack the demonstrators with pepper spray, rubber bullets and tear gas. Two hundred and thirty-six students are arrested and two photographers injured, as the city's left-wing mayor defends the actions of the police. The reason for the protests is an increase in the price of bus tickets in São Paulo, but the students are also questioning why the state has put $12 billion into the 2014 World Cup instead of into education and healthcare. Many banners bear the question '*Copa pra quem?*' Who's the World Cup for?

The following day, other students hold sympathy protests that mobilise over a hundred thousand people around the country. The international media's sports reporters are commandeered away from the last rounds of training sessions to report live from the riots. The Confederations Cup, intended to be the government's definitive sign that Brazil is ready to host the 2014 World Cup and the 2016 Olympics, suddenly seems to be giving the opposite impression. Outside the national stadium, Mané Garrincha in Brasília, where the opening match between the host nation and Japan is to be played, tyres are being set alight and the police task force is obliged to fence off a three-kilometre-wide area around the stadium with anti-riot fencing, tanks and tear gas platoons.

It looks as though Brazil has been taken over in a military coup.

I've barely had a chance to take in Brazil's formation against Japan before Neymar smashes a long shot on the half-volley, straight into the left corner. It's a genuine *golaço*, and Neymar himself is so surprised that his goal drought is over that he postpones his well-practised dance moves by the corner flag and hugs his teammates first. Two minutes into the second half, Corinthians' Paulinho strikes to make it 2-0, and in the last minute of the match, late substitution Jô, of Atlético Mineiro, makes the score 3-0.

The much-admonished, frequently booed-off team have played convincingly for the first time in several years. And even though Neymar has just signed for Barcelona, and Jô was a professional in Europe for five years, the Brazilians feel it's their three 'home players' who scored the goals.

Two days later, something unusual happens in Rio.

Over the last twenty years, only a few thousand people have turned up to even the biggest demonstrations in Rio. In other Brazilian cities, people have sourly commented that it's impossible to stage a revolution in a beach resort – the golden sands are too tempting. But when Rio's residents see how the demonstrations in São Paulo and Brasília have gained pace, anger boils over in the country's most famous city too.

Brazilians can't believe their eyes when the first images are dispatched from Globo's helicopter. The whole of the enormous Avenida Rio Branco, which runs through the centre of the city, is filled with hundreds of thousands of *cariocas*, Rio residents, chanting against the city's politicians. Banners are printed with slogans such as: 'We don't need more football. We want schools and healthcare', 'Water and drainage now!', 'End corruption!' and 'Politicians who commit crimes must be punished'. It's the biggest demonstration Brazil has seen since President Fernando Collor de Mello was toppled in 1992.

The people in power are shocked. More than anything else, they are surprised by the fact that it's the middle classes who've taken to the streets.

Personally, I'm not that surprised. The Brazilian middle class is one of the world's most betrayed. A Brazilian pays a larger proportion of their income in tax than a Swiss, and higher VAT than a Swede, but gets no more in the way of public services than an African. Brazil is in eighty-eighth place in UNESCO's education rankings, after Bolivia and Ecuador, which are South America's poorest countries. Public healthcare is just as bad: infant mortality is higher, and average life expectancy shorter, than in Colombia, which has been living with a civil war for several generations. To give their children a future, middle-class parents have to send them to private school. To ensure the family's health, they have to take out health insurance. The fact that the Brazilian government are good at collecting taxes, but appalling when it comes to offering acceptable services, can primarily be put down to two things: corruption and incompetence. Money disappears along the way and the authorities do nothing about it.

No one was complaining as long as all sections of society were doing better. But now the middle class is worried that an old Brazilian spectre will rise again: inflation. The middle classes fear that their income will be drained away, and, as a result, they have less patience with the cheating and wastefulness of politicians. They've also noticed that the cost of living has increased significantly since Brazil was granted the honour of hosting the 2014 World Cup and the 2016 Olympic Games. Many have had to leave the areas they live in as rents have doubled, and a three-course meal in São Paulo is no longer any cheaper than in Stockholm or London. High taxes make cars and computers significantly more expensive than in the USA and Europe. The fact that the government has also passed a bill improving the working conditions for domestic servants, the biggest labour sector in Brazil, has meant that the traditional solution to the Brazilian middle-class's privations – exploiting the uneducated underclass – is no longer as accessible.

In the capital Brasília, the students take their protest a step further and march on Congress. For several hours the demonstrators stand outside Oscar Niemeyer's modernist building, shouting slogans. One student manages to force a barricade and climb up on to the roof of the Congress building. Soon, she and several hundred other demonstrators are dancing on the building that's become synonymous with corruption in Brazil.

The Brazilian team are set to play their second group-stage match in Fortaleza in north-eastern Brazil, and follow the TV footage from Rio and Brasília in their hotel. After training the following morning, Brazilian reporters ask the players what they think of the protests.

'From living in England, I know that standards in Brazil could be much higher,' the Chelsea defender David Luiz says.

Star striker Hulk agrees. 'We come from the lower classes and feel an urge to be out there on the streets. We know that people have a reason to be there.'

The fact that the new, young players disregard the football association's ban on the expression of political opinions surprises everyone. Scolari is surprised, too, but he doesn't deal out any reprimands, instead concluding calmly that 'it seems as though the players' silence is over'. Two hours before it's time to attempt revenge on Mexico for the Olympic final in London, Neymar posts a picture of the Brazilian flag on Instagram, and describes how his father struggled so that he and his sister could have a good upbringing. Neymar writes that he wants to see 'a fairer, safer, healthier and more honourable Brazil', and asks people to raise the Brazilian flag, which features the words '*Ordem e progresso*', order and progress. Neymar finishes: 'From this match on I'll run on to the pitch strengthened by the protests.'

In the same way, the fans and demonstrators are strengthened by the footballers' support. When the team line up in the new World Cup stadium, Castelão in Fortaleza, the stands explode.

Never before has a Brazilian crowd joined in so fiercely with the national anthem. When FIFA's short version finishes and the music falls silent, the spectators continue to sing the rest of the anthem unaccompanied. It's a historic moment. Football, which those in power once used to sedate the people, has now awoken them. In the stands, supporters hold up banners saying 'Where do our taxes go?', 'We want FIFA-standard schools' and 'This protest isn't against the team – it's against the corruption'. Romário follows the match from his villa in Brasília, and tweets '*O gigante acordou*', the giant has awoken, a nod to the second verse of the Brazilian national anthem, which starts with the phrase '*Deitado eternamente em berço esplêndido*', a description of the sleeping giant Brazil 'resting in eternal splendour'.

Eight minutes into the match, Neymar makes it 1-0 with a volley. It's his second *golaço*, and the final floodgates burst. The audience spontaneously sing the national anthem and David Luiz is so psyched up that he breaks his nose colliding with the captain Thiago Silva. In the final minutes, Neymar tricks two defenders with a single movement, and finds himself unmarked in the penalty area. Instead of taking a shot at goal, he passes to the substitute Jô, who scores his second goal in two matches. Neymar wins the man of the match award, and says: 'We played for the people.'

Two days later, renewed protests take place. Now, even working-class people join in. Children, students, adults and pensioners gather outside the Candelária cathedral in downtown Rio, where the democracy movement's protests against the military dictatorship used to start. To FIFA's chagrin, the demonstration takes a new route. Instead of going along Avenida Rio Branco, the 300,000-odd demonstrators head up Avenida Presidente Vargas, named after Getúlio Vargas who encouraged the working classes to celebrate their citizenship through football. At the other end of Avenida Presidente Vargas lies the Maracanã.

The mayor holds a crisis meeting with the police, and decides to stop the demonstration before it reaches the stadium where Spain's international stars are getting changed after humiliating Tahiti 10-0. The police force roll out their most infamous vehicle – 'O Caveirão', the Big Skull – an armoured bus with apertures for firearms, which is used in the invasion of favelas – and park it across the avenue. The military police fire hundreds of tear gas canisters and rubber bullets towards the crowd of demonstrators, unleashing the worst riots Rio has experienced in several years. Angry demonstrators smash the windows of the council offices and banks. Pelé encourages the people to 'concentrate on the football rather than protesting' and is met with a wave of popular derision.

By this point, I've left Rio to watch Brazil's third match in Salvador, Brazil's third biggest city. Here, too, the police's attempts to beat down the protests result in violence. The difference is that the demonstrators turn their rage on FIFA. Just as the police think the situation has calmed down, the demonstrators turn up outside the Sheraton where the FIFA dignitaries are staying. The demonstrators try to invade the hotel and throw stones at the FIFA buses transporting the journalists to and from the stadium. Their banners say 'FIFA Go Home!' and one of the teams is said to be thinking of quitting the championship. In Brasília, the students go a step further once again, and invade the moat around the glass-clad foreign ministry. The students smash window panes and throw in Molotov cocktails. Firefighters manage to fight the flames, but the TV footage is beamed round the world, showing the police and authorities losing control of the protests in Brazil.

The whole Confederations Cup teeters on a knife edge, and

FIFA advise their staff not to wear their corporate polo shirts or have their accreditation cards on show when they're outside the stadiums. In an attempt to lay the blame on the host nation, FIFA president Sepp Blatter says: 'It was Brazil who wanted to host the World Cup. We haven't forced anyone. And to arrange a good championship you have to build stadiums. Brazil knew that.'

The president Dilma Rousseff tries to put the brakes on the criticism by giving a speech to the nation, in which she says that she 'hears the street's calls for change'. She promises that the profits from the oil field will go directly to the education system and that six thousand doctors will be imported from Cuba to improve the public health system.

The attempts to calm the protests down don't work, and, ahead of Brazil's last group-stage match against Italy, large parts of Salvador are closed off. Special corridors are created to funnel spectators through to the World Cup venue, Fonte Nova, constructed on the site of the former stadium, which was on the point of collapse. Three kilometres outside the stadium, I and all the others have to show our tickets in order to pass the barricades. The riot police, with their visors, black shields and machine guns, line the streets long before the start of the match.

Instead of hanging around in front of the stadium, I walk up a steep alleyway to one of the favelas crowding the hills around Fonte Nova. The contrast is evident. This area is home to many of the black population who make up 80 per cent of the residents of Salvador, the city that was Brazil's first capital.

It smells of *acarajé* and *abará*, Afro-Brazilian dishes made of dried shrimp and fried beans, and music by Gilberto Gil and Carlinhos Brown spills from the houses. I sit down outside a house where an old black lady is setting out an informal serving area with eight stools and two plastic tables. I order dried shrimps and two beers at a dollar a can, and ask whether the lady is worried that FIFA will shut her little café down – within a one-kilometre radius, the only people allowed to sell food are official sponsors of FIFA. She shakes her head.

'This is my home and I'm the only one who can decide who I want to sell food to. FIFA doesn't make the decisions here.'

On the other side of the alley, a woman has carried out her TV and placed it on a chair in front of her house. This is where she and her friends will be watching the match. On the hill above Fonte Nova I can't find anyone who even knows anyone who has a ticket.

'I guess we'll hear it if any goals are scored. Especially if Dante scores them,' says the neighbour.

The centre-back Dante is everyone's favourite up here in the hills. He's Salvador's very own prodigal son, a down-to-earth guy brought up in the Afro-Brazilian religion *Candomblé*, which worships African gods and in difficult times conducts *macumba*, an Afro-Brazilian ritual which calls up spirits using cigar smoke, cachaça and onions. Dante has also made a typical Brazilian football journey – not that of the super-talents, but, rather, a slog that resembles the kind thousands of Brazil's teenage football players have embarked on. A journey of that kind might end in Romania, or Norway, in Cyprus or a Brazilian state league. Or nowhere at all.

For Dante, things started to get serious at the age of sixteen when he moved from Salvador to the richer states of São Paulo and Rio Grande do Sul, where he first played for a small club, and then for the slightly larger Juventude. From there, an agent sent him to Lille in France. After that he played at Charleroi and Standard Liège in Belgium, before he made it to the Bundesliga and Borussia Mönchengladbach. That was further than many had thought his talent would take him, but after a few more years he was acquired by Bayern Munich for $6 million – a very agreeable sum for the German giants. Dante immediately took a regular spot, and during his first season he won the Champions League, the Bundesliga and DFB Cup. Simultaneously, his dream of playing in the World Cup on home turf was coming to life. At the start of 2013, the twenty-nine-year-old was selected for his first ever international match.

When Dante found out the manager Scolari had picked him for the Confederations Cup squad, and that the team would be playing one of their group-stage matches in Salvador, he imme-diately bought sixty tickets for his relatives. The chance of them actually getting to see him play, however, was small. Thiago Silva and David Luiz are the regular centre-backs, and it was they who'd played the first two matches in the Confederations Cup. But eight minutes into the match against Italy, David Luiz receives a yellow card for a tackle from which Luiz himself comes out worst. He starts limping, and after twenty minutes he lies down on the pitch. The team of doctors run on and bandage his thigh. In the thirty-fourth minute he can stand it no longer. The thing no one had expected takes place: Scolari sends on the prodigal son, to the delight of his family.

Despite several good chances, the Brazilian forwards can't get a hold on Italy, and concern grows that Brazil will end up in group two, and be forced to play the reigning World Cup holders Spain in the semi-final. In injury time in the first half, Dante joins the attack as a free-kick is taken. Fred heads the ball straight at Buffon, and it rebounds. Then it seems as if the *macumba* forces take over: the ball heads straight for Dante, who makes it 1-0. In his first competitive match for the team, after twelve minutes on the pitch, the prodigal son has scored his first goal for Brazil. The celebrations from the surrounding hills can be heard all the way down in the stadium.

In the second half, Neymar spins a free kick into Buffon's right corner, and even the British journalists, who've stubbornly persisted in called Neymar a 'YouTube chancer', are applauding. Brazil play their best match in the tournament, and sally forth to a 4-2 victory.

Suddenly, it seems as though nothing can go wrong for this new team, so recently tipped for defeat. Their relationship with the Brazilian people develops into an impassioned dance. The players support the people's efforts, and the people feel for the first time in a decade that the national team is theirs. This is a team playing attractive football, where almost half the players are from Brazilian clubs and reflect the diverse Brazilian population. The Pentecostal church followers, who dominated during Dunga's time, have been mixed with Catholics and those who follow Afro-Brazilian religions. Even the samba is back. Not since Ronaldinho drummed rhythms in the players' bus during the 2002 World Cup has there been so much singing in the team. Dante is brilliant at playing the *cavaquinho*, the little samba guitar that the ukulele is based on, and together with Real Madrid's Marcelo, Barcelona's Dani Alves and PSG's Lucas, he has formed a quartet to liven up boring flights and hotel stays with samba classsics.

In the semi-final, Brazil will face Uruguay in Belo Horizonte. Grey-haired journalists take the ghost of *Maracanazo* out of the closet once again. Scolari brushes off the questions at a press conference:

'There is no psychology in this match. What happened in 1950 was that a team lost. In football, one of the teams has to win, and on that occasion Uruguay were better. In no way does that affect today's match. On the other hand, Cavani has the best shot in Italy, Luis Suárez is one of the best players in the Premier League and Forlán was man of the tournament in the 2010 World Cup. We have to have respect for these players. Not for historical events.'

Then a smile plays at the corner of the hard-boiled manager's mouth.

'We might play for a draw, and go into extra time, maybe even penalties. But we'll win. Do you know why?'

Dramatic pause.

'Because this is Zagallo's match,' Scolari says, pointing at FIFA's match calendar.

The semi-final is the thirteenth match of the tournament.

The match hangs in the balance at 1-1. Then Scolari makes his most daring substitution of the championship. In the sixty-fourth minute, he takes off Hulk and sends on twenty-year-old Bernard. When Atlético Mineiro's young idol runs into his own home stadium, the newly renovated Mineirão explodes, giving his team an extra burst of energy. Four minutes before full time, Paulinho heads in to make it 2-1, and Brazil are through to the final.

At the same time, politicians start to listen to the almost two million people who've taken part in the demonstrations. Before the final, the Senate approves a draft bill stating that corruption is to be classed as a serious offence, and, for the first time, the Supreme Court sends a parliamentarian to prison: the politician is sentenced to thirteen years for embezzling almost $4 million.

One of the focuses of the protests has also been to stop 'PEC 37', a proposed bill in the Congress which will take responsibility for investigating politicians suspected of corruption away from the public prosecution authority. The members of Congress would prefer the police to investigate them.

The Brazilian public prosecution authority is known for being one of the country's least bribeable bodies. It reports rural land-owners who keep their workforce under conditions akin to slavery to the police. It investigates livestock farmers who clear rainforest in Amazonas. It sues public hospitals that close Accident and Emergency units during carnival because all the doctors have taken their annual leave simultaneously. As a result of its position, many employees of the public prosecution authority have received death threats.

The Brazilian police are the exact opposite. Citizens can buy protection and order assassinations, cocaine and prostitutes from the police. You can also buy your way out of jail if you are arrested. If the police started investigating the country's democratically elected representatives, it would mean politicians no longer had to worry about being banged up. Therefore, before the protests started, the majority of Congress's 513 members in the second chamber were behind the proposed law. During the protests, many change their minds: 430 vote against 'PEC 37'. Only nine maintain their previous position. It's obvious the politicians have got scared.

Even the football bigwigs are uncertain of the new lie of the land. They don't know where they stand with the players, supporters and the media. In the middle of the tournament, I meet Brazil's most famous football writer, Juca Kfouri, former editor-in-chief of the football magazine *Placar*, which coined the term 'Democracia Corinthiana' during a debate with Sócrates and Washington Olivetto. Today he writes a column in the *Folha de São Paulo*, and runs Brazil's most read football blog. Kfouri doesn't deal in myths, as most other Brazilian football columnists do, and he's one of the few Brazilian football journalists who dare criticise the football association. It was Juca Kfouri's revelations that CBF had invoiced for a friendly against Portugal for $5 million more than they should have that led to Ricardo Teixeira's departure. Most other Brazilian journalists are afraid they won't be accredited for the next international match, or that they'll be refused an interview with a player, if they write something critical.

I ask Kfouri what he thinks of the recent protests.

'Fantastic! They're running scared now. Just look at the association's new chairman. No one wants to sit next to him at matches.'

Kfouri's talking about a behind-the-scenes squabble ahead of Brazil's match against Italy, in which the former enemies, Brazil's sports minister Aldo Rebelo, and FIFA's general secretary Jérôme Valcke, chose to watch the match together in a different VIP box from the one in which CBF chairman José Maria Marin was sitting. It may have been that Rebelo and Valcke wanted to avoid becoming targets for the booing and protests that some expected Marin to attract.

'Then Marin flew home straight after the match. Imagine – CBF has a chairman who doesn't even dare to hang out with the players in the hotel after a win.'

I ask what he sees as the decisive factor behind the fact that 'the giant has awoken'. The sixty-three-year-old sports writer runs his hand through his wavy hair.

'When people saw the new stadiums built with taxpayers' money, they were angry and started thinking: "If we can build these beautiful stadiums, why do we have the worst hospitals and schools on the continent?" And when the politicians deflected the blame, saying it was FIFA who demanded that the stadiums be that modern, the people got even angrier and demanded that public schools and hospitals should also be FIFA-standard. These Pharaonic stadiums were the straw that broke the camel's back.'

I fly back to Rio, a city that's pulsating: Spain have knocked out Italy on penalties in the second semi-final, and everyone is wondering how the new Brazil will stand up against the world's best. It's also time for The Return. For the first time, the team are to play a competitive game at the newly renovated Maracanã. But there are major concerns about what's going to happen with the protests. During the demonstrations, Brazil's biggest stadium, which was once jointly financed by 20,000 *flamenguistas* and *tricolores* buying five-year and life-long season tickets, has become the very image of politicians' corruption and wasteful treatment of public funds.

In other Brazilian states, the political post responsible for leisure and sports is one of the least attractive. Minimal budgets, fights over leisure centres, and low prestige make career-minded politicians seek other routes. In the state of Rio de Janeiro, with sixteen million residents, it's the exact opposite. Here, the job of sports and leisure secretary is one of the most sought-after, a trampoline to spring you right into national politics. The reason is that the state owns the Maracanã, and the sports and leisure secretary is the director of the Maracanã. Without any major interference, the sports and leisure secretary can apparently gain power and influence through the operation of the stadium. Presiding over expensive renovation work has been a key part of that.

The first time the Maracanã underwent a total renovation was ahead of FIFA's Club World Cup in 1999. The top sections got plastic seats, and audience capacity was reduced from 150,000 to 103,022, meaning that the stadium lost its position as the world's largest. The next time the Maracanã was closed for renovation was before the Pan-American Games in 2007. The remaining terraces disappeared, and the roof awning that covered the upper-most sections was repaired. New toilets were installed, and the pitch was dug up and lowered by a metre in order to improve visibility. The cost of these initiatives was around $150 million.

The sports and leisure secretary at the time was Eduardo Paes. The year after the Pan-American Games, he had enough money to stand in the mayoral elections. He gathered his last votes in Zona Oeste, the poorest part of Rio, where the former sports and leisure secretary treated residents to food on election day. Eduardo Paes won by a margin of 1.6 per cent over the Green Party candidate Fernando Gabeira.

Now that Eduardo Paes was Rio's mayor, he could decide that the Maracanã needed to be renovated again, this time for the 2014 World Cup. The temple to football was closed for two years, and the new seating was changed again for something even newer, the recently renovated concrete roof was torn down and a new roof made of plastic netting was constructed, and the pitch was dug up again so that a new, more modern drainage system could be installed. Together with the renovation for the Pan-American Cup, the politicians spent $700 million on getting the Maracanã up to scratch for the 2014 World Cup. That's almost twice as much as it cost to build the Allianz Arena in Munich from the ground up.

The sports and leisure secretary who's been responsible for the World Cup renovations is Marcia Lins. She's a former TV Globo journalist who was Eduardo Paes's deputy when he was sports and leisure secretary. At a press conference, where she let it be known that the world's biggest soft drinks company had recycled the plastic bottles for the Maracanã's seats, I asked her why the state had used so much of public funds to renovate a stadium that's already been renovated, at the same time as hospitals and schools were falling apart.

'The Maracanã is our Eiffel Tower, our Statue of Liberty,' she answered. 'Together with the Christ the Redeemer statue, it's our biggest icon. It's obvious that the state should pay for the renovation. I'm sure the French government would have done that if the Eiffel Tower needed to be renovated.'

When the renovation of the Maracanã was finished, fury was again sparked in the football republic. The rights for the running of the stadium were sold to a consortium headed by the mining magnate Eike Batista, one of Brazil's richest men. Although the consortium hadn't invested a cent in the renovation, they were given the right to run the Maracanã until 2046. The only thing the state will recover for its $500 million, the price of the latest renovation, is a rent of $2.5 million a year. Over thirty-plus years, the total won't even amount to an eighth of the cost of the investment.

At the opening of the new stadium came the next shock. The sports and leisure secretary's eagerness to turn the Maracanã into Brazil's Eiffel Tower had been so strong that large parts of the world's most legendary temple to football had been renovated out of existence. The characteristic ellipse-shaped stands have been changed, and now bear a closer resemblance to an ordinary rectangular stadium in the UK. The new plastic roof blocks the view, so that superstitious supporters will no longer be able to look to the statue of Christ on the mountain before important penalty shoot-outs. Even the underground dressing rooms are gone. And crowd capacity has been reduced further, to 73,531 seats, less than half the original capacity. Instead, the sports and leisure secretary has delighted the business world:

the new Maracanã has 110 luxury suites, twelve escalators and six lifts. When Romário heard what the sports and leisure secretary had done with the stadium that had been his home ground with Flamengo, Fluminense and the national team, he accused her of defacing the Maracanã: 'The soul is gone, only the shell remains.'

Before the final of the Confederations Cup, I warm up at Praça Saens Peña, a square in Tijuca, a kilometre from the Maracanã and a stone's throw from the block where TV commentator Galvão Bueno grew up. Over the last few years, this area has been experiencing an upswing as a result of the pacification of the favelas that crown the surrounding hills. Furthermore, the high rents in Zona Sul have led many people from the middle classes to move out here. Nowadays, there are plenty of sushi restaurants, fancy shops, clubs and bars in Tijuca. Because of the beer ban around the Maracanã, this is also where the supporters are meeting before the match. But today it's not the fans who've set their stamp on the square, it's the riot police on their horses. The first demonstration started at ten this morning. The second sets off at 2 p.m. The third starts its protest against the privatisation of the Maracanã at 5 p.m., two hours before the match is due to start.

It's clear that the balance of power has shifted since the record demonstration in which 300,000 Rio residents wandered peacefully up Avenida Presidente Vargas. The police's violent responses on that occasion have scared off the families, who've opted to stay at home today. Just like at the first demonstrations against the increased bus prices, it's the students who are the voice of the people. No more than five thousand have gathered. They are pitted against 18,000 police and soldiers who have been ordered out to make a human shield around the Maracanã.

The balance of power on the football pitch that day is seen as being just as unequal. Spain haven't been beaten in twenty-nine matches, and landed in Brazil as reigning world and European champions. It makes no difference that Marcelo and Dani Alves have revealed all the weaknesses of their clubmates at Real Madrid and Barcelona to their colleagues on the Brazilian team – for the first time ever, *A Seleção* are not the favourites to win a match at the Maracanã.

Two whole hours before the match is due to start, the world's most expensive football stadium is filled to capacity. The authorities have forbidden bars, restaurants and local shops from selling beer within a kilometre radius of the Maracanã, but have approved the sale of beer inside the stadium. As a result, long queues snake from the bars. Budweiser, one of FIFA's main sponsors, are rubbing their hands at the authorities' contradictory decision. Just like in Salvador, the black population are nowhere to be seen in the crowd, despite the fact that they represent half of Brazil's population. Only the white middle classes have managed to get hold of tickets to the final. The toilets smell of lemon, and the black cleaners hand out paper towels to the visitors. Everything's clean and tidy, but the smell of football has been wiped away. It feels like a lot of Fla–Flu derbies will be needed before the Maracanã gets its magic back.

Another thing that's surprising is that the bust of Garrincha is gone. Ever since the wake in 1983 it has stood in the centre of the main ramp leading into the arena. *Botafoguenses*, and others, have developed a habit of rubbing Garrincha's bronze head before the match, reminding themselves that the world's best right-winger came from Rio. Now it's Pelé, from rival state São Paulo, whose statue will stand in the Maracanã instead. The sports and leisure secretary has commissioned a statue that depicts the moment at which Pelé jumps up and punches the air after the goal that made it 2-1 against Czechoslovakia in Mexico in 1970.

On the pitch, the *sertanejo* duo Victor and Léo, king of samba Arlindo Cruz, and pop god Jorge Ben Jor are entertaining the crowds. Outside the stadium, the Big Skull has been driven up to stop the demonstrators reaching the stadium. Tear gas canisters detonate at the students' feet, and the organisers turn up the music so the riots can't be heard inside the stadium. On the streets, the students are shouting for bread, while the fans inside are waiting for the circus.

When the two teams are out, the yellow-clad mass stands up and sings the Brazilian national anthem. Just as in Fortaleza, before the match with Mexico, the spectators ignore FIFA's short version and carry on singing their anthem unaccompanied when the music has finished. And the players do too. It's obvious that something has changed. The hard-to-impress spectators at the Maracanã, who have caused the football association to move important qualifiers to other cities ever since the qualifying rounds for the 2002 World Cup, embrace the new national team with open arms.

A minute and thirty-five seconds into the match, Hulk chips a ball over to Fred, who trips but still manages to score lying down to make it 1-0. The players jump over the advertising hoardings and disappear among substitutes, coaches and spectators from the lowest rows in a giant group hug. The classic chant *Sou brasileiro com muito orgulho*, I'm a proud Brazilian, with which the Maracanã crowd haven't graced the national team for many years, echoes around the stands.

Brazil continue to dominate, and Spain's only real chance in the first half is a counter-attack in the fortieth minute, as Barcelona's Pedro outwits Júlio César, but is then himself outwitted by David Luiz, who flings himself across the goal at full pelt to prevent the ball from crossing the line. The Maracanã celebrates the centre-back as though he's scored a goal himself. Soon afterwards, Oscar runs from the centre of the pitch and exchanges passes with Neymar until a chance arises. Santos's wunderkind shows once again why he's the youngest player since Pelé to wear the number ten shirt. His shot catapults into the nearest corner of the net. In five matches, Neymar has now scored four *golaços*.

The Maracanã is boiling over. *A Seleção* are leading 2-0 against the reigning world champions, the supporters are waving their favourite yellow shirts around with their chests bared, and the whole audience is yelling '*O campeão voltou*', the champions have returned. Two minutes into the second half, Neymar jumps clean over the ball and lets it roll on to thirty-year-old Fred, who almost nonchalantly slips it beyond Iker Casillas to make it 3-0. When Spain get a penalty in the fifty-third minute and Sergio Ramos shoots wide, it's obvious that the world champions are being outclassed. Even steady centre-back Piqué is off balance, and when Neymar dribbles past him on the counter-attack, the Spaniard has no more weapons left apart from tripping his clubmate over. Piqué is sent off, and when the camera zooms in on his girlfriend Shakira's reaction in one of the VIP boxes, the audience sing the chorus to her hit song 'Loca'. Even irony has found its way back to the Maracanã. For the last half an hour, Scolari's new national team have such dominant possession that the most insulting chant, used for the first time in the newly opened Maracanã in 1950, when Brazil beat Spain 6-1, gains pace. Every time the Brazilians pass, the Maracanã roars '*Olé!*', and Galvão Bueno stands up in the Maracanã's biggest TV booth, with Ronaldo beside him as pundit, and shouts out to a hundred million viewers: 'Who would have expected this? That Brazil would play the world champions to cries of "*Ole!*"'

Ten minutes before full time, the students storm the police barricades and reach the stadium. Police helicopters sweep over the Maracanã and the police task force goes on the tear gas offensive outside the fence. One of the students responds with a Molotov cocktail which hits a police officer. Once again, Brazil has become a vibrant mix of heaven and hell. Outside the Maracanã, the streets are ablaze with rioting; within the stadium, we're witnessing samba football. Seldom has Brazil experienced so much *emoção*. When the referee blows the whistle for full time, the tear gas has reached the stands, where it blends with the scent of lemon from the toilets.

An hour after the final whistle, a proud, confident and jovial Scolari takes a seat behind the table in the pressroom, and states that from now on other teams will have to respect Brazil once again.

'Now we know we have a team who can stand up against any opponents. Of course, much remains to be done, but we no longer need to feel inferior ahead of matches against Germany, Spain and Argentina.'

A journalist asks what the Brazil manager thought of the atmosphere at the Maracanã.

'Well, what can I say? It was totally exceptional. You saw yourselves the players' reactions when the audience were roaring "The champions have returned".'

When the journalists meet the players after the final, Júlio César is one of the happiest. After the 2010 World Cup in South Africa, he lost his place in the team and was close to quitting. It was his wife, Ronaldo's ex-girlfriend, who convinced him to continue. Júlio César ended up at Queens Park Rangers, and it wasn't until Scolari took over the team that he was once more entrusted to keep goal. Between 1998 and 2005, the Maracanã was Júlio César's home ground with Flamengo, but never before has the thirty-three-year-old goalkeeper walked out of the dressing room looking as happy as he did on this day. He smiles widely, and gives a long row of high fives to the Brazilian journalists. Then he can't hold back any longer.

'All due respect to Spain, but in football there's a hierarchy. No one else but Brazil is five-times world champion.'

BRAZILIAN CLUB FOOTBALL

STATE CHAMPIONSHIPS

The area of Brazil is almost as large as that of Europe. Therefore the first state championships started almost half a century before the nationwide championship. Today, there are almost thirty state championships, with vastly different numbers of teams and levels of quality. The two biggest by far are:

Campeonato Paulista
NICKNAME: 'Paulistão' FOUNDED: 1902
RUNS: From the third week in January until mid-May
FACTS: The Campeonato Paulista is divided up into three divisions, of which the highest division consists of twenty teams who play each other once. The eight best-ranked teams go through to a play-off round in which every phase consists of a home and an away match. As the state of São Paulo has almost as many residents as Argentina, the Paulista is like a national league in itself. It has the biggest spectator figures in Brazilian football, and in 2013 the goal average was 2.73 goals per match. The record for paying spectator numbers is held by Corinthians, from the

261

1977 final at Morumbi: 146,082.
MOST TITLES: Corinthians (27), Palmeiras (22), São Paulo FC (21), Santos (20)

Campeonato Carioca
NICKNAME: 'Carioca' FOUNDED: 1906
RUNS: From the third week in January until the first week in May
FACTS: The Campeonato Carioca is divided into two rounds. The first round, Taça Guanabara, consists of sixteen teams divided into two independent groups in which every club plays each other once. The two best teams in each group go through to a play-off in which the winner qualifies for the Carioca final. The other round, Taça Rio, is played in the same way. The winners of these two championships face each other in a final in which the victor becomes Carioca champion. Record spectator numbers: In 1963, 194,604 attended the final between Flamengo and Fluminense.
MOST TITLES: Flamengo (32), Fluminense (31), Vasco (22), Botafogo (20)

SÉRIE A
NICKNAME: 'Brasileirão' FOUNDED: 1971
RUNS: From the end of May until the beginning of December
FACTS: In 2004, the highest division was reformatted to follow the European model: the teams meet each other twice, and the team with the most points wins (previously, the league ended in a play-off). Up until 2004, the number of participating clubs varied from almost one hundred (1979) to sixteen (1987). Today there are twenty teams in the league. Every year, four teams go down to Série B and four come up.
MOST TITLES: Flamengo and São Paulo FC (6), Corinthians (5), Palmeiras, Vasco and Fluminense (4)

SÉRIE B
NICKNAME: 'Segundona' FOUNDED: 1960
RUNS: From the end of May until late November
FACTS: During the 1980s, the second division was called Taça da Prata, the Silver Cup, and was a colourful championship, where the rules governing how clubs were promoted to Série A changed constantly. For three seasons, 1973, 1979 and 1993, the championship was cancelled because of organisational problems, and the 1986 and 1987 seasons are not acknowledged by the Brazilian football association.
MOST TITLES: Coritiba, Goías, Paysandu and Paraná, with two titles each

COPA LIBERTADORES DA AMÉRICA
NICKNAME: 'Libertadores' FOUNDED: 1960
RUNS: From the last week in January to the start of July
FACTS: Libertadores is South America's Champions League, featuring the thirty-eight best clubs on the continent. Argentinian and Brazilian clubs are guaranteed five places in the tournament, and clubs from Bolivia, Chile, Colombia, Ecuador, Paraguay, Peru, Uruguay and Venezuela have three places each. Every year, Mexico's clubs are also offered three places in the tournament. The championship is organised by the South American football association, Conmebol. Argentinian clubs have a total of twenty-two victories, Brazilian clubs have seventeen and Uruguayan clubs have eight.
MOST TITLES: Independiente (7), Boca Juniors (6), Peñarol (5), Estudiantes (4), São Paulo FC (3) and Santos (3)

INTERCONTINENTAL CUP/FIFA CLUB WORLD CUP
NICKNAME: Club World Cup FOUNDED: 1960/2005

RUNS: Second week in December

FACTS: The Intercontinental Cup was created in 1960 by UEFA and Conmebol, to determine the world's best club. The winner of the European Cup faced the winner of the Libertadores. As a result of the violent play of Argentinian clubs, many European clubs boycotted the match during the 1970s. From 2005 onwards, FIFA has organised the championship, which has been expanded to also include the best clubs from Africa, Asia, Oceania and North and Central America.

MOST TITLES: Brazil (10), Argentina (9), Italy (9), Uruguay (6), Spain (6)

BRAZIL'S WORLD CUP TOURNAMENTS

1930 URUGUAY
Group stage (2nd, eliminated)
Brazil vs Yugoslavia   1-2
Brazil vs Bolivia   4-0

Brazil's top scorer: Preguinho (3).

1934 ITALY
Last sixteen:
1*Brazil vs Spain   1-3*
Brazil's scorer: Leónidas.

1938 FRANCE
Last sixteen
Brazil vs Poland   6-5
(after extra time, 4-4 at half-time)

Quarter-final:
Brazil vs Czechoslovakia   1-1

Replay
Brazil vs Czechoslovakia   2-1

Semi-final:
Brazil vs Italy   1-2

Match for third place:
Brazil vs Sweden   4-2

Brazil's top scorer: Leónidas (7) (top scorer in the competition).

1950 BRAZIL
Group stage (1st):
Brazil vs Mexico   4-0
Brazil vs Switzerland   2-2
Brazil vs Yugoslavia   2-0

Final group stage:
Brazil vs Sweden   7-1
Brazil vs Spain   6-1
Brazil vs Uruguay   1-2

Final positions: 1. Uruguay, 2. Brazil, 3. Sweden, 4. Spain.

Brazil's top scorer: Ademir (9) (top scorer in the competition).

1954 SWITZERLAND
Group stage (1st):
Brazil vs Mexico   5-0
Brazil vs Yugoslavia   1-1

Quarter-final:
Brazil vs Hungary   2-4

Brazil's top scorers: Didi, Julinho and Pinga (2 each).

1958 SWEDEN
WINNERS! The 1958 World Cup tournament was the first in which all the leading football nations participated. In the important third match against reigning Olympic champions the Soviet Union, the seventeen-year-old Pelé and the unconventional dribbler Garrincha had their World Cup debuts. Garrincha hit the post and Pelé the crossbar in the first minute, and thus two future international stars introduced themselves.

Pelé and Garrincha played the rest of the tournament, in which Brazil scored eleven goals in three matches. Pelé scored one goal in the quarter-final, a hat-trick in the semi-final and two goals in the final. Six Brazilian players were selected for the team of the tournament, and 1958 was the first time a team from the dominant football continents of Europe and South America had won a World Cup outside its own continent.

Group stage (1st):
Brazil vs Austria   3-0
Brazil vs England   0-0
Brazil vs Soviet Union   2-0

Quarter-final:
Brazil vs Wales   1-0

Semi-final:
Brazil vs France   5-2

Final:
Brazil vs Sweden   5-2

Brazil's top scorer: Pelé (6).

1962 CHILE

WINNERS! As reigning world champions, Brazil automatically qualified and were clear favourites, not least thanks to Pelé and Garrincha being four years better. But Pelé's involvement was short-lived: he managed to score one of the goals in the 2-0 victory in the first match, but he injured himself against Czechoslovakia, and hobbled round the edge of the pitch for the rest of the match. Even without Pelé, however, Brazil were a powerful team. In the following match against Spain, who had enlisted the former Hungarian legend Ferenc Puskás, Pelé's replacement, Amarildo, was the big player of the match – with two goals he turned Brazil's weak position into victory.

The star of the tournament was still Garrincha. In Pelé's absence he was the one who secured Brazil's success, with two goals in the quarter-final and two more in the semi-final – before he was sent off. Garrincha escaped without a ban, and was allowed to play in the final, where Brazil successfully defended their title, despite falling behind early, just as they had against Sweden four years earlier. Once again, four Brazil players were selected for the team of the tournament. Brazil and Italy (1934 and 1938) are still the only teams to have defended a World Cup title successfully.

Group stage (1st):
Brazil vs Mexico   2-0

Brazil vs Czechoslovakia   0-0
Brazil vs Spain   2-1

Quarter-final:
Brazil vs England   3-1

Semi-final:
Brazil vs Chile   4-2

Final:
Brazil vs Czechoslovakia   3-1

Brazil's top scorers: Garrincha and Vavá (4 each) (top scorers in the competition).

1966 ENGLAND
Group stage (3rd, eliminated):
Brazil vs Bulgaria   2-0
Brazil vs Hungary   1-3
Brazil vs Portugal   1-3

Brazil's top scorers: Pelé, Garrincha, Tostão and Rildo (1 each).

1970 MEXICO
WINNERS! The Brazilian football supporters' memory of the fiasco in England was wiped out in the qualifying round, in which Brazil went undefeated through the six matches with a goal difference of 23-2.

The tournament proper continued in the same style. Brazil's World Cup winners of 1970 are probably the best in the history of the competition: they won six consecutive matches, with a goal difference of 19-7, and treated spectators to blinding football along the way. The captain Carlos Alberto scored the tournament's final goal, a thundering shot given extra pace by the thin air of Mexico City, which is still seen as one of the most beautiful World Cup goals ever.

Group stage (1st):
Brazil vs Czechoslovakia 4-1
Brazil vs England 1-0
Brazil vs Romania 3-2

Quarter-final:
Brazil vs Peru 4-2

Semi-final:
Brazil vs Uruguay 3-1

Final:
Brazil vs Italy 4-1

Brazil's top scorer: Jairzinho (7).

1974 WEST GERMANY
Group stage, first round (2nd):
Brazil vs Yugoslavia 0-0
Brazil vs Scotland 0-0
Brazil vs Zaire 3-0

Group stage, second round (2nd):
Brazil vs East Germany 1-0
Brazil vs Argentina 2-1
Brazil vs Holland 0-2

Match for third place:
Brazil vs Poland   0-1

Brazil's top scorer: Rivelino (3).

1978 ARGENTINA
Group stage, first round (2nd):
Brazil vs Sweden   1-1
Brazil vs Spain   0-0
Brazil vs Austria   1-0

Group stage, second round (2nd):
Brazil vs Peru   3-0
Brazil vs Argentina   0-0
Brazil vs Poland   3-1

Match for third place:
Brazil vs Italy   2-1

Brazil's top scorers: Dirceu and Dinamite (3 each).

1982 SPAIN
Group stage, first round (1st):
Brazil vs Soviet Union   2-1
Brazil vs Scotland   4-1
Brazil vs New Zealand   4-0

Group stage, second round (2nd):
Brazil vs Argentina   3-1
Brazil vs Italy   2-3

Brazil's top scorer: Zico (4).

1986 MEXICO

Group stage (1st):

Brazil vs Spain   1-0

Brazil vs Algeria   1-0

Brazil vs Northern Ireland   3-0

Last sixteen:

Brazil vs Poland   4-0

Quarter-final:

Brazil vs France   3-4

(after penalties, 1-1 at full time).

Brazil's top scorer: Careca (5).

1990 ITALY

Group stage (1st):

Brazil vs Sweden   2-1

Brazil vs Costa Rica   1-0

Brazil vs Scotland   1-0

Last sixteen:

Brazil vs Argentina   0-1

Brazil's top scorer: Careca (2).

1994 USA

WINNERS! The 1990 World Cup in Italy didn't leave much cause for celebration for the Brazilian fans. The result was the worst since 1966, and it was a defensive, dull Brazil who were unsuccessful.

The new manager Carlos Alberto Parreira intended to change

things. However, Dunga, the symbol of Brazil's new pragmatic approach, was still in the team, and the '94 team would have been no more fun to watch than the '90 team, if it hadn't been for the creative pair of forwards Romário and Bebeto.

The final against Italy is considered one of the dullest ever. After 0-0 and penalties, Brazil salvaged their fourth World Cup title, with the lowest goal average for a winning team in World Cup history – 1.57 goals a match.

Group stage (1st):
Brazil vs Russia   2-0
Brazil vs Cameroon   3-0
Brazil vs Sweden   1-1

Last sixteen:
Brazil vs USA   1-0

Quarter-final:
Brazil vs Holland   3-2

Semi-final:
Brazil vs Sweden   1-0

Final:
Brazil vs Italy   3-2
(after penalties, 0-0 at full time)

Brazil's top scorer: Romário (5).

1998 FRANCE
Group stage (1st):
Brazil vs Scotland   2-1

Brazil vs Morocco   3-0
Brazil vs Norway   2-3

Last sixteen:
Brazil vs Chile   4-1

Quarter-final:
Brazil vs Denmark   3-2

Semi-final:
Brazil vs Holland   4-2
(after penalties, 1-1 at full time)

Final:
Brazil vs France   0-3

Brazil's top scorer: Ronaldo (4).

2002 SOUTH KOREA/JAPAN

WINNERS! Brazil had their worst qualifying round ever, losing six matches and coming third in the group, thirteen points behind Argentina.

In the World Cup tournament itself, however, they had seven straight wins. In the quarter-final, Ronaldinho gave England's keeper nightmares after his free-kick from the wing sailed into the top corner. After the second victory of the tournament against Turkey, Ronaldo scored two goals in the final against the World Cup's best player, Oliver Kahn, thereby securing the title for Brazil and becoming the leading scorer in the competition.

Group stage (1st):
Brazil vs Turkey   2-1
Brazil vs China   4-0
Brazil vs Costa Rica   5-2

Last sixteen:
Brazil vs Belgium   2-0

Quarter-final:
Brazil vs England   2-1

Semi-final:
Brazil vs Turkey   1-0

Final:
Brazil vs Germany   2-0

Brazil's top scorer: Ronaldo (8) (top scorer in the competition).

2006 GERMANY
Group stage (1st):
Brazil vs Croatia   1-0
Brazil vs Australia   2-0
Brazil vs Japan   4-1

Last sixteen:
Brazil vs Ghana   3-0

Quarter-final:
Brazil vs France   0-1

Brazil's top scorer: Ronaldo (3).

2010 SOUTH AFRICA

Group stage (1st):

Brazil vs North Korea   2-1

Brazil vs Ivory Coast   3-1

Brazil vs Portugal   0-0

Last sixteen:

Brazil vs Chile   3-0

Quarter-final:

Brazil vs Holland   1-2

Brazil's top scorer: Luis Fabiano (3).

ACKNOWLEDGEMENTS

There's really only one person to thank for this book. It was Tobias Regnell who took the initiative on the project, spurred me on and steered it home: without your comments, corrections and saves this would never have become the book it did. Thanks, Tobias! As an editor, your big heart and quick mind have been invaluable.

But there are other people who deserve my thanks too. Mainly my readers, who patiently went through manuscripts, pointing out errors and inconsistencies. Bo Reimer, Martin Assarson, Kristian Bengtsson, Henrik Ystén, Federico Moreno, Helena Malmström, Sujay Dutt and Rafael Maranhão. Thanks for all your time and knowledge! Other people I want to thank are my wonderful wife Regina Brandão da Silva, my best Botafogo buddy Afonso Machado, and my wise therapist Potiguara Mendes da Silveira Jr. My colleagues and friends who have supported me along the way have also been important: Rogério Pacheco Jordão, Martin Curi, Alois Gstoettner, Andrew Downie, Chris Gaffney, Bobo Karlsson, Andreas Behn, Nicolas Behr, Fredrik Gertten,

Richard Martinsson, Erick Omena, Ingo Ostrovsky, Radames Vieira, Rodrigo Chiquetto and Leticia Alcântara. I would also like to thank my agent Rita Karlsson and Nichola Smalley who did the translation.